THE BATTLE OF VITTORIA.
LOOKING TOWARDS THE PASS OF PAMPLUNA

Peninsular Sketches

by

Actors on the Scene.

Edited by
W. H. Maxwell, Esq

Author of "The Life of the Duke of Wellington"
"Stories of Waterloo" etc.

Revised edition by S. Monick

IN TWO VOLUMES.

VOLUME II

Text © 2002 S. Monick
This edition © The Naval & Military Press Ltd 2002

First published in 2002 by
The Naval & Military Press Ltd
Unit 10, Ridgewood Industrial Park,
Uckfield, East Sussex TN22 5QE
www.naval-military-press.com

All rights reserved. No part of this book may be reproduced, stored in a retrieval system, or transmitted in any form or by any means without the prior written permission of the publisher, nor be otherwise circulated in any form of binding or cover other than that which it is published and without a similar condition being imposed on the subsequent publisher.

Printed and bound in Great Britain by Antony Rowe Ltd, Eastbourne

CONTENTS

OF

THE SECOND VOLUME.

	PAGE
MARCH TO MADRID, AND RETREAT FROM BURGOS	1
THE BATTLE OF VITTORIA	28
ADVANCE FROM VITTORIA	55
THE BATTLES OF THE PYRENEES	78
THE BRITISH CAVALRY ON THE PENINSULA	97
THE ACTION IN FRONT OF BAYONNE	133
"TAKE THE HILL BEFORE DARK!"	150
REMINISCENCES OF BAYONNE	163
A NIGHT IN THE PENINSULAR WAR	187
RECOLLECTIONS OF THE LATE WAR IN SPAIN AND PORTUGAL	205
RECOLLECTIONS OF THE PENINSULA	243
DOLORES: AN INCIDENT IN THE PENINSULAR WAR	260
JOURNEY TO HEAD-QUARTERS NEAR BURGOS	270

CONTENTS.

	PAGE
SEVEN WEEKS' CAPTIVITY IN ST. SEBASTIAN, IN 1813	286
ARROYO DE MOLINOS	312
THE TWENTY-NINTH AT ALBUERA	321
OUT-POST ANECDOTES, ETC.	332
MARSHAL BERESFORD	337
THE PYRENEES, IN 1813	343
THE 40TH REGIMENT IN THE PYRENEES	347
MILITARY RETRIBUTION	349
ANECDOTE OF BAROSSA	356
ANECDOTE OF SIR WILLIAM INGLIS	358
SANTAREM	359
VENTURINHO DO POÇO	367
ESCAPE AT ALBA DE TORMES	372
THE HEAVY CAVALRY AT SALAMANCA	373
CAPTURE OF THE ENEMY'S PICKET AT BLANCHEZ SANCHEZ	380

PENINSULAR SKETCHES.

MARCH TO MADRID, AND RETREAT FROM BURGOS.

IN the meantime, the second division had moved, in the middle of September, across the Guadiana, through Truxillo Jaracejo, towards Almarez, and then crossed the Tagus, by a pontoon bridge, and continued its movement on the right of that river, passed Talavera de la Reyna, and arrived, on the 30th, at Toledo, occupying both banks of the Tagus. Lord Hill pushed forward his advance to Yepes and its vicinity, taking the command of the right wing of the army, composed of the second, third, fourth, and light divisions, besides cavalry and artillery. For my part, I had no sooner contrived to get out of bed at Salamanca, than I began to pace up and down the room, and in a very few days gained sufficient strength to be enabled to inhale the fresh air in the cool of the evening; while walking slowly along, I met the staff doctor of our division, who expressed much regret that he had not been aware of my being sick in that town, and offered every assistance in his power; I expressed my thanks, but informed him that I intended to join my regiment. He asked me if I was mad, and insisted on my giving him a promise not to think of prosecuting so wild a scheme for the present; which I was necessitated to acquiesce in, from a fear that he would effectually stop my rambles; however, two days afterwards, I presented myself to the medical board, which sat daily to examine officers; the group of medicos were seated round a table, and having eyed them particularly, I experienced great relief at finding the worthy doctor did not form one of the party. I felt considerable agitation, from a fear that they would not sanction my departure, which gave me a colour; in fact I reported myself in perfect health, and obtained permission to proceed to rejoin the army with a strong detachment who were about to depart for that purpose. At five o'clock next morning, the day before I was to recommence my journey, my servant entered my quarter, and announced that my mule had been stolen during the night, out of the stable, and that my horse had been running about loose, with the door wide open. This unwelcome intelligence caused me to tremble so violently that I sunk down on the bed, nor do I ever recollect being so agitated in my life, for I had no means left to supply its place, and I could not have walked, in my weak state, half a league; fortunately, an officer who had just come from England to join us, relieved my anxiety, by offering to carry my baggage on one of his animals.

At daylight the next morning we started; the spangled dew still hung on the trees, the morning breeze refreshed my body and mind, and with exhilarated spirits, I felt as if new life and fresh vigour had been conveyed throughout my frame. The dead French soldier was still stationary in the wood, and in exactly the same position already described. On re-entering Alba de Tormes, I passed the apothecary's shop with exultation, which only three weeks before I had entered in such a miserable plight. When we passed through Arevalo, one of the narrow streets leading to the Plaza was choked up with cars from Burgos, crammed to overloading with exhausted, speechless, and wounded Highlanders, covered with hot sand, and many of them slumbering unto death; their pallid countenances portrayed the speedy dissolution of their lingering sufferings, while their sable plumes and torn tartans hung loosely on the pointed stakes, which formed the temporary sides of the rude vehicles. I searched in vain, through every narrow avenue, and amongst numerous convents and monasteries, for the house of the young lady who had been so attentive to me in that town, as I well recollected the high walls of one of those fabrics inclosing one side of the garden; I was, therefore, in hopes that in some spot of difficult access, I should find the fair object of my solicitude. The whole of the following day (during our halt) was passed, however, in fruitless search.

Continuing the march, our little column consisted of three hundred and fifty men, and when within sight of the distant villages, which were surrounded by extensive plains, the church bells rang merry peals: almost the whole of these places had been entrenched by temporary works, and the churches loopholed by the French posts of communication, to protect their small detachments from being destroyed or cut off by the Guerillas, or surprised by the infuriated peasantry. Shortly before we reached the Guadarama mountains, we struck into the high road to Madrid; for many miles there was scarcely a house to be seen. At length we came to a Posada, but the casa had been thoroughly gutted, and it was impossible for the owners of it to procure anything for us to eat. The country bore a very solitary aspect until we began to ascend the pass by the paved road, cut in a zigzag direction up the face of the mountain, on the top of which stands a stone fountain. The prospect from this spot is very grand, commanding a distant view of Madrid, the palace of the Escurial, and of the rugged mountains extending towards Segovia, which are covered with snow during the greater portion of the year.

The poor village of the Guadarama is situated in a valley at the foot of the grand pass. Towards evening, our horses being in some degree refreshed, we rode into the park of the Escurial, which is of considerable extent, and lies adjacent to the village, producing pretty good pasturage, but infested by prowling wolves and wild boars. The trees are generally of small growth, consisting of oak, carob, ash, and cork. The front of the palace of the Escurial looks towards the mountains of the Guadarama, and is built of a grey granite, in the shape of a gridiron. This culinary utensil is represented in the books of mass, on the doors, and various other parts of the building, which is perforated by innumerable windows. The length of the edifice is six hundred and forty feet, breadth five hundred and eighty, and sixty feet high. The pantheon of the palace is octagon, composed of marble; about fourteen niches are occupied by embalmed kings and queens, with a variety of other curiosities worthy the observation of the traveller. Returning towards the village, the old man of the house assured us the extraordinary edifice we had explored was nothing to the wonder and astonishment we should experience at the grand bull fights of Spain. The tears rolled down his furrowed cheeks as he ran about the room, which was paved with red tiles, representing the wild Andalusian bull staring with surprise on first entering the arena; then getting astride of a chair, he showed us how the Piccadoré received the bellowing bull on his lance, and the way he was frequently tossed, mangled, and killed, by the infuriated animal; then again, skipping and dancing about the room to represent the men insinuating the pointed darts and crackers into the animal's neck, and finally the graceful Matador, with a red cloak over one arm, and a short sword in his hand, making his obeisance with a profound bend to the señoras and cavalleros who excite him by countless *vivas*, and the waving of their white hands, and whiter pocket-handkerchiefs, to dispatch the staggering bull at one thrust. At length the ancient cavallero became so much exhausted by his exertions and feelings, that he fell back motionless in his chair, exclaiming, "Oh, los ladrones Franceses! they have eat up all our Andalusian bulls, killed our poultry, got all our *mothas* with young, and knocked all our Santa Marias from the altars and out of their sacred niches by the road-side."

During this rodomontade, we remained quiet spectators, quaffing the excellent wine which our host had extracted from its concealed deposit. Taking our departure the next morning, two of us being some short distance behind the detachment, at a very lonely spot we observed a Spaniard of most ferocious aspect, with huge mustachios and a capacious sombrero, clad in a leathern jacket, like a cuirass, with a short broad sword by his side, and a brace of pistols in his broad belt, which was buckled round his waist. We were instantly convinced that he was a robber; however, saluting him as we passed, which he returned by a cold and distant bend of the head, the few baggage animals being in sight, we thought it necessary to warn the soldiers in charge to be on their guard, although, generally speaking, the British might pass all over the country without danger; yet some robberies had been committed in Spain and Portugal, also by banditti. This day we halted at the village of Rosas, about two leagues from the capital. The country was bare and hilly, and even when within half a mile of Madrid, the traveller might fancy himself in a bare wilderness, as the town stands isolated in the midst of a rugged plain, skirted on the north side by distant mountains, without the least signs of traffic, with the exception of a few mules or asses loaded with chopped straw, the usual forage (instead of hay) given to animals, all other vegetation being parched up, and even the shallow river of the Manzanares having ceased to flow.

After the short absence of six weeks, having travelled, as already described, more than two hundred and thirty miles, and recovered from my fever, I rejoined our first brigade quartered in Madrid, as well as the third division; the second brigade was stationed two leagues from the town, in support of those troops cantoned in the line of the Tagus. I received the welcome information, that since I had quitted the division they had not seen the enemy. The troops were quartered in the various convents and monasteries, and the officers were billeted on the most splendid houses; many of them had white papers stuck on the windows, to denote that the former occupiers of them had followed the fortunes and court of El Rey Joseph, thereby deserting their country's cause.

One of my friends, whom I had left under a tree, I found occupying the house of a marquis, and decorating and perfuming himself before a splendid toilette, previous to making his bow to the beautiful and attractive object of all his desires, who had invited him to spend that evening at her house. He described to me their proud entry into Madrid as a conquering army, and how the variegated drapery hung from the windows, the acclamations of the people, and all the beauty of the place welcoming them, striking guitars, tambourines, and castanets, with eyes beaming love and admiration in a manner indescribable, known and felt only by those who have won the battle, and had been wandering under the heaven's bright blue canopy for sixty days, and traversed hundreds of miles over burning plains. Another officer reposed his limbs on a bed of down, enveloped by white satin curtains edged with long gold bullion, encompassed by mirrors, the whole surmounted by a gilded helmet, adorned with a noble plume of ostrich feathers; the rest of the furniture in this superb mansion was composed of the most costly materials.

Madrid is a compact town. The lower windows of all the monasteries and houses are defended by iron bars. Many of the streets are spacious, and the whole of them are remarkably clean. The Plaza Major is a square of lofty houses, many of them stained of various colours. The windows are very close together, out of which hang mats and drapery of a variety of striped patterns, to shade the rooms from the mid-day sun. This is the principal market for vegetables and other commodities, and invariably presents a bustling and busy scene. The royal palace is of a square form, and surrounds an interior court-yard, which has two gateways. The grand staircase rises out of the yard near the principal entrance. It is a most splendid work, wide and lofty, leading into the principal suite of rooms magnificently furnished. As we passed through them, I noticed the man in charge locking the doors after us. When, therefore, the curiosity of the admiring spectators was satisfied, we were ushered into another, and again made prisoners for the time being. A picture, beautifully executed, represented Napoleon in his younger days crossing the Alps, at the head of his bare-footed army, and was considered, by those who had seen him, to be an exact likeness. The face was extremely handsome. The Callé Major and Alcala are the principal streets of the town. The latter is wide and spacious, lined by large buildings, leading direct into the Prado, which is much admired for its broad walks divided into avenues by rows of trees, and runs the whole length of one side of the town, being terminated at each end by gates leading from it. On the north side stands the Bueno Retiro, encompassed by temporary works, (which had been thrown up by the French,) gardens, and pleasure grounds.

The fountains stand at certain distances from each other in the middle of the walks, and are framed after antique models. The water from one of them is esteemed the best in the town. The broad walk in the centre is adorned by these cascades, and is crowded every evening by the best company. It is here the stranger may examine with advantage the costume, style, and gait of the Spanish ladies, whose dress is composed of a mantilla or veil, gracefully thrown over the head, a long-waisted satin body, black silk petticoats, fringed from the knee downwards, white silk stockings, with open clocks, kid shoes of white or black. They carry a large fan in their little hands, which they open and shut as they glide along. It serves to shade them from the sun, or to salute their different acquaintance as they pass, which they do by shaking the fan rapidly, and simpering an affable smile.

At sunset the bells of the convents and churches give notice for offering up the evening prayer to the Virgin. Instantaneously the crowd becomes stationary, the men take off their hats and remove the cigars from their mouths, the señoras cover their faces with their fans, while they inwardly mutter a short prayer. At the expiration of a few minutes the profound silence is broken, when all again are in motion. In this place, dedicated to pleasure, our time was so divided, as to be occupied night and day either in dancing or at the tertullias. Public balls were also held twice a week at the Callè de Baños and Principe.

The officers of our division were anxious to display their powers as actors to their beloved señoritas; therefore, among other things, they were occupied in ordering dresses, and studying their theatrical parts. "The Revenge" was fixed upon as the tragedy to astonish the Spaniards. Captain Kent, of the Rifle Corps (95th), played the part of Zanga in "*El Teatro del Principe*" with due solemnity, and the piece went off in silence, until he began to move his sinewy arm and clenched fist backwards and forwards, like the pendulum of a clock cased in a black silk stocking or glove, encircled by a shining bracelet, which caused the muleteers in the gallery to roar with laughter; the señoras tittered, and held their fans to their faces. During the remainder of the evening, poor Zanga was treated more like a comic than a tragic character; and whenever he raised his arm, which he had frequent occasion to do, the same round of salutations greeted him on all sides, such as "*Arré Mulo*," &c. &c. At the conclusion of the piece, a Spaniard and a girl danced a bolero in inimitable style. Both of them were habited in male attire; the black hair of the female was clubbed up behind, and tied with a bunch of ribbons hanging down her back; she wore a richly embroidered silk jacket, white kerseymere breeches fitting tight to the shape, white silk stockings, shoes, and buckles. She rattled the castanets exquisitely, and beat admirable time with her pretty little feet.

About the 20th of October, our division was hastily concentrated, and first moved to some lonely villages, and then to Alcala, one of the principal universities of Spain. On the night of the 21st, the general-in-chief raised the siege of

Burgos,* and slowly retired on the Douro, followed by General Souham. Joseph and the Duke of Dalmatia had also formed a junction, and were making various demonstrations on the line of the Tagus. On the 22nd, the second division were put in motion on that river to observe the enemy's movements. On the 24th, the third division, which had continued in Madrid, moved towards Pinto, on the road to Aranjuez, in support of the fourth and second divisions. On the 26th, the second division crossed to the right bank of the Tagus, and extended its left on the Jarama. On the same day, we marched four leagues and a half from Alcala, and entered Arganda, which is situated on the high road from Valencia. The enemy continued to make such a variety of movements, that it was impossible to ascertain positively whether he would attempt his grand push on the south or east side of Madrid, which obliged Lord Hill to show front on two sides of a square for the protection of the great roads leading towards the capital, across the rivers Tagus, Jarama, and Hanares.

At ten o'clock at night (of the same day we had

* "To defile an army across bridges within musket range of the castle batteries was an operation that required both rapidity and silence. All was secretly prepared for the attempt. The wheels of the gun carriages were muffled with straw, and after dark the position was quietly abandoned. Although the night was moonlight, such was the good order observed by the troops, that the first division passed over without losing a man, or provoking the fire of the place."
—MAXWELL'S LIFE OF WELLINGTON.

entered Arganda,) the bugle horns sounded the assembly, which never occurred without the most urgent necessity, as it was not customary for the horns to sound when manœuvring near the enemy, except under peculiar circumstances. The orderlies usually passed round, and gave the word to pack up and accoutre, no further questions being asked either by officers or soldiers, and all repaired to the alarm post, and patiently awaited further orders, and so often without an enemy, owing to the variety of marches and countermarches in war, that such orders had ceased to be a novelty or any surprise to us. The division soon fell in. I had to precede the column on duty with another officer, who was mounted on a sorry lank pony, which, on being touched on the near or off side, kicked out with one leg at every mule that passed him in the most singular manner. I never recollect laughing more heartily. The muleteers cursed and swore, and particularly one who received a severe kick on the leg. This class of men wear a large hat, or pocket-handkerchief of various colours tied tight round the head, with the corner hanging down their backs, and a sort of red Moorish sash round the loins, dark blue or green velveteen breeches, open at the knee, and leather gaiters, with innumerable buttons up the sides, open in the middle, so as to show the calf of the leg to advantage. The mules are very gaily caparisoned, with bells at the head, and the backs closely shaved; the tails tied up in bunch, with red or other coloured worsted binding, and when loaded, the men sit on the top astride, singing boisterously. They usually bivouack in the woods when the day's journey is finished, and allow their mules to browse about all night, and cover themselves with a tarpauling. These muleteers robbed the English army of hundreds of mules during the war. I lost two myself; and during the time the light division were quartered in Madrid, the ladrones caused false keys to be made to fit the stable-doors, and actually, in the middle of the day, took the animals clear off, which were never afterwards heard of. At the end of a tedious night march, the division bivouacked in the morning on a rising ground, about a mile from Alcala, watching the right bank of the Hanares, and the cross-road leading from Arganda. The enemy, however, did not make their appearance, and at night we entered the town. The troops lay on their arms under the piazzas, which run through nearly all the principal streets. The inhabitants were so fearful that we might become engaged in the streets, that they illuminated the town for three successive nights.

On the 30th, we crossed the Jarama at a bridge near St. Fernando, which was already mined ready to blow up, and continued our retreat on Madrid. A slight affair also took place more to the right, at Puente Largo, between the van of the enemy and our troops, who had formed a junction with us from Cadiz. The general-in-chief on the same day made a movement to his left towards Ruêda, on the left of the Douro, causing the bridges to be destroyed right and left on that river, to guard his flanks, enable him to keep open his communication with his right wing at Madrid, and to cover its rear and left flank while retrograding from that place, through Arevalo to Salamanca.

Towards nightfall, as we approached Madrid, a slight rain fell, and when within a league of the town, the whole of the dismounted cannon taken from the enemy in the Bueno Retiro were blown up with a tremendous explosion, which quite convinced us that a retreat was decided on. We hastily traversed by column of companies the long walks of the Prado, which reverberated with the tramping of the soldiers' footsteps, and on passing the last gate of the town without a halt, we observed the bright fires of a portion of our army in bivouack on the distant hills, on the road leading to the Guadarama, which completed the gloomy thoughts of many who had formed attachments, and had, until this moment, cherished hopes of once again passing a short time in the society of the fair objects who had captivated their hearts in Madrid. We filed to the summit of the comfortless bleak hills, and as our baggage did not reach us until two hours before daylight, we passed a tolerably uncomfortable night. At nine o'clock in the morning, with gladdened hearts, we received orders again to advance on Madrid, but our anticipations were of short duration, as we merely halted without the walls to cover the troops who had been marching all night from the direction of Arganda and Aranjuez.

Many of the ladies came on the walks to take their last farewell, and just as we were moving off, forming the rear-guard, in the afternoon of the 31st, a beautiful girl, lightly clothed, refused to leave her lover, an English officer in the Portuguese Caçadores, who dismounted, and tied his silk handkerchief round her neck, and placed her sideways on his horse. Towards evening the wind blew keenly, and I saw her enveloped in a soldier's great-coat. Many females left their homes in a similar manner with the French officers, and travelled about with the army, on horseback, and astride, clad in uniform of the Polish lancers, or hussars, splendidly embroidered, with crimson trowsers, made very wide, in the Cossack fashion. The ladies of Spain frequently ride astride, with pantaloons, and Hessian boots, with a habit buttoning up before and behind, and when they are on horseback it is unfastened and hangs down on each side, to conceal their legs from view. On the 1st of November, we bivouacked in the park of the Escurial, where two wild boars galloped through the lines, and caused great confusion; a soldier of the 52nd was overturned by one of them, which bounded over him without doing any further damage.

During the retreat, the enemy did not press us, nor were our marches unusually long; in fact, everything went on so regularly, that several days' march passed with merely the usual incidents. The whole army from Burgos and Madrid were now in junction, the left marching on the heights of St. Christoval to cover Salamanca, and the right on Alba de Tormes, to take up a line of defence on the right bank of the Tormes. On the evening of the 7th, our division reached within a league and a half of Alba, where it drew up, until temporary defences were constructed, to resist the enemy at that small town. The country was perfectly open, without a house or tree to be seen, and I was contemplating the dreary prospect, and regretting the loss of my blanket placed under the saddle of my horse, which I had sent to the rear sick on the previous morning. As the night closed on us, the rain began to pour down in torrents; we were without food, or a particle of wood to light fires. Before daybreak we stood to our arms, looking out for the enemy: what a moment for an engagement! our clothes completely soaked through. At about eleven o'clock, the order came to retire, when we filed through the narrow streets of Alba, and crossed the bridge, where we found sappers hard at work, mining, and laying barrels of powder to blow up the centre arch if necessary. The river Tormes had swollen considerably, owing to the torrents from the mountains, therefore the fords became difficult and uncertain. Continuing our march on the left of the river, we entered a dripping wood, half-way to Salamanca, when we found our baggage waiting for us. The division being dismissed, all the trees were filled with soldiers, cutting and tearing down huge branches to build huts.

In a short time, great fires blazed up in every direction, while the soldiers encircled them with joyful countenances. Having been disencumbered of our drenched clothes, and rations being served out, we set to work making dumplings; before dark the canteens were laid, with smoking tea, rum, hot puddings, and beef. This was, indeed, a relishing and luxurious meal. The whole of the spirits being exhausted, a heavy slumber (under a tottering hut) put an end to our carousal. The next morning, before daylight, we were again under arms, and moving towards Salamanca to occupy that town with the first division and some Spaniards. Every morning we assembled an hour before daybreak, without its walls, waiting the approach of the enemy. I noticed the Spanish officers, invariably covering their mouths before the sun had risen, with their cloaks, and blowing the smoke of their cigars through their noses.

The Duke of Dalmatia moved slowly and with great caution, and evidently wishing, if possible, to force us to retire without coming to blows. His army had been collected at vast trouble, and enormous marching; many of his troops had marched within the last three months and a half, over eight hundred miles of ground. On the 10th, the enemy made a strong reconnoissance in front of Alba de Tormes, but after a heavy firing of artillery, they drew off at finding they could make no impression. On the 12th, some musketry was distinctly heard in the direction of the position of San Christoval. Our division had been dismissed as usual early in the morning, but was again formed, and ordered to crown those heights, where we remained the whole day, the alarm having been occasioned by a few guerillas firing at the French cavalry.

On the 14th, we all left Salamanca, and moved by the left bank of the Tormes, on the road towards Alba de Tormes, the enemy having crossed the river by some fords, two leagues above that town. As soon as this movement was ascertained by the General-in-chief, he made a reconnoissance under a fire of cannon, and found the enemy strongly posted on the left of the Tormes, at Monzarbes; the second division remained near Alba. In the evening our advance fell back, and the whole army was collected in the neighbourhood of the Arapiles, and showed front in the same direction as at the previous battle; it was supposed during the night by every one, that a great action would be fought on the following day. The country was illuminated for miles around from the quantity of fires which marked the line of our bivouack. All hands caroused until nearly midnight, being fully determined to make themselves happy previously to the supposed approaching struggle; then stretching themselves under the trees or around the fires, they tranquilly slept until an hour before daybreak, when we formed, and stood to our arms, and were again dismissed. At noon the baggage animals were ordered to the rear, and soon after we observed great masses of our army, moving in dense columns from the right by *echelon* of division towards the great forest. The enemy had laboured hard to strengthen Monzarbes, as a *point d'appui*, and under cover of which they continued to extend their left at a distance, to outflank our right, and to threaten our communications with Ciudad Rodrigo. About two o'clock in the afternoon, our division followed the movements of the army. The rain had begun at mid-day, and now fell in torrents, and we passed a miserable night under the trees. As soon as the road was distinguishable in the morning we were again on the march, ankle deep in mud, which tore the shoes from off the soldiers' feet; in this manner we trudged along the whole day; towards evening we saw the enemy on our right flank, when a little cannonading took place. One hour after nightfall, we drew up under the trees, hungry, and in the most miserable plight; the fires were kindled with difficulty, and while roasting on one side, we were shivering and perishing on the other, the rain still pouring down most unmercifully, as if the very flood-gates of the heavens had opened on us, for we were literally flooded.

On the morning of the 17th, not having received any orders to move, we were in groups, roasting acorns to satisfy the cravings of hunger, when an officer, who had rode a short way to the left, came unexpectedly on the French heavy horse, who were stealing through the wood, and would have made a prisoner of him, had it not been for the speed of his English horse, which was at full gallop as he passed us, calling out, "The enemy's cavalry," "Fall in," "Join the ranks." The division were only waiting for orders to move off, and instantly seized their arms and debouched from the wood, and formed contiguous columns, with our horse-artillery filling up the intervals. A few of the enemy's horse, with polished helmets, and covered with white cloaks, appeared moving backwards and forwards amongst the trees looking at us. Two officers of infantry, mounted on English horses, went to reconnoitre them, when the enemy tried to decoy them into the thicket. A troop of light horse were formed on our left flank, with sloped swords, but they did not throw out any skirmishers to feel the enemy. After a short time the division retired, and crossed a narrow rivulet, and reformed. One company of our regiment was left amongst some old houses on the margin of the stream, when some French dragoons slowly came forward to look at us; one in particular went to our right, as if he intended to cross the stream, when a German hussar, (I believe an orderly,) went towards him and challenged the Frenchman to single combat, provided he would cross the water. The Frenchman laughed, and made a similar proposal to him, as he approached quite close to the edge of the water, and the German advanced, but instead of fighting, they entered into a jocular conversation, and parted very good friends. Our division again went to the right about, and moved off to the rear; fortunately the road continued very wide, which enabled us to march in column of quarter distance, with screwed bayonets, and ready to form squares. The soldiers of the division bore the wet and privation with unexampled fortitude, nor did they lose their organization for a moment. At three o'clock in the afternoon, things began to look black; we heard that all the baggage had been captured, and that Lieutenant-General Sir E. Paget was taken prisoner; all this having occurred on the very road which it was absolutely necessary for us to traverse.

The Duke of Wellington at this time joined us, and continued riding on the left flank, and quite close to our column, and could not well join the main body of his army, as the enemy's horse scoured the road, and all our cavalry had retired. It was one of the chances of war, and could not be wondered at in a forest of such an amazing extent; the army were three days passing through it. The French heavy horse continued to accompany us on each flank amongst the trees, and frequently spoke to the soldiers in the ranks. We made two halts, to keep the men fresh, and in good order to engage, and then resumed a quick march, but not so rapid as to cause any soldiers to be left behind. The column preserved a profound silence; not a shot was discharged, for had we begun to fire, the noise would have brought the enemy from all quarters, who could not be aware of our isolated march.

Just before we reached a break in the forest, at four o'clock, it was absolutely necessary to detach a few skirmishers to prevent the audacious French horse from almost mixing in our ranks. The enemy's infantry were now coming up, mixed with their cavalry. Owing to the reverberation in the wood and dense atmosphere, the report of each musket sounded as loud as a three-pound mountain gun. The Duke of Wellington made a sweep round the column, to examine for the best fighting ground, while a lively firing of musketry took place close on the left, and in rear of our column, intermixed with the shouting of our assailants and the whizzing of bullets. As we emerged from the forest, to our surprise, we were saluted on the left by a number of the enemy's cannon, posted on a high hill, just above San Munoz. The division broke into double time across the plain, about half a mile, and made for the ford of the river Helebra. The second brigade branched off to the right to cross elsewhere, to extend a line of defence behind its banks. The seventh division was already formed in close columns on the other side of the river, near San Munoz, and suffering terribly from the effect of the round shot.

Two squadrons of our heavy dragoons came forward to protect us over the valley. We had no sooner reached the river, than we plunged in up to our middles in water, under a sharp fire of artillery, and we were obliged to scramble up the steep bank, having missed the ford, by which the troops were thrown into a momentary malformation; and while forming up in a hurried manner behind the horse-artillery, who were drawn up to protect the ford, the Duke of Wellington rode up in front of the left of Number 1 company, and looked placidly at them, saying, " The emeny must not cross here." At this moment a round shot carried away one of our officer's legs, and knocked a German hussar from his horse, leaving his hands hanging by a few shreds or sinews: notwithstanding, he got up and walked off, with an agonized countenance, and his head bent forward, resting on his breast.

The three companies of our regiment, who had been left in the opposite wood, now issued out at full speed, pursued by the enemy, and were obliged to run the gauntlet across the plain, with the round shot of both armies flying over their heads. The second brigade, which had already formed on our left, were keeping up a sharp fire of musketry to oppose the French crossing the river. A Portuguese regiment was stationary in close column, two hundred yards behind us. I saw three cannon-balls strike in precisely the same spot, carrying away a number of men each time. The firing of artillery and musketry continued until after dark, and then gradually died away, when the soldiers of the contending armies approached the river for water, and amicably chatted to each other in their different languages. The French infantry wore broad-toed shoes, studded with nails, wide trowsers of Spanish brown, a brown, hairy knapsack, a broad, leather-topped cap, decorated with a ball, shining scales, and fronted by a brazen eagle, with extended wings.

In action they usually appeared in light grey great coats, decorated with red or green worsted epaulettes, belts outside, without any breast-plates, with short sleeves, slashed at the cuff, to enable them to handle their arms, and prime and load with facility. Their flints were excellent, but the powder of their cartridges coarse; that of the British army was remarkably fine, but their flints were indifferent. During this day, the rain had held up for eight hours, but after dark again fell heavily. Beef was served out without biscuit; our cooking was speedily made, as we toasted it on ramrods. After another wretched night, about two hours before daybreak, the soldiers began to clean their arms, by the light of the fires, to prepare for the coming morning. Day broke, but the enemy made no attempt to molest us, and for two tedious hours we continued without any order to move, owing to a stream four hundred yards behind us, which detained the other division some hours in crossing it. As we moved off, the dead and the dying lay under the trees, (the trunks of many of them in flames,) pale and shivering with their bloody congealed bandages, imploring us not to leave them in that horrible situation, in the middle of the forest in the depth of winter.

However, to attempt to afford them assistance was impossible, every individual had enough to do to drag himself along. After three days' privation, the stream we had to cross was only a few yards wide, but so deep that the soldiers were forced to cross it by single files over a tree which had been felled and thrown across; had the enemy been aware of such an obstacle, we should have had a terrible struggle at this point; but the French army had suffered so much during the pursuit, that they could no longer follow, and became glad of a halt, and we equally glad to get rid of such disagreeable neighbours. Numerous soldiers from the other divisions of the army, (which retired in three columns,) fell out, and kept up a heavy firing, right and left, in the wood at wild pigs, or any other animal they could see. Many hundreds of these exhausted men fell into the hands of the enemy, and when they arrived at Salamanca, El Rey Joseph gave the English prisoners a pesetta each. During this day's march the weather was fine, but the road was overflown, and up to the men's knees for many miles. Two hours after dark, we drew up on a bare hill, clear of the forest; the atmosphere became frosty, but there was scarcely any wood to be obtained, and we spent another shivering night (without rations), gazing at the starry heavens, and counting the dreary hours.

Early on the 19th we moved off. The 20th Portuguese regiment, 900 strong, which had come from the South with Colonel Skerret, and had been attached to our division the morning we left Madrid, could only now muster 300 men in the ranks, owing to the cold, and not being accustomed to campaigning. The light division still continued in wonderful good order, and reached Rodrigo on that day, and bivouacked a mile from the walls of the town, without suffering scarcely any loss, except from the enemy's balls the day they were engaged.

Six divisions of the army entered Portugal for winter cantonments; the second division crossed the Sierra de Gata, and took up its quarters in the vicinity of Coria, in Estremadura, and the light division remained near Rodrigo, on the left bank of the Agueda; the head-quarters of the first brigade being at Gallegos, and that of the second brigade at Fuente de Guinaldo.

THE BATTLE OF VITTORIA.

EARLY in May 1813, the light division, commanded by Major-Gen. Baron C. Alten, formed line in the plain, near Gallegos, with one regiment of the German Hussars, and a brigade of horse artillery, for the purpose of passing in review before the Duke of Wellington, who appeared on the ground encircled by a numerous and brilliant staff.

During the winter, we had been cantoned by regiments on the Spanish frontier, on the left of the Agueda, in the different villages, during which period we, as well as the whole army, had received various reinforcements from England, the greater proportion of whom had taken up their quarters in Portugal, and near Coria, in Estramadura. The 10th, 15th, and 18th Hussars had recently landed at Lisbon, and also the household brigade, consisting of two regiments of Life Guards, and the Royal Horse Guards. Every effort had been made by the General-in-chief to make the infantry as effective as possible, and the great depôt was removed from Belem to Santarem. Previous to our advance, the great coats belonging to the soldiers were delivered into store, it being considered that the blanket was a sufficient covering for them at night, the more particularly as tents were served out for the use of the whole army, in the proportion of three to each company, to be carried by the mules, that had formerly conveyed the iron camp-kettles for cooking; instead of which, a light tin kettle, between every six men, was substituted, to be strapped on their knapsacks, and carried alternately on the march. Each man was provided with a reasonable supply of necessaries, including three pairs of shoes, and an extra pair of soles and heels, in his knapsack.

The daily allowance of rations for soldiers and officers consisted of one pound of beef, one of biscuit, and a small allowance of rum or wine: the former was invariably preferred by the old soldiers, although frequently much adulterated by the mischievous capitras.* The left of the army being already in motion from the interior of Portugal, second and light divisions concentrated on the 20th of May; the former crossed the Sierra de

* A muleteer, so called from having the charge of five mules, for the use of which he received five dollars daily, and one for himself. The biscuit, rum, and reserve ball-cartridge, were carried by the mules;—under charge of these men the lean Barbary bulls and bullocks followed the different divisions on their line of march, the whole originally provided by, and under the superintendence of, commissaries.

Gata, near Baños, the following morning, which brought it in communication with our right; our division forded to the right bank of the Agueda the same day, and encamped on the skirts of the extensive forest situated between Rodrigo and Salamanca. The German Hussars rode up, smoking their pipes, and singing some delightful airs, their half squadrons at intervals joining in chorus. We had heard that the hussar brigade was to supersede these veterans, and to act with our division: the whole of us left our canvass, and lined the road to greet our old friends and companions of out-post duty. The hussars became so much affected by our cheering, that tears rolled down many of their bronzed faces. "Oh!" said they, "we are always glad to see the old *lighty* division, who will ever live in our hearts."

On the third day we had arrived near San Munoz, and encamped on the river Huebra; many of the forest trees were covered with beautiful blossoms, and the plumaged tribe hopped from branch to bough, while here and there a solitary skeleton lay bleached, and reminded us of those starved, drenched, and wounded victims, the recollection of whose cries for help still rang in our ears, as we had marched past them on our retreat from Burgos and Madrid the previous winter. Now, how changed the scene! the inmost recesses of this extensive wood resounded with many voices, and a long line of animated troops continued to thread its mazes and winding roads. On this day the household brigade of cavalry came up;

their horses' backs were in a very bad state, owing to the heat of the weather. In the evening, while sitting at our tent door, we observed one of the Germans making up his fat horse for the night, and afterwards employing himself in sharpening his sabre with a stone. "That man," remarked an officer, "seems to be preparing for single combat."

Early on the 26th, we halted on the verge of the wood, within a short distance of Salamanca; our cavalry and some guns pushed onwards, and crossed to the right bank of the Tormes by two fords above the town, where they found three thousand French infantry preparing to retrograde. Our cavalry made a demonstration to charge them, but the enemy presented so firm a front, and then retired in such good order, that it was thought advisable not to attempt to break them, until a few discharges of artillery should have shaken the resolution of these veterans, which it failed to accomplish. They at length formed a junction with a part of the French troops retiring from Alba de Tormes.

Our dragoons were then drawn off, and the enemy continued to retreat without farther molestation. In the afternoon our division moved forward, and took up their ground in a wood immediately overlooking the left bank of the Tormes, a league below Salamanca. The next morning, as there had not been any order for the troops to move, I mounted my horse, and in company with some other officers rode into Salamanca. The inhabitants expressed their congratulations on seeing us again, although our reception was not of that warm character shown towards us in the preceding summer; and it would have been out of all reason to expect to find countenances decked with joy, when contending armies had trampled down and destroyed their corn over a fertile plain of many leagues in extent.

On entering the great square, we observed the principal inhabitants, full-dressed, flocking towards the cathedral, a very handsome stone structure, where we alighted, and, following the crowd through the grand entrance, found a great multitude waiting the arrival of the Duke of Wellington, who soon entered, escorted by a numerous retinue of Spanish generals and other staff officers, in a variety of uniforms magnificently embroidered. I was much struck at the simplicity of the Duke of Wellington's attire, who wore a very light-grey pelisse coat, single-breasted, without a sash, and a white neck-handkerchief, with his sword buckled round his waist, underneath the coat, the hilt merely protruding, with a cocked-hat under his arm. He stood with his face towards the altar during the prayer offered up for the success of our arms, (for during this time the divisions of our centre were branching off and marching over dusty plains towards Miranda de Douro, to support the extreme left, under Lord Lynedoch, which had crossed to the right bank of the Douro, east of Lamego, and had passed through the different defiles of Tras os Montes, and was marching on the right of that river through Leon towards Carvajales and Tabara to out-flank the enemy;) the deep-toned organ played some fine pieces during the ceremony; at the conclusion, the ladies, by way of a benediction, dipped their delicate fingers into a marbled basin at the door, and sprinkled us with holy water.

At daylight, on the 28th, we forded the Tormes, and continued a forward movement along a winding road, through a rich valley compassing the base of a hill, on the summit of which stood a number of videttes belonging to the household brigade; and although the men and horses looked gigantic, and bore a fine appearance, still the idea of out-post duty for the heavy cavalry caused much merriment in the ranks. At the expiration of a long march, we encamped in the vicinity of Aldea de Figueras, on the high road to Toro, where we halted four days; the second division, under Lord Hill, besides Portuguese and Spanish auxiliaries, were encamped half a league to our right, for the purpose of keeping in check and watching the movements of the enemy stationed on the right of the Douro, and also at Pollos and Ruêda, situated about two leagues from Tordesillas, on the left bank of the river, where the French still remained in some force hovering on our right flank. Under all these circumstances, it became necessary to be vigilant, as the left and centre of the army were now moving to pass the river Esla, under the immediate orders of the general-in-chief, who had left Salamanca to join them and to superintend this delicate movement in person, which he had caused to be executed for the purpose of turning the enemy's right, and to threaten his northern line of communications.

Owing to this manœuvre, the French army was thrown on two sides of a square, and only possessed the option of extending a line on the Esla, by throwing their left forward against Lord Hill at the moment when he was separated from the bulk of our army, (thereby making Madrid the base of their operations.) However, El Rey Joseph had not concentrated his army, and shewed no inclination to keep open his communication with that capital; and therefore gave up the line of the Esla and the Douro without a blow.

The passage of the Esla having been effected on the 31st, without opposition, the Duke of Wellington moved on Toro, where he arrived on the 2nd of June, and the hussar brigade fell in with a strong body of the enemy's heavy horse between that town and Morales, where they overthrew the French after a very vigorous charge, and made upwards of two hundred prisoners. Our division on this day made a forced march over a bare country, halted to cook during the heat of the day, then again resumed its movement, and reached the vicinity of Toro in the evening, and encamped among some luxuriant. well-watered vegetable gardens on the left bank of the Douro, the sight of which proved very refreshing after a long, sultry, and weary march; and it was most gratifying to observe with what zest and relish the officers and soldiers devoured the raw cabbages, onions, and melons.

The next morning our division crossed the fine stone bridge, the centre arch of which had been blown up and entirely destroyed. The soldiers, therefore, in the first instance, descended by ladders placed close together, communicating by planks thrown across to the steps of the opposite ladders, by which the men again ascended, thereby surmounting the obstacles with little difficulty, and then marched through Toro, which is situated on high ground on the right bank of the river, and commands a fine prospect for some leagues over the surrounding country.

The artillery and baggage forded one hundred yards above the bridge, without difficulty, the water being only knee-deep at this season of the year. We encamped half a league from the town. In the afternoon I walked in to see the prisoners, who had been taken by the English hussars on the previous day, all of whom bore a very martial appearance, and many of their countenances were so covered with hair that it was difficult to distinguish their features: one man, in particular, had a long red beard which reached down to his middle; he wore a brass helmet, surmounted with tiger's skin. One hundred of these French dragoons, who had not been wounded, were assembled to march to the rear. Their officer maintained a profound silence, and looked angry and highly indignant, with a large stick over his shoulder, stuck through the middle of a four-pound Spanish loaf. The whole of the captured, raw-boned horses, were huddled together in a court-yard, and bore evident marks of bad provender, escort duties, marches, and counter-marches; and nearly the whole of them had the most horrible sore backs, almost frying in the sun, while innumerable flies settled on and irritated the poor animals. A number of English medical officers were busily employed dressing the wounds of the French cavalry; some of them were of a most shocking description, from sabre cuts on their heads and faces. A Frenchman, of enormous stature, lay extended with a dreadful thrust from a pike, which had been inflicted by a cruel Guerilla, some hours after he had surrendered himself a prisoner. A medical officer was on his knees trying to bleed him, and held his wrist, moving his arm gently, having made an incision in hopes of causing the blood to flow; but every effort to save his life was useless; the dying soldier nodded thanks to the doctor, and soon after expired.

On the 4th, the whole army being concentrated,* it moved in three columns, the centre in the direc-

* The British army was composed of eight divisions of infantry, as usual. The first, of two brigades of Guards, two of the King's German Legion; the second, three brigades of British and three of Portuguese; the third, two of British and one of Portuguese; the fourth, fifth, sixth, and seventh, the same; the light division of two brigades. Total, seventeen brigades of British infantry, two of Germans, ten of Portuguese, besides other detachments. The cavalry consisted of four brigades of heavy, and four of light dragoons, and two of Portuguese.

tion of Palencia. The country was beautifully diversified, studded with castles of Moorish architecture, realizing the description in the chivalric days of Ferdinand and Isabella. The sun shone brilliantly, the sky was of heavenly blue, and clouds of dust marked the line of march of glittering columns. The joyous peasantry hailed our approach, and came dancing towards us, singing and beating time on their small tambourines; and when passing through the principal street of Palencia, the nuns, from the upper windows of a convent, showered down rose-leaves on our dusty heads; and the inhabitants declared, by way of compliment, that the Oxford Blues were nearly as fine as the Spanish Royal Horse Guards. Our division took up their ground close to the town, and on the exact spot where the French had bivouacked the same morning. Continuing our advance towards Burgos, on the 12th, the right of our army made a demonstration to attack the enemy, who had taken post there, while our division brought up its left shoulders, and hovered, with the hussar brigade, on their right flank; the left of our army halted, until the effect of this movement was ascertained, by which the enemy were again thrown on two sides of a square. The day was remarkably cold and cloudy. Towards morning, on the 13th, we heard a great noise, which we considered distant thunder, but it was soon known that the enemy had blown up part of the works of the Castle of Burgos, and had retreated. The left of our army was now pushed on in echelon, to turn by a flank movement the line of the Ebro, while our right and centre hung on the enemy's rear, ready to engage them in support of this movement. The country here was extremely wild and mountainous.

On the 15th we descended by a narrow pass, about a league in extent, which had the appearance of being scarped. The road was extremely rugged, and, winding suddenly, we found ourselves in the valley of the Ebro, which extended some distance to our right. The beauty of the scenery was far beyond description, and the rocks rose perpendicularly on every side, without any visible opening to convey an idea of any outlet. This enchanting valley is studded with picturesque hamlets and fruitful gardens, producing every description of vegetation. We crossed the river by the Puente Arenas, where we saw a number of sturdy, thick-legged women, loaded with fresh butter from the mountains of the Asturias. I had not tasted that commodity for more than two years, therefore it will be unnecessary to describe how readily I made a purchase, and carried the treasure in front of my saddle until we had encamped; but, as ill luck would have it, there was not any biscuit served out on that day; notwithstanding, I could not resist nibbling at such a luxury. The next morning we ascended by a most romantic winding road for a league, and obtained a view of the tents of the fifth division, who had made a *détour* to outflank the enemy, and to secure the passage of these narrow defiles. While passing a village, I asked several of the inhabitants to sell me some bread; a shake of the head was the only answer returned. I at last caught a glimpse of a priest, and, as I was determined to have bread to eat with the fresh butter, I made towards him, saluted him by a most gracious bend, pulled out a pesetta, and requested he would procure me a loaf. He very good-naturedly acquiesced, and soon again made his appearance with a three-pounder, and also returned half my money. He seemed pleased, so was I; and more courteous salutes having been exchanged between us, I rejoined the ranks. Travelling onwards, we perceived a large building on the side of a hill, with something white waving at each window, which, on a nearer view, we perceived to be a convent, and the nuns shaking their white handkerchiefs to greet our approach. On taking up our ground for the day, the baggage made its appearance, and ample justice was done to the bread and butter by myself and companions.

On the 18th, while advancing, left in front, along a narrow road, shrouded by overhanging woods and high mountains, a hussar informed us that the enemy were at hand. On reaching a more open space, we observed a brigade of the French drawn up behind a rivulet, and their front covered by a few houses. Two battalions of the rifle corps, supported by the 52nd, instantly attacked them, and after some smart firing the enemy gave ground. During this skirmish, our regiment turned off the road to the left, and formed line on a hill, as a rallying point in case of need, when, to our astonishment, we observed the head of another column of the French issuing, by a road parallel to us, out of an opening between two perpendicular rocks, and in rear of our second brigade already engaged. The other regiments composing our brigade scrambled over the rocks to endeavour to attack their left, which the enemy perceiving, turned off the road, and made for a hill. The 52nd brought up its left shoulder, and actually formed line facing to the rear, at a run, and encountered the enemy on the crest of the hill, who, the moment they met that regiment, turned round, and throwing off their packs, fled to the mountains, keeping up a running fight. The second brigade was now engaged front and rear.

During this desultory fusillade, the baggage belonging to the French division debouched from the already described outlet. The whole of the enemy's escort huddled together, and made a most desperate resistance amidst the rocks, while their affrighted animals ran loose, and were seen on the highest pinnacles of precipices. Nearly the whole fell into our hands, besides three hundred wounded and prisoners. The position of the division became singular after the fight, with its centre at the village St. Millan, and keeping a look-out to the front and rear. The enemy had also attacked the left of our army, near Osma, in hopes that, by causing such a delay, it would enable these two brigades, marching from Frias, to form a junction with their main body.

On the 19th, we moved forward, and at about ten o'clock in the morning, part of the fourth division became engaged with the light troops of the enemy. Our division then made a short *détour*, and turned the left of the French, who precipitately retired towards Vittoria. The next day we halted, and the army took up a line on the river Bayas, after long and arduous marching. The Duke of Wellington approached the river Zadora, which covered the enemy's position, for the purpose of examining the ground they occupied, and pointing out to different generals the various debouches, and their necessary line of attack in the event of the French continuing to occupy the same ground on the following day.

On the 21st, we stood to our arms, and moved forward in darkness some time before daybreak. A heavy shower of rain fell; but, as morning dawned, the clouds dispersed, and the sun arose with fiery splendour. A towering and steep ridge of mountains ascended abruptly from the valley on our right, which the Spaniards climbed early in the morning at first unopposed. The ascent was so steep, that, while moving up it, they looked as if they were lying on their faces, or crawling. They were supported, and soon followed across the river Zadora, and through the town of Puebla de Arlanzon, by part of the second division, for the purpose of attacking the left of the enemy, who were posted on the heights above Puebla de Arlanzon and Sabijana de Alva, where the contest began, at nine o'clock, amongst deep ravines, rocks, and precipices. The second division becoming heavily engaged with the enemy under all these disadvantages, it could only maintain the ground already won, and the firing seemed to die away in that quarter. Our right centre, composed of the light and fourth divisions, continued to advance, as also the great bulk of our cavalry. At about ten o'clock, on ascending a rising ground, we observed the French army drawn out in order of battle, in two lines, their right centre resting on a round hill, their left centre occupying a gentle ascent, and their left hid from view on the heights of Puebla. The river Zadora ran at the foot of this formidable position, and then took a sudden turn, embracing and running parallel to their right flank, towards Vittoria.

El Rey Joseph, surrounded by a numerous staff, was stationary on the hill, overlooking his own right and centre.* The French army was unmasked, without a bush to prevent the sweeping of their artillery, the charging of their cavalry, or the fire of their musketry, acting with full effect on those who should attempt to pass the bridges in their front, and which it was absolutely necessary to carry before we could begin the action in the centre. When within a short distance of the

* "Wellington chose an eminence in front of the village of Arinez, commanding the right bank of the Zadora, and continued there observing the progress of the fight, and directing the movements of the divisions, as calmly as if he were inspecting the movements of a review."—MAXWELL's LIFE OF WELLINGTON.

river, five of the French light horse advanced on the main road to look-out, and were overtaken by an equal number of our dragoons, when they wheeled about and attempted to make off, without effect; they were assailed on the near side, when three instantly fell from their saddles, covered with sabre wounds, and their affrighted horses gallopped at random.

The light division left the road when within one mile of the river, and drew up in contiguous close columns behind some shelving rocks near Olabarre, with the hussar brigade dismounted on the left; the fourth division made a corresponding movement, by branching off to the right, and took post opposite their intended point of attack; the greater part of our heavy cavalry and dragoons remained in reserve, to succour the central divisions, in case the enemy should advance before the third and seventh divisions should have taken up their ground on the enemy's right flank. The first and fifth divisions, with two brigades of Portuguese, a Spanish division, and two brigades of dragoons, were making a *détour* from Mergua, to place themselves on the line of the enemy's retreat, towards St. Sebastian; the sixth division remained some leagues in the rear of our army to guard the stores at Medina. General Clausel's division was manœuvring on our right, but not sufficiently near on this day to give much cause of apprehension.

All the movements of our army required the nicest calculations, both for the attack and defence; for at this time the four great columns advancing were separated by difficult rocks and a rugged country, interspersed with deep gulleys, narrow roads, and scattered hamlets. The enemy were again under the painful necessity, for the third time in one month, of manœuvring on two sides of the square; and the first cannon fired by Lord Lynedoch, at Abechucho and Gamarra Major,* must have been to Joseph and Marshal Jourdan, (his Major-General,) like a shock of electricity: all in an instant was riot and confusion in the Vittoria; the baggage stuck fast, blocking up all the roads, and even the fields.

At half-past eleven o'clock the Duke of Wellington led the way by a hollow road, followed by the light division, which he placed unobserved amongst some trees, exactly opposite the enemy's right centre, and within two hundred yards of the village of Villoses, which we understood was to be carried at the point of the bayonet. I felt anxious to obtain a view, and, leisurely walking between the trees, I found myself at the edge of the wood, and within a very short distance of the enemy's cannon, planted with lighted matches ready to apply to them. Had the attack begun here, the French never could have stood to their guns so near the thicket; otherwise, the riflemen would have annihilated them. The General-in-chief was now most anxiously looking out for the third and seventh divisions to make their appearance. We

* We could not see the extreme right of the enemy stationed near the Arunnez, in front of Abechucho and Gamarra Major.

had remained some time in the wood, when a Spanish peasant told the Duke of Wellington, that the enemy had left one of the bridges across the Zadora unprotected, and offered his services to lead us over it. Our right brigade instantly moved to its left by threes, at a rapid pace, along a very uneven and circuitous path, which was concealed from the observation of the French by high rocks; and reached the narrow bridge which crossed the river to Yruna. The first Rifles led the way, and the whole brigade following, passed at a run, with firelocks and rifles ready cocked, and ascended a steep road of fifty yards, at the top of which was an old chapel, which we had no sooner cleared, than we observed a heavy column of French on the principal hill, and commanding a bird's eye view of us; however, fortunately, a convex bank formed a sort of *tête de pont*, behind which the regiments formed at full speed without any word of command. Two round shots came amongst us; the second severed the head from the body of our bold guide the Spanish peasant. The soldiers were so well concealed, that the enemy ceased firing. Our post was most extraordinary, as we were at the elbow of the French position, and isolated from the rest of the army, within one hundred yards of the enemy's advance, and absolutely occupying part of their position on the left of the river, without any attempt being made by them to dislodge us. Scarcely the sound of a shot, from any direction, struck on the ear, and we were in momentary expectation of being immolated; and, as I looked over the bank, I could see El Rey Joseph, surrounded by at least five thousand men, within five hundred yards of us. The reason he did not attack is inexplicable, and, I think, cannot be accounted for by the most ingenious narrator.

Major-General Sir James Kempt expressed much wonder at our critical position, without being molested, and sent his aid-de-camp at speed across the river for the 15th Hussars, who came forward singly and at a gallop up the steep path, and dismounted in rear of our centre. The French dragoons coolly, and at a very slow pace, came within fifty yards, to examine, if possible, the strength of our force, when a few shots from the rifles induced them to decamp. I observed three bridges, within a quarter of a mile of each other, at the elbow of the enemy's position. We had crossed the centre one, while the other two, right and left, were still occupied by the French artillery; at the latter, the enemy had thrown up an earth entrenchment.

We continued in this awkward state of suspense for half an hour, when we observed the centre of the enemy drawing off by degrees towards Vittoria, and also the head of the third division rapidly debouching from some rocks on our left near Mendoza, when the battery at Tres Puentes opened upon them, which was answered by two guns from the horse artillery on the right of the river. Some companies of the rifle corps sprang from the ground, where they lay concealed, and darted forward, opening a galling fire on the left flank of the enemy's gunners, at great risk to themselves of being driven into the water, as the river ran on their immediate left, while the French cavalry hovered on their right; however, so well did this gallant band apply their loose balls, that the enemy limbered up their guns, and hastily retired; and the third division, at a run, crossed the bridge of Tres Puentes, cheering, but unopposed.*

The enemy withdrew the artillery from the bridges in their centre at two o'clock P.M., and were forming across the high road to Vittoria. The third division had no sooner closed up in contiguous columns than Sir Thomas Picton led them forward in very handsome style in column by a flank movement, so as to place them exactly opposite the French centre. The fourth division directly after crossed the river by the bridge of Nanclara, and were hurrying forward to support the right flank of the third division; the seventh

* The French did not defend any of the seven bridges across the Zadora, except the two, North and N.N.E. near Vittoria, although it was their original intention to do so. The able manœuvres of the general-in-chief threw the French generals into doubt: they knew not whether to defend their left, their right, or their centre, so they gave up one after the other, in conformity to the threatened attacks of the Duke of Wellington. Which was exactly what he wished, and most accommodating of his opponents, leaving this intended great battle without beginning or without end; for the French infantry were not half beaten, before disjointed orders and crowds of baggage blocking up the different roads, completed their confusion past all remedy.

division also crossed the bridge of Tres Puentes, supported by the second brigade of the light division, and faced the small village of Marganta. Our heavy horse and dragoons had deployed into line, on the other side of the river, so as to communicate with the rear of the second division, (in the event of their being driven back from the mountains,) or to support the centre of the army in case of any disaster. They made a brilliant display of golden helmets and sparkling swords glittering in the rays of the sun.

Three divisions being in motion, the centre and left supported by the light division, and the Hussar brigade, the battle began by a terrible discharge on the third division, while they were deploying into line. We closed up to them, behind a bank; when with loud huzzas they rushed from behind it, into the village of Ariyez, with fixed bayonets, amidst flashing small arms and rolling artillery, and after a bloody struggle, carried it. The enemy's artillery was within two hundred yards of us, ploughing up the ground in our rear: fortunately, the bank nearly covered us, during the time it was necessary to remain inactive, to support the front attack if needful. A Portuguese regiment, attached to our brigade, had been detached for a short time, and rejoined in close column; but just before they reached the cover, some round shot tore open their centre, and knocked over many men; and such was the alarm of a Portuguese officer, by the whizzing of balls and bursting of field shells, that he fell into an officer's arms, weeping bitterly. For ten minutes at this point, what with dust and smoke, it was impossible to distinguish any objects in front, save the shadows of the French artillerymen serving the guns, and the shouts of troops while forcing their way into the village. The smoke had no sooner cleared away, than we came on the bodies of many dead and gasping soldiers stretched in the dust. The sharp fire of musketry and artillery in the centre, announced it to be the point of contest. The advance of the second division had been severely handled on the mountains to our right, but they were now getting on as speedily as the nature of the ground would admit; it being composed of deep ravines, and such natural obstacles, as almost to delay their progress unopposed.

The first and fifth divisions were engaged at Gamarra Major and Abechucho, in front of the bridges over the Zadora. The villages were carried after a smart action, by which a position was gained, threatening the enemy's line of retreat by the high road to France, running N.N.E. some distance close on the left of the river. The bridge was attempted, but was found to be impracticable, until our centre had forced the enemy to give up Vittoria. The different divisions in the centre were exposed to a desultory fire, while passing the villages of Gomecha and Luazu de Alva, and over broken ground, forming lines, columns, or threading the windings of difficult paths, according to the nature of the country, or the opposition of the enemy. The fourth division pushed back the left centre of the French, and were fighting successfully, and performing prodigies of valour, among crags and broken ground. The seventh division now came in contact with the enemy's right centre, which resisted so desperately, and galled them from a wood and the windows of houses with such showers of bullets, that victory for a short time was doubtful; however, the second brigade of the light division coming up fresh and with closed ranks, assisted by the seventh division, broke through all opposition at a run, and routed the enemy at the point of the bayonet. The four divisions of the centre continued to gain ground, shooting forward alternately, leaving the killed and wounded scattered over a great extent of country. At six o'clock in the evening, by a sort of running fight, with hard contests at certain points, the centre of the army had gained five miles in this amphitheatre. For Lord Hill's corps was on the mountains, and Lord Lynedoch was still on the right of the Zadora.

The Duke of Wellington was in the middle of the battle, vigorously driving the enemy, to finish that which the wings had so well begun: first, Lord Hill's movement in the morning caused the enemy to weaken his left centre; then Lord Lynedoch's attack induced them to give up the front line of the Zadora without hardly a shot being fired. At half-past six we were within one mile of Vittoria, situated in a fruitful valley, when the French army now drew up, and shewed such an imposing front, that our left centre, facing Ali, were completely kept at bay, owing to the blazing of one hundred pieces of cannon vomiting forth death and destruction to all who advanced against them. This roaring of artillery continued for more than an hour on both sides with unabated vigour: the smoke rolled up in such clouds, that we could no longer distinguish the white town of Vittoria; the liquid fire marked the activity of the French gunners. During this momentous struggle, the left centre of the French covered a bare hill, and continued for a considerable time immoveable; while, pouring their musketry into the now thinned ranks of the third division, it was doubtful whether the latter would be able to keep their ground, under such a deadly fire from very superior numbers: however, they maintained this dangerous post with heroic firmness, having led the van throughout the thick of the battle. At this period of the action, it was absolutely necessary to strain every nerve to win it before nightfall. The fourth division, on our right, shot forward against a sugar-loaf hill, and broke a French division, who retired up it in a confused mass, firing over each other's heads, without danger to themselves, owing to the steepness of its ascent. I was laughing at this novel method of throwing bullets, when one struck me on the sash, and fell at my feet, thereby cooling my ardour for a short time: however, when a little recovered from the pain, I picked it up, and put the precious bit of lead into my pocket.

The scene that now presented itself was magnificently grand: the valley resounded with confused sounds like those of a volcanic eruption, and was crowded with red bodies of infantry and the smoking artillery, while the cavalry eagerly looked for an opening to gallop into the town. On one side of the field rose majestically the spiral and purple-capped mountains, rearing their pinnacles on high; on the other ran the glassy waters of the Zadora: the departing sun threw his last beams to light up the efforts of those struggling in dangerous strife for the deliverance of Spain. The enemy sacrificed all their cannon,* with the exception of eight pieces, while withdrawing the right of their army behind the left wing, under cover of this tremendous cannonade, which was the only chance yet left them to quit the field in a compact body. This movement being executed in strange confusion in and about Vittoria, their left wing retired by echelon of divisions and brigades from the right, while delivering their fire; and finally, their last division quitted the field with nearly empty cartridge-boxes, and taking the road towards Pamplona. The greater portion of our army then brought up its left shoulder, or rather wheeled the quarter circle to its right, which movement brought us on the road to Pamplona. The French managed to drag the eight pieces of artillery across the fields for nearly a league; but, coming to marshy ground, they stuck fast, and three of them rolled into a

* According to official returns of the artillery and ordnance stores captured at Vittoria, 151 brass guns, 415 caisons, 14,249 rounds of ammunition, 1,973,400 ball cartridges, 40,668 pounds of gunpowder, 56 forage wagons, and 44 baggage wagons, fell into the hands of the conquerors.—Ed.

ditch, with mules struggling to disentangle themselves from their harness. Two pieces the enemy carried clear out of the action, leaving their numerous cannon behind them, owing to the roads being so blocked up with wagons. The dark shades of evening had already veiled the distant objects from our view, and nothing of the battle remained, saving the lighting flashes of the enemy's small arms on our cavalry, who continued to hover and threaten their rear guard. The road to Pamplona was choked up with many carriages, filled with imploring ladies, wagons loaded with specie,* powder and ball, wounded soldiers, intermixed with droves of oxen, sheep, goats, mules, horses, asses, milch cows, *filles de chambre*, and officers. In fact, such a jumble surely never was witnessed before; it seemed as if all the domestic animals in the world had been brought to this spot, with all the utensils of husbandry, and all the finery of palaces, mixed up in one heterogeneous mass.

Our brigade marched past this strange scene (I may assert) of domestic strife in close column, nor did I see a soldier attempt to quit the ranks, or shew the most distant wish to do so; our second brigade had not yet joined us, when we bivouacked a league from Vittoria, on the road towards Pamplona. The half-famished soldiers had no sooner disencumbered themselves of their

* Some excesses were committed, although the greater part of the booty, as usual, was bagged by the followers of the army.

knapsacks, than they went to forage; for even here the sheep and goats were running about in all directions, and large bags of flour lay by the side of the road; in fact, for miles round the town, the great wreck of military stores was scattered in every direction.

Night put an end to the contest: the growling of artillery ceased, the enemy were flying in disorder, the British army bivouacked round Vittoria, large fires were kindled and blazed up, and illumined the country, over which were strewed the dead and suffering officers and soldiers: strange sounds continued throughout the night, and passing lights might be seen on the highest mountains and distant valleys.

ADVANCE FROM VITTORIA.

On the morning of the 22nd of June, 1813, the atmosphere was overcast, and being without either cloaks or blankets to cover us, our uniforms were very damp, owing to the heavy dew which had fallen during the night; notwithstanding, we arose from the ground exceedingly refreshed, and gazed around, in mute amazement, at the prodigious wreck of plundered Spain, for beneath the French caissons, tumbrils, and brass cannon, lay scattered *los doblones de oro, of the same virgin gold* which had been extracted in former times from the peaceful incas of the New World, by those vindictive Spanish adventurers, whose avaricious veins boiled at that epoch with the hot blood of the Moors.

At nine o'clock the rolling of the tenor and bass drums, and the clank of cymbals, beating the marching time, announced that the leading regiments of the division were in motion for the purpose of following the enemy. During the rest of the day we marched through a valley, enclosed by highlands, but did not overtake the enemy; the corn was trampled down in many places, which shewed they had moved in three columns, wherever the ground would admit of it. Soon after dark, the division bivouacked in a wood; a drizzling rain began to fall, and we lay down under a tree to enjoy a nap, until the arrival of our sumpter mules, heavily laden with flour and live stock, which we had industriously scraped together from the refuse of Vittoria's field. At midnight we were awoke, with keen appetites, by the well-known neighing of the horses, and braying of donkeys; but none of the baggage animals came our way, and during our anxious and broken slumbers the night passed away, and the morning was ushered in by a sweeping rain, which thoroughly saturated the troops before they began their march. As I chanced to be for the duty of bringing up any stragglers who might happen to lag behind, and my hungry messmate being also for the baggage guard, (of those who had come up,) we journeyed together along the sloppy road, when the conversation naturally turned on the splendid victory gained over the French legions two days before, and how gladdened the people of England would be on the receipt of such a piece of glorious intelligence, little imagining that the greater portion of the victors would willingly lay down half their laurels for a good breakfast. At the close of the evening we came to the remains of a French bivouac, consisting of doors and window shutters torn from a neighbouring village by the enemy, and propped up to screen them from the inclemency of the weather.

The sole person to be seen was a draggle-tailed old woman, with a ragged petticoat, who, without noticing us, or once raising her eyes, continued to pursue her interesting employment in stirring up the mud with a stick, (which was interspersed with fragments of books and French novels,) or handling the broken fragments of earthenware pots. Our curiosity was so much excited, that we reined in our steeds to watch the progress of the wrinkled and copper-coloured old dame, who, stretching out her bronzed and shrivelled arm, at last laid hold of a whole utensil, and, as she hastily splashed off, I caught a glimpse of a chicken, resting on one leg, behind a shutter, which somehow or other had escaped the ramrod of the enemy, and the hawk-eyed soldiers of the pursuing column. Unsheathing my sabre, I jumped to the ground, and sprang forward either to grasp or maim the destined prize; however, the ground was in such a slimy state, that my speed availed not; on the contrary, it hastened my fall. My companion, disdaining to take warning at my mishap, must needs himself begin a hot pursuit; however, the practical part soon convinced him of the slippery obstacles, as he soon lay sprawling on his face, plastered with mire: suffice, the bird escaped, and we resumed our wet saddles, in a condition and appearance nowise enviable. Soon after dark we came to a river, but, as the enemy had not had a sufficient time to blow up the bridge, they had set fire to many of the houses in the main street of the town, (which were still in flames,) in hopes of blocking up the way with the burning rafters, which they had hurled from the roofs of the houses, with the object of preventing our artillery from passing through, and harassing their retreat. The rain, still falling in torrents, by degrees extinguished the red embers of the smoking ruins, and prevented the place from being entirely consumed to ashes. The soldiers of the division crowded the houses, and huddled under cover wherever they could find shelter. We were obliged to content and squeeze ourselves into a small hovel, where the smoke found egress through the broken roof; the floor was composed of slabs of rocks, in some places rearing their primitive heads amid flints and loose stones. During the night a ration of meat and six ounces of mouldy biscuit was served out, which was greedily devoured by the victorious troops. It was in vain that we scraped into a heap the stones of this Macadamized lodge, for the purpose of lying down; for bumps and holes only increased our difficulties, and we were forced to ascend a broken ladder into a wretched loft, swarming with vermin, to prick for a soft plank, whereon to stretch our chilly limbs.

At dawn, on the 24th, we were again on the road; the weather cleared up, and the cheerful rays of the sun sparkled in the crystal drops, which fell on our heads as we glided beneath the wet foliage. Having advanced a few miles, we found the enemy's rear-guard posted at a bare and steep pass, which covered the high-road, two leagues from Pamplona. The column having closed up, two battalions of the rifle corps (supported by the horse artillery*) pushed forward, and after a sharp skirmish, they succeeded in pushing back the French rear-guard; the guns then galloped up the road, and plied the round shot with such effect, that they succeeded in dismounting one of the only two cannon which the enemy had extricated from Vittoria's entangled field. They had rolled the gun over a steep bank on the right of the paved causeway, on which were regular league stones, and the first I had noticed in Spain. One round shot had struck down seven of the enemy on the left of the road; some of them were dead; others, still alive, with either legs or arms knocked off, or otherwise horribly mutilated, were crying out in extreme anguish, and imploring the soldiers to shoot them, to put an end to their dreadful sufferings. A German hussar, in our service, assured them that they would be kindly treated by our medical officers. "No, no!" they vociferated, "we cannot bear to live. Countryman, we are Germans, pray kill us and shorten our miseries." Continuing onwards, we soon after drew up on the slope of a hill, within sight of Pamplona,† the capital of Navarre; it is well fortified

* Lieutenant-Colonel Ross of the Horse Artillery, as usual, commanded this troop.

† Pamplona, the ancient Pompeiopolis, founded by Pompey the Great, and consequently a place of much antiquity, is,

with a strong citadel, and situated near the banks of the river Arga, in a fertile plain abounding with wheat, the ears of which we rubbed between our hands to satisfy the cravings of hunger. Just before our arrival the enemy's scattered army had clustered beneath the ramparts of the fortress, where they were in hopes of entering to obtain rest and provisions; but the place was so scantily supplied that the gates were ordered to be barred against all intruders. From this place an excellent road branches off in a north-westerly direction to Tolosa; but as Lord Lynedoch, with his corps, was marching direct on that town, by the great road to France, it was of no avail to the main body of the enemy, who were obliged to continue their retreat into France by Roncesvalles and other roads, merely leaving a rear-guard in the valley of Bastan.

The following morning we filed over a rugged and flinty mountain, south-west of Pamplona, from the summit of which we almost commanded a bird's-eye view into the very heart of the town, garrisoned by four thousand of the enemy. This place, well-provisioned, should have been fixed on for the grand base of Joseph's defensive and offen-

in modern days, an extensive city, and one of the strongest fortified places in the Peninsula. Situated on a perfect level, it is not commanded by any domineering ground. The citadel, built at the southern extremity of the works, is from the exterior scarcely perceptible, the parapets being level with the surrounding plain, and consequently, in a great measure, it is protected from the effects of breaching batteries.—ED.

sive movements; for had he made it the pivot of his operations, and opened his line on Aragon, (and the strong holds in Catalonia, held by the Duke of Albufera,) his flanks would have been secured by the Ebro and the Pyrenees, and have thrown our army on two sides of a square, entangled between two strong fortresses and the labyrinths of the Pyrenees. Most probably such a movement would have kept the war from the immediate frontier of France, whence fresh troops, under favourable circumstances, could debouch and attack our left face, as from political reasons the time had not arrived for the decided invasion of that country; besides, if it had, such an invasion could not have been executed, so long as the enemy hovered in force on our right flank.

Continuing our route, we crossed the Arga and entered the town of Villalba: our baggage at last came up, and the Casa in which we were quartered was enclosed by a good garden, well stocked with vegetables, which was considered a piece of good fortune in those days. This day, the 25th, Lord Lynedoch overtook General Foy, retiring from the vicinity of Bilboa, who, on hearing of the unhappy extent of the French disasters at Vittoria, made an effort to block up the passage through Tolosa, but the victorious English broke through all obstacles, and continued to advance. In a few days the small garrison of Passages surrendered themselves prisoners; thus it was that the left wing of the army had hardly halted since issuing from the bowels of Portugal, until the precipitous bank of the river

Bidassoa (which divided France and Spain) put a stop for a time to its memorable march and victorious career.

On the 26th, we had an idea that we should halt, but during the day we were again under arms, marching by an excellent road running S.S.E. leading direct on Tafalla, accompanied by the third and fourth divisions, with a proportion of cavalry and artillery to endeavour to cut off General Clausel's corps, which had approached Vittoria the day after the battle; but he also being made acquainted with the total rout of El Rey Joseph, immediately countermarched on Logrono, thence to Tudella;* during the movements of the right and left wings of the British army, Lord Hill, with the centre, showed front, and masked Pamplona.

The weather now cleared up, but continued variable during the whole summer, the seasons here being totally different from the dry and scorching heats in the more southern provinces, where the sun-burnt mountains and vast plains are covered, at this time of the year, with a parched vegetation, or the remains of many cindered forests.

Continuing our movement we became once again extricated from the mountainous regions, which

* Where he gained information of our movements, which forced him to follow the right bank of the Ebro, until he reached Saragossa, where, crossing the river, and leaving a small garrison behind, he moved towards the pass of Jaca, and entering France on the first of July, he at last succeeded, after a round-about march, with the loss of the greater part of his *materiel*, in forming a junction with the French army.

had every where enclosed us for more than a fortnight. The country was now open, and highly cultivated, with groups of bold peasantry lining each side of the way, and greeting us by crying, *Viva los Coluros, y viva el Réy Fernando séptimo;* and while moving in the direction of Tudella, our enthusiastic hopes were raised to the highest pitch, at the probability of reaching the venerable and renowned city of Saragossa; but our line was all at once changed, and by a forced march we entered the province of Aragon, passing through a barbarous-looking country, barely peopled, the forlorn *Pueblos* lying wide asunder, the poor dwellings being mostly constructed of dried mud, and plastered over with the same substance; at the expiration of five days we reached Sanguessa, and encamped. Here we halted one day,* and while promenading the town in the evening, the soft notes of music floated in the air, and on a nearer approach to the place whence the sounds issued, we were agreeably saluted by the scraping and cheerful notes of violins. A crowd of Spaniards had assembled round the door of the *Casa,* and on being questioned by another officer and myself whether the ball was public, "Oh si señores," an-

* There was a great scarcity of wood in the neighbourhood of this place, and as the third division followed ours, Sir T. Picton cast his eye on a pile ready cut, and as soon as he had dismissed his division, sent a regular party, with a *val,* to secure it, when, lo, it had vanished! The gallant general being informed of the circumstance, exclaimed, in a laughing tone,—" Oh! I had forgot that we were so near the plundering light division."

swered they, "es muy público," so, bustling up the stone steps, and feeling our way along a dark passage, we found ourselves, on opening a massive door, amongst many señoritas, with a scarcity of cavalleros. A staff-officer who was the promoter of the dance, expressed his gladness at so opportune an arrival. Although a friend, we apologized to him for the apparent intrusion; but he was a man of no ceremony, and declared it to be a lucky mistake, which turned out to be the case, for we beat good waltz time during the whole night, to the great satisfaction of the señoritas, and on reaching the camp the following morning the tents were already struck, and the troops moving off on their return to Pamplona. What with the overpowering rays of the sun, the rising clouds of dust, and our overnight's exertion, we were so overcome, that had it not been for the kindly arms of the soldiers, we should have dropped from off our horses, while fast asleep, dreaming of black-eyed señoras, waltzing, and precipices.

In two days we reached Pamplona by a more direct road, but the men began to flag, owing to irregular and poor feeding; besides which, we had been marching for thirty-two days, with only two regular halts, since quitting our camp between Toro and Salamanca; therefore, those plagued and suffering from sore feet, were under the painful necessity (unless totally unable to proceed) of going on until they got well again. I have often seen the blood soaking through the gaiters, and over the heels of the soldiers' hard shoes, whitened with the dust.

PENINSULAR SKETCHES. 65

The general-in-chief having cleared his right flank, and again condensed his right and centre round Pamplona, he debouched thence on the 4th July, for the purpose of taking possession of the passes of the Western Pyrenees, and pushing the enemy's van-guard out of the valley of Bastan into France, which was executed by part of the second division on the 7th. Our division, forming the left centre of the army, flanked this movement. Our route at first lay through verdant and luxuriant valleys, abounding with apple orchards, groves of chesnut trees, and small fields of Indian corn; from thence we ascended by broken roads, over rugged mountains, which were cracked in many places, into vast chasms, overhung with oak trees of enormous magnitude, whose ponderous and wide spreading branches cast their dark shadows over the dried water-courses and natural grottoes, formed by the intricate mazes of the underwood, entwining around the peaked and overhanging rocks. The third day, after leaving Pamplona, we descended from the mountains into the compact little town of St. Estevan, situated on the rocky and woody bank of the clear stream of the Bidassoa, over which a good stone bridge communicates with the opposite side of the river: here we halted, with full leisure to explore the lovely scenery, which on every side encircled this secluded valley. Our curiosity was much excited by the peculiar method of washing in this part of the country, the women squatting, or rather sitting on their bare heels, with their lower garments tightly pulled about them, whilst others stood in the river rinsing the linen, with their only petticoat tied in a knot very high up betwixt their legs, displaying the most perfect symmetry; and it was morally impossible to refrain from admiring the natural and graceful forms of these nymphs.

The dress of the Basque peasantry is totally different from other provinces, and many of the females possess very fair complexions, and are extremely beautiful, being a happy mixture of *las brunas y las blondas;* their hair is combed back without any curls, and plaited into a long tail, which hangs down below the hips; their jackets are of blue or brown cloth, and pinned so exceedingly tight across the breast, that the bosom seldom swells to any size; the only woollen petticoat worn by them is of a light or mixed colour, reaching to the middle of the calf of the leg; and, with the exception of the bosom being so compressed, they are divinely formed, and are remarkably nimble of foot, and always carry their little merchandise on the top of the head; they seldom wear shoes or stockings, except on Sundays and saints' days.

The males go bare-necked, and wear a blue cap, or bonnet, precisely similar to those worn in the highlands of Scotland, with bushy hair hanging in ringlets on their shoulders. In hot weather they usually carry the short blue, or brown jacket, slung over the left shoulder, and with long and rapid strides, or at times, breaking into a short run, they traverse the steep acclivities with their shoes and stockings frequently slung on a long pole, which they either carry sloped over the shoulder, or grasped in the middle like a javelin, and used for the purpose of assisting them in scaling or descending the crags, or frightful precipices. Their waistcoats are double-breasted, without a collar; the breeches are of brown cloth, or blue velveteen, fitting tight over the hips, (without braces,) and reaching to the cap of the knee, where they are usually unbuttoned, to give full play to the limbs. A red sash is twisted round the loins. They are a gaunt, sinewy, and remarkably active race of men, of sallow complexions; their limbs are admirably proportioned, and they are as upright as a dart.

After a rest of two days, we marched towards Vera by a narrow road, running parallel on the right bank of the Bidassoa, the greater part of the way being blocked up with large stones, or fragments of rock, which had tumbled from the overhanging cliffs, rent in many places into terrific chasms, partly choked with huge trunks or roots of trees, through which overwhelming torrents gushed from the mountains during the heavy rains, forming vast cataracts, and often swelling the river into a foaming and angry torrent; its rocky bed is fordable at this time of the year, and varies from thirty to more than a hundred yards in breadth. Owing to the badness of the road, a company of infantry was employed in clearing away obstacles, or lifting the wheels of the cannon, with handspikes, over the loose fragments or projecting slabs of rock, which at every few paces impeded their progress for three leagues. During the march we passed near the bridges of Sunbilla, Yanzi, and Lazaca, which cross the river to where some Spanish sentinels were posted on the cliffs, who called out to us, " *Mira ustedes, mira los Franceses,*" and, on casting our eyes upwards, we observed three of the enemy's *chasseurs à cheval,* looking down on us as if from the clouds: part of the division had been already detached, for the purpose of keeping a look-out up the narrow road to the right leading to the heights of Etchalar. Just before we reached the mouth of this contracted defile, a buzz from the head of the column proclaimed the enemy's infantry to be at hand, and the musketry had no sooner commenced than an officer, who had been amusing himself by the perusal of a volume of *Gil Blas,* hastily placed it under the breast of his grey pelisse; almost at the same instant a musket ball buried itself in the middle of the book, and displaced him from his horse, without inflicting any further injury; it is a curious fact, that the exact pattern of the silk braiding of the pelisse* was indented in the leaden bullet. Our front being speedily cleared of the enemy's skirmishers, the firing ceased, and we entered a pleasant valley, within half a mile of Vera,

---

* Many of the officers of our corps wore red and grey pelisses, similar to those of the hussars. The bullet which I have described was afterwards shewn as a curiosity, and I examined it myself; the silk braiding had been carried into the compressed leaves of the book, and remained twisted tight round the ball.

which on this road is the frontier town of Spain, and is situated at an elbow, on the right bank of the Bidassoa: it has a good church with a lofty steeple, and consists of one long straggling street, a quarter of a mile in length, and immediately at the foot of the mountain De Comissari, over which a steep road, three yards broad, crosses the summit, which is called the *puerto de Vera*, and leads N.N.E. to St. Jean de Luz, in France; two other roads, if they may be so designated, branch off right and left from Vera, the first running easterly along the valley, (parallel with a small rivulet which empties itself into the Bidassoa,) and passes between the great rock of La Rhune and the opposite mountain of St. Bernard, to St. Barbe and Sarré, into France; at this point the rugged defile is very narrow, and almost causes a complete break or separation in the Western Pyrenees. The other road from Vera runs across the Bidassoa, over a narrow stone bridge, four hundred yards from the town, to Salines, thence branching off through gloomy forests, and over steep mountains to Oyarzun, Passages, and St. Sebastian.

From Salines there is also a narrow rugged pathway, which traverses N.N.W. by the winding current, on the left bank of the Bidassoa. It is intersected with loose stones, and in many places ascends the steep and difficult declivities over the naked rock, and finally enters the great road beyond Irun, which leads across the Bidassoa (where the enemy had broken down the bridge) into France, thence passing over the Nivelle to

St. Jean de Luz, and on to Bayonne, a distance of about twenty-four miles from Irun, which is the frontier town of Spain by that route.

The right of the enemy immediately opposed to us, rested on a nearly perpendicular rock, at the elbow of the Bidassoa, and overlooking the small market-place of Vera; so much so, that, if inclined, they might have smashed the roofs of the houses at the west end of the town by rolling down upon them huge fragments of rock. This post was decorated with a variety of fancy flags, or strips of cloth, of various colours, tied at the top of long poles, while groups of French tirailleurs, who encircled them, sounded their small shrill trumpets, and jocosely invited us to the attack.

Their centre or reserve, composed of black columns, crowned the heights on each side of the Puerto de Vera, and also the wooded heights extending to the base of the rock of La Rhune, on which their left was stationed in an old ruin. The ground having been fully examined, and the pickets properly placed, we re-entered the mouth of the pass, and having cut down two or three small fields of Indian corn, and stored it up as provender for the animals, we encamped on the stubble close to the river. The day was fine, but during the night the rain descended in torrents, and continued to fall so heavily for two days as to swamp the ground on which our tents were pitched; and it was with the utmost exertion that we could keep them upright, owing to the frequent gusts of wind tearing the pegs out of the liquid mud. In these damp and chilly regions the tents proved of incalculable service to the army. The weather again clearing, our first brigade ascended the bare heights of Santa Barbara, the second brigade occupied a rising ground to protect the entrance of the defile leading to St. Estevan, and the pickets were pushed into the town of Vera, (within half a stone's throw, and beneath those of the enemy,) and into the farm houses in the valley, enclosed by orchards, which produce an abundance of small tart apples.

The stupendous and lofty chain of the Western Pyrenees being now taken up for the purpose of covering Pamplona and St. Sebastian, the second division occupied the various rugged paths and passes winding up the steep sides of the mountains near Roncesvalles and Maya; the seventh division those of Etchalar; the light division the heights of Santa Barbara, and the road leading to St. Estevan, opposite to Vera; and the first division and Spaniards guarding the left bank of the Bidassoa to the sea-coast. The latter troops helped to block up the numerous gaps all along the crest of the position, such as mountain paths, goat tracts, and dried water-courses, as well as the numerous fords across the Bidassoa. This extended position is about thirty-eight miles in extent as the crow flies, (running north-west from Roncesvalles to Fontarabia, which is situated near the mouth of the Bidassoa, where this river empties itself into the sea,) but necessarily following the rugged and zigzag flinty roads, along the winding or crooked valleys, or over difficult mountains, intersected with deep glens, chasms, craggy defiles, tremendous precipices, and through almost impenetrable forests, the distance may be fairly calculated at sixty miles for troops to march from right to left.

On the 13th, the Duke of Dalmatia came from the north for the purpose of taking the command of the French army.* The 15th being the anniversary of Napoleon's birth-day, the enemy at night illuminated their bivouack, by ingeniously festooning the branches of the trees by thousands of paper lamps, which produced a very bright glare, and of course presented a very novel appearance. Two days after this, the fifth division began to dig the trenches at St. Sebastian, for the purpose of erecting batteries to batter *en breche*. The third and fourth divisions, which had been kept in the neighbourhood of Pamplona in reserve, and also to assist the Spaniards in drawing a line of circumvallation round that place, for the purpose of hemming in and starving the garrison into a surrender, now moved forward, leaving a Spanish corps to guard the lines. The former went to

* "On the 1st of July, Soult was appointed lieutenant to the Emperor. His powers were plenary, amounting even to the removal of Joseph; and by force, if such an alternative should be required. That, however, *was unnecessary*. The fugitive monarch was weary of the mockery of a throne; and he willingly retired from the command of an army which had always been borne with dissatisfaction, and, under it, had experienced nothing but dishonour and defeat."—MAXWELL'S LIFE OF WELLINGTON.

Olaque, and the latter to Biscarret; the sixth division was at St. Estevan; these three divisions being the reserve, and ready to succour at those points where their assistance might be required. The cavalry and artillery were cantoned in rear of the centre and left of the whole army.

One evening, while reclining on the parched and sun-burnt turf at the tent-door, our milch goat nibbling particles of hard biscuit out of my hand, on looking round, I was much struck with the beauty of the scenery. The azure sky was reddened, and glowing with a variety of brilliant tints, reflected from the glare of the setting sun, whose bright rays gilded the rugged peaks of the towering and great bulging mountains which everywhere enclosed us; a long line of grey-coated French sentinels lined the opposite ridge, and one of their bands was playing a lively French air. In the valley below us, the little active Basque boys and girls were pelting each other with apples* between the hostile armies, while

* This was a usual pastime amongst them throughout the mountains, which abounded with vast quantities of apple trees. One day another officer and myself were enjoying a rural walk, when we met two of our friends, whom, for amusement, we pelted with apples, and drove them at full speed out of the orchard. All of a sudden we were assailed by a number of the Basque boys, led on by a girl, who had witnessed our sport at a distance; and although we piqued ourselves as being pretty good throwers, we found it a difficult matter to contend with them, from their dexterity in dealing out such irritating blows on our faces and legs; and being ashamed to ask for quarter of such diminutive and

the straggling and half-starved Spanish soldiers (who dare not pluck the fruit) pretended to enjoy the sport, but in reality were picking up the apples, and carefully depositing them in their small forage bags. In the back ground sat our tanned and veteran batman,* employed in mending a pack-saddle after a long day's forage, and casting an eye of affection towards his animals, which were tied round a stake, feeding, with ears turned back, on some fresh heads of Indian corn.

In the meanwhile my messmate was conversing with, and drawing a caricature of, a dowdy woman,† (from the Asturias,) loaded with an oblong

---

laughing antagonists, we made a last effort, and succeeded in hitting one of their leaders on the bare heel, when they all ran away, to our exceeding satisfaction. My companion had been a cadet at the Royal Military College at Marlow, and declared that he had never experienced a warmer rencontre in his more juvenile affrays at that place.

* The batmen of the army were hard-working and privileged characters, and after unloading at the end of harassing marches, they were obliged to go a great distance in search of forage, (armed with a sickle,) ready to cut down even rushes or any thing they could lay their hands upon, for their famished animals. If all happened to be right, after a long day's journey, when questioned by the anxious officers, (no matter of what rank,) they would negligently turn away, and scarcely give any answer; but if one of their horses or mules happened to be lame, or suffering from a sore back, or had cast a shoe, they would fret, fume, curse, swear, throw the ropes about, and give such a catalogue of evils, as to terrify the master that all was going to rack and ruin.

† These hardy women are in the habit, thus heavily loaded, of walking thirty or forty miles a day.

basket of fresh butter, with her arms akimbo, and her nut-brown knuckles resting on hips which supported no less than four short, coarse, woollen petticoats; from underneath branched out a pair of straddling legs of enormous circumference, the feet being wrapped in brown hairy skins, by way of sandals. My contemplative mood was all at once interrupted by an officer of the rifle corps riding up, who, with a mysterious air, whispered me, by way of a profound secret, that he had become acquainted with a Spanish family, residing in the town of Vera, and offered to introduce me, provided that I would agree to limit my attention to the eldest daughter, *Maria Pera*, who he acknowledged was endowed with very ordinary attractions, whereas her sister, *Ventura*, of seventeen, possessed charms of a far superior description. As a matter of course, not wishing to throw any impediments in the way of so liberal an offer, I readily acquiesced in the proposal, and forthwith accompanied him to the destined casa; for such I may justly nominate it, as I may affirm that this introduction was subsequently the means of the life of a wounded brother officer being preserved, owing to the kind attentions of its inmates, who watched over his mattress night and day, until he was out of danger; his hurt was so severe, that when a doctor was asked how he found the patient, he replied, "Pretty well; but no man can ever recover from such a wound."

On alighting from our horses we entered the house, and having ascended the staircase, we found *el padre, el madre, y las dos hijas* seated in a spacious apartment, with the casements open, and a French sentinel, who was posted on a projecting grey rock, so thoroughly overlooking the house, that we could almost fancy he could overhear the lamentations of the anxious parents, who, devoutly crossing themselves, prayed that the siege of St. Sebastian might be speedily brought to a conclusion, to enable them to return to their house at that place, and secure the valuable plate and property, which they had been forced to abandon in great haste, to escape being confined in that town during the siege. Having passed some hours with them in a very agreeable manner, we took our departure, with a promise of shortly renewing our visit.

The left and main body of the French army being now concentrated on a line at the foot of the Pyrenees, in the vicinity of Forage and St. Jean Pied de Port in France, with its right wing occupying the mountains from the Rock of La Rhune to Vera, thence by the right of the Bidassoa to Andaye, and flanked by the Bay of Biscay—(this ridge immediately covers the country in front of St. Jean de Luz and Bayonne)—preparatory to offensive movements, the French marshal issued a flaming proclamation to his troops, in which he reminded them that the standards of Britain waved aloft, and that its army, from the summits of the Pyrenees, proudly looked down on the fertile fields of France, an evil which he attributed to the want of decision in the late French commanders. " Let us, then," said the marshal, " wipe the stain off our faded laurels, by chasing the English beyond Vittoria, and there celebrate another triumph to the many victories which have so often decorated your brows, in all parts of Spain, and on many a hard-fought day."

THE BATTLES OF THE PYRENEES.

THE Duke of Dalmatia, on the 25th of July, 1813, assaulted the passes in the neighbourhood of Roncesvalles,* and the Count d'Erlon that of Aretesque, four miles in front of Maya. The result of this day's combat obliged Generals Sir L. Cole, Byng, and Morrillo, to fall back from Roncesvalles; owing to this retrograde, the British army were taken in reverse. The fifth division at daybreak had stormed the breaches of St. Sebastian without success, two thousand men had fallen, or were made prisoners at the various points of contest; and Lord Hill fell back during the night from the pass of Maya. So far everything seemed propi-

* Pamplona is thirty-five miles from the extremity of the principal pass at Roncesvalles, forty-five from that of Aretesque in front of Maya, and fifty-five *miles from the* pass of Vera: all these points it was necessary to occupy on the right of the Bidassoa, which clearly demonstrates the advantage the enemy possessed by attacking principally at Roncesvalles.

tious to the views of the French Marshal. Under all these circumstances, General Campbell, (who was stationed with a Portuguese brigade at the pass of Los Alduides,) finding his flanks laid bare, retired from that post, and during the 26th formed a junction with General Sir T. Picton, who, by a flank movement to the right, had marched from Olacque to Lizoain, for the purpose of succouring the troops falling back from Roncesvalles.

During these operations, Lord Hill had taken up a strong position at Irrueta, sixteen miles from the pass of Aretesque, where he opposed for the time being the further progress of the Count d'Erlon. This position covered the flank of Sir T. Picton's column retrograding from Zubiri, and prevented the Count d'Erlon from uniting with the Duke of Dalmatia, and also enabled the sixth division to march direct to the rear from San Estevan, and to unite at the well-arranged point *d'appui*.

Five miles in front of Pamplona, where, on the 27th, the General-in-Chief joined those troops which had retired from Zubiri under the command of Sir T. Picton, Generals Sir L. Cole, Byng, Campbell, and Morrillo, were drawn up on a strong ridge in front of Pamplona, and flanked by the rivers Arga and Lanz. Sir T. Picton was in a manner thrown back on the left of the Arga, in front of Olaz, and supported by Lord Combermere with the cavalry in reserve, for the purpose of preventing the enemy from taking the right of the army in reverse by the road from Zubiri. The enemy, who had followed the march of the troops by that road, had no sooner arrived opposite the third division, than by an oblique prolongation to their right, they began to extend their line across the front of the General-in-Chief under a fire of small-arms, by which manœuvre they succeeded in cutting off Lord Hill's retreat by the Maya road running through Ortiz; he therefore, having passed through Lanz, edged off diagonally in a westerly direction, and by an oblique march formed a junction with the seventh division (from St. Estevan) at Lizasso, thence to co-operate, if possible, with the left of the General-in-Chief, whose position in front of Pamplona was about eighteen miles from that place. During these various movements, Lord Lynedoch, with the first and fifth divisions and a corps of Spaniards, remained stationary on the left bank of the Bidassoa, for the double purpose of covering St. Sebastian (the siege of that place was now converted into a blockade, and the battering train embarked at the port of los Passages,) and watching General Villate, who lined the opposite bank of the river, to be in readiness to assume the offensive, for the purpose of raising the siege of St. Sebastian, or hanging on Lord Lynedoch's rear, in the event of the Duke of Dalmatia gaining a victory at Pamplona, or succeeding in cutting off in detail the various divisions of the British army, now thrown into echelon, and extending from the banks of the Bidassoa in front of Irun, to seven miles in an easterly direction beyond Pamplona;

a distance of at least seventy miles for the army to unite to either flank (between two fortresses, whose ramparts were garnished with the cannon and small-arms of the enemy,) on an irregular quarter circle: amid multifarious barren rocks, towering mountains, and extensive forests, over whose inhospitable regions it was necessary amongst other things to convey provisions, ammunition, and biscuit bags, for the daily consumption of the moveable divisions, an operation attended with great difficulty under such circumstances. Although the right of the army had been retiring for two days, the light division still tranquilly remained unmolested in front of Vera; but on the morning of the 27th, on finding that the seventh division had quitted the heights of Echalar and uncovered our right flank, the first brigade quietly descended from the heights of Santa Barbara, and the whole division concentrated behind the defile on the road to Lazaca, the pickets being left to mask this movement and form the rear-guard. As soon as the division had got clear off, the pickets evacuated the farm-houses in succession from the right, and lastly, at ten o'clock, A.M., quitted the town of Vera within pistol-shot of the enemy's sentinels; who pretended not to notice this retrograde, probably being apprehensive of bringing on an action without being able at this point to display a sufficient force to assume offensive movements, and also conjecturing that the division might meet with a reception little anticipated on reaching the neighbourhood of Pamplona. The

Duke of Dalmatia at this moment was still pursuing the troops from Roncesvalles and Zubiri, and actually within a few hours of the vicinity of Pamplona, two days' march behind the second and seventh divisions, and three in rear of the right division, and even threatening to intercept the sixth division from San Estevan.

As I was left with the pickets at Vera, I had a good opportunity of witnessing the *sang froid* of the French outposts; they made no forward movement; and as I was loitering behind within a short distance of the bridge of Lazaca, over which the troops had crossed to the left bank of the Bidassoa, I observed the Spanish family, (with whom I had recently become acquainted,) with rapid strides trudging along the flinty road, having rushed from their only dwelling through fear of the French, the instant they perceived the sentries retiring from their posts. They now presented real objects of commiseration, clad in thin shoes and silk stockings; the glossy ringlets were blown from off the forehead of La Senorita Ventura, and a tear from her dark blue eye (shaded with raven eyelashes) rolled down her flushed cheek, into the prettiest pouting lips to be imagined; a mantilla loosely hung across her arm, fluttering in the breeze, and a black silk dress hanging in graceful folds around her delicate form, gave her, with all her troubles, a most enchanting appearance. El Padre accepted the offer of my horse, and sticking his short legs into the stirrup leathers, composedly smoked a cigar. The mother took my arm, the other I offered to Ventura, who smilingly declined, saying, "It is not the fashion for *las Senoritas* to take the arms of *los Caballeros*," but politely offered her hand; while crossing the bridge, here, said the little heroine, "Why do you not call back *los Soldados*, and tell them to *tirar las balas a este puente?*" I endeavoured to explain that our flank was turned, and all the grand manœuvres of an army; little to her satisfaction, for she could not comprehend any other than the front attack.

On entering the town, the family stopped at a large stone mansion of a relation, where they intended to take up their abode for the present: the parents urged my departure, through fear that I might fall into the hands of the enemy. I then took my farewell of them, as I thought for the last time, and galloping through the town, soon came within sight of the division, threading its march up a steep defile, enclosed on all sides by an extensive forest. Towards evening we encamped, one league and a half W.N.W. of San Estevan, on the mountain of Santa Cruz, from whence we still commanded a view of the French bivouack. Here we halted during the night. On the following day, the battle of Pamplona took place, thirty miles in our rear, and being entangled amongst the mountains, we did nor hear of the event until three days afterwards. The combat began in a singular manner: the sixth division, under General Pack, while on its march over a rough country, intersected by stone walls, within a few miles of Pamplona, suddenly encountered the grey-coated French columns in full march, debouching from behind the village of Sauroren for the purpose of out-flanking the left of the fourth division. The consequence of these two hostile bodies clashing was, that the enemy's van were driven back by a hot fire of musketry. The French, being foiled in this manœuvre, turned their grand efforts against the front of the heights on which the fourth division was stationed. The valour of the red regiments shone transcendant, and the Duke of Wellington repeatedly thanked the various corps, while recovering breath to renew fresh efforts with the bayonet, in driving the enemy headlong from the crest of the rugged heights; thus forcing them, after a most sanguinary and furious contest, to desist from farther offensive movements on that position.

The general-in-chief could only collect, at the end of three days, two brigades of the second division, General Morillo's, and part of the Count d'Abisbal's, Spaniards, and the three reserve divisions, to oppose the Duke of Dalmatia, which clearly demonstrates the great difficulty of occupying such a vast and difficult range of country. The first, second, fifth, seventh, and light divisions, were too far distant to join in the action of the 28th; and even the third division, only a few miles to the right of the field *of action*, could not take part in it, as the enemy had a corps of observation opposite Sir T. Picton, backed by a numerous train of artillery and a large body of cavalry, in readiness to engage him, should the sixth and fourth divisions lose the day.

The light division continued in position at Santa Cruz during the whole of the 28th, having completely lost all trace of the army; and during these doubtful conjectures, at sunset we began to descend a rugged pass, near Zubieta, to endeavour to cut in upon the road between Pamplona and Tolosa, as it was impossible to know whether Lord Lynedoch, by this time, was not even beyond the latter town; and to add to our difficulties, the night set in so extremely dark that the soldiers could no longer see each other, and began to tumble about in all directions; some became stationary on shelvings of rock, or so enveloped in the thicket, that they could no longer extricate themselves from the trees and underwood. The rocks and the forest resounded with many voices, while here and there a small fire was kindled and flared up, as if lighted in the clouds by some magic hand. For myself, I at length became so exhausted and out of temper, at the toil of lugging along my unwilling steed, that in a fit of despair I mounted, and, keeping a tight rein, permitted the animal to pick its own steps. The branches of the trees so continually twisted round my head that I expected every minute to find myself suspended; at last the trusty horse made a dead stop, having emerged from the forest into a small hamlet, where I encountered a few harassed soldiers, inquiring of each other where the main body had vanished to, or what direction to pursue, for they no longer knew whether they were advancing or retiring; and, without farther ceremony, began to batter, with the butt-end of their firelocks, the strong and massive doors of the slumbering inhabitants, demanding, with stentorian voices, if any troops had passed that way; a difficult question for people to answer who had just risen from their mattresses, and now timidly opened their doors, in considerable alarm, being apprehensive that we had come at midnight hour to rob and plunder them. At last a resolute Spaniard* threw a large capote over his shoulder, and stepping forward said, " Senores Caballeros, only inform me whence you came or whither you are going, and I will be your guide;" but we were so bewildered, owing to the crooked path and intricate windings of the forest, that no one could take upon himself to point towards the direction of the bleak mountain we had come from, or the name of the place we were going to; as a matter of expediency, therefore, we patiently awaited the coming morn.

---

* It was a frequent custom, when in want of a guide, to employ a peasant, who received a dollar at the end of his day's journey. These *Pizanos*, being accustomed to pastoral lives, were well acquainted with every inch of ground or by-path for leagues around their habitations, as well as the various fords across rivers and tributary streams; which depend on the season of the year, or the quantity of rain that might happen to fall at uncertain periods on these mountains.

At daybreak,* a scene of complete confusion presented itself, the greater part of the division being scattered over the face of a steep and woody mountain, and positively not half a league from whence they had started on the previous evening. As soon as the various corps had grouped together, they followed the only road in sight, and soon met a mounted officer, who directed them towards Leyza: near that place one half of the division were already bivouacked, having reached the valley before the pitchy darkness had set in. It was now the third day since we had retired from Vera, and General Baron C. Alten became so uneasy, that he ordered some of the best mounted regimental officers to go in various directions to ascertain, if possible, some tidings of the army, with which he had had no communication for three days, and were now isolated amongst the wilds of the Pyrenees, on the left of the river Bidassoa, half-way between St. Sebastian and Pamplona. At six o'clock the same evening we again broke up, and marched two leagues in the direction of Arressa, and then bivouacked in a wood, with an order not to light

* On the 29th, at the end of four days' fighting both marshals desisted from hostilities in front of Pamplona. The French employed themselves in edging off to their right to assist the Count d'Erlon, who had followed the march of Lord Hill by Lanz. The Duke of Wellington, on the other hand, was drawing in the seventh division to ensure a communication with Lord Hill, and also watching his adversary's movements, to take advantage of what might accrue on the morrow.

fires, to prevent any of the enemy's scouts or spies ascertaining our route. Two hours after nightfall, the troops were again put in motion, and I was left in the forest with directions to continue there all night, to bring off in the morning any baggage or stragglers that might happen to go astray. At daylight on the 30th, I collected together a few women who dared not again encounter another toilsome night-march, along the verge of precipices. It was a droll sight to see this noisy group defiling from the forest, many dressed in soldiers' jackets, battered bonnets, and faded ribbons, with dishevelled locks hanging over their weather-beaten features, as they drove along their lazy *borricas* with a thick stick; and when the terrific blows laid on ceased to produce the desired effect, they squalled with sheer vexation, lest they might be overtaken, and fall into the hands of the enemy's light horse. Having travelled for two hours as a sort of guide to these poor women, I perceived an officer at some distance in front, and on overtaking him, he expressed the greatest joy at seeing me, and declared that he had been wandering for some hours in the most agitated state of mind, not knowing whither to bend his footsteps. The division had drawn up again during the night, and having laid down on the flank of the column, he had fallen into a profound slumber, out of which he had awoke at broad daylight, with the rays of the sun shining full on his face; and when somewhat recovering his bewildered recollections, he wildly gazed around for the column which had vanished, and springing on his feet, hallooed with all his might; but no answer was returned. A solemn silence reigned around, save the fluttering of the birds amongst the luxuriant foliage of the trees; the morning dew no longer bespangled the sod, nor did the print of a single footstep remain to guide his course: at length, in a fit of desperation, he hastily tore a passage through the thicket, and luckily reached the road, and at random sauntered along in no very pleasant mood, until I overtook him. Soon after this we heard to our left sounds like those of distant thunder; as the sky was perfectly serene, we concluded that the noise must be caused by a heavy firing of musketry.* On reaching Arriba, we found most of the doors closed; however, we succeeded in purchasing a loaf, and

* This firing was near Lizasso, where the enemy endeavoured to turn Lord Hill's left flank by the road to Buenzu; and while the Count d'Erlon was striving to execute this movement, the light division, unknowingly, were marching on his right flank. However, the general-in-chief being still in position in front of Pamplona, finding that the Duke of Dalmatia had weakened his left and centre, to support the Count d'Erlon, immediately counter-manœuvred, and attacked the right of his opponent with the sixth and seventh divisions, the left with the third division, and then pierced the centre of the enemy with the fourth division and General Byng's brigade of the second division, and before sunset pushed back the enemy beyond Olacque: by this attack the left flank of the Count d'Erlon became uncovered, which obliged him to fall back, during the night, towards the pass of Donna Maria, to avoid falling into the snare originally intended for his adversary.

then seated ourselves on the margin of a clear mountain-stream, where we devoured it, and then solaced ourselves with a hearty draught of the refreshing beverage; this stream looked so inviting, that we threw off our clothes and plunged into it. Notwithstanding the cooling effects of the bath, the feet of my companion were so much swollen, owing to previous fatigue, that with all his tugging he could not pull on his boots again; fortunately mine were old and easy, so we readily effected an exchange, and then followed the road across a high mountain, from whose summit we saw the division bivouacked to the right of the broad and well-paved road (near Lecumberri) which leads from Pamplona to Tolosa; from this position we could march to either of those places, being half-way between them. Here the division awaited the return of its scouts the whole of the following day.

The French army being completely worn out, and having suffered terribly in killed and wounded, continued to retreat during the 31st,* followed by

* "Soult's situation was now so critical, that a terrible disaster was about to close an expedition that had been marked by a succession of defeats; and accident alone averted it. He was in a deep narrow valley, and three British divisions, with one of Spaniards, were behind the mountains overlooking the town; the seventh division was on the mountain of Donna Maria; the light division, and Sir Thomas Graham's Spaniards, were marching to block the Vera and Echalar exits from the valley; Byng was already at Maya, and Hill was moving by Almandoz, just behind Wellington's own position. A few hours gained, and the French must surren-

five divisions of the British in three columns, by the roads of Roncesvalles, Maya, and Donna Maria. On the evening of the same day, although obliquely to the rear of the pursuing columns, we received orders, if possible, to overtake the enemy, and attack them wherever they might be found. Accordingly, in the middle of the night we got under arms and began our march; towards the middle of the following day, (the 1st of August,) having already marched twenty-four miles, we descended into a deep valley between Ituren and Elgoriaga, where the division drew up in column to reconnoitre the right flank of the enemy, who were still hovering in the neighbourhood of San Estevan. After an hour's halt, we continued our movement on the left of the Bidassoa, and for three hours ascended, or rather clambered, the

der or disperse. Wellington gave strict orders to prevent the lighting of fires, the straggling of soldiers, or any other indication of the presence of troops; and he placed himself amongst some rocks at a commanding point, from whence he could observe every movement of the enemy. Soult seemed tranquil, and four of his *gens d'armes* were seen to ride up the valley in a careless manner. Some of the staff proposed to cut them off; the English general, whose object was to hide his own presence, would not suffer it; but the next moment three marauding English soldiers entered the valley, and were instantly carried off by the horsemen. Half an hour afterwards the French drums beat to arms, and their columns began to move out of San Estevan towards Sumbilla. Thus the disobedience of three plundering knaves, unworthy of the name of soldiers, deprived one consummate commander of the most splendid success, and saved another from the most terrible disaster."—NAPIER.

rugged asperities of a prodigious mountain, the by-path of which was composed of overlapping slabs of rock, or stepping stones; at four o'clock in the afternoon a flying dust was descried, glistening with the bright and vivid flashes of small arms, to the right of the Bidassoa, and in the valley of Lerin. A cry was instantly set up—" The enemy!" the worn soldiers raised their bent heads covered with dust and sweat. We had nearly reached the summit of this tremendous mountain, but nature was quite exhausted; many of the soldiers lagged behind, having accomplished more than thirty miles over the rocky roads intersected with loose stones; many fell heavily on the naked rocks, frothing at the mouth, black in the face, and struggling in their last agonies, whilst others, unable to drag one leg after the other, leaned on the muzzles of their firelocks, looking pictures of despair, muttering in disconsolate accents that they had never fallen out before.

The sun was shining in full vigour, but fortunately numerous clear streams bubbled from the cavities and fissures of the rocks, (which were clothed in many places by beautiful evergreens,) and allayed the burning thirst of the fainting men;— the hard work of an infantry soldier at times is beyond all calculation, and death by the road-side frequently puts an end to his sufferings,—but what description can equal such an exit? At seven in the evening, the division having been in march nineteen hours, and accomplished nearly forty miles, it was found absolutely necessary to halt the second brigade near Aranaz, as a rallying point; being now parallel with the enemy, and some hours ahead of the vanguard leading the left column of our army, our right brigade still hobbled onwards; at twilight we overlooked the enemy within stone's throw, and from the summit of a tremendous precipice; the river separated us; but the French were wedged in a narrow road, with inaccessible rocks, enclosing them on one side, and the river on the other. Such confusion took place amongst them as is impossible to describe; the wounded were thrown down during the rush, and trampled upon; and their cavalry drew their swords, and endeavoured to charge up the pass of Echalar, (the only opening on their right flank,) but the infantry beat them back, and several of them, horses and all, were precipitated into the river; others fired vertically at us, whilst the wounded called out for quarter, and pointed to their numerous soldiers supported on the shoulders of their comrades in bearers, composed of branches of trees, to which were suspended great coats clotted with gore, or blood-stained sheets, taken from various habitations, to carry off their wounded, on whom we did not fire.

Our attention was soon called from this melancholy spectacle to support the Rifle corps* while they repulsed the enemy who had crossed over the bridge of Yanzi to attack us, to enable the tail of

* One of the first I saw wounded was Captain Perceval, of the Rifle corps. "Well," said he, "I am a lucky fellow, with one arm maimed and useless by my side from an old wound, and now unable to use the other."

their column to get off: night closed on us, and the firing ceased; but, owing to our seizing the bridge, we cut off the whole of their baggage, which fell into the hands of the column of our army following from San Estevan.

In this way ended the most trying day's march I ever remember. On the following morning, soon after daylight, we filed across the bridge of Yanzi, held by our pickets, and detached a small force to guard the road towards Echalar, until the troops came up from the direction of San Estevan, which had hung on the enemy's rear for the then three previous days. Continuing our march, we once more debouched by the defile opposite Vera, where the French sentinels were still posted, as if rooted to the rocks on which they were stationed the day we had taken our departure. As soon as the second brigade came up, we again ascended the heights of Santa Barbara, where we found a French corporal, with a broken leg, his head resting on a hairy knapsack, and supported in the arms of a comrade, who generously remained behind to protect the life of his friend from the *cuchillo* of the Spaniards. As soon as he had delivered him to the care of the English soldiers, he embraced the corporal, saying, "*Au revoir, bon camarade Anglais*," and throwing his musket over his shoulder, with the butt-end *en l'air*, he descended the mountain to rejoin the French army on the opposite range of heights. Of course, no one offered to molest this *simple soldat*, who easily effected his escape. As our pickets could not enter the valley until our right was cleared, and the enemy pushed from the mountain of Echalar, as soon as another division attacked those heights, the first Rifles moved on and clambered the mountain of St. Bernard, supported by five companies of our regiment. The soldiers had been for two days without any sustenance, and were so weak that they could hardly stand; however, an excellent commissary had managed to overtake us, and hastily served out half-a-pound of biscuit to each individual, which the soldiery devoured while in the act of priming and loading as they moved on to the attack.

The summit of the mountain was wrapped in a dense fog; an invisible firing commenced; it was impossible to ascertain which party was getting the best of the fight; the combatants were literally contending in the clouds. When half-way up the side of the mountain, we found a man of the Rifles lying on his face, and bleeding so copiously that his haversack was dyed in blood: we turned him over, and being somewhat recovered before he was carried off, he told us, in broken monosyllables, that three Frenchmen had mistaken him for a Portuguese, laid hold of him, thrust a bayonet through his thigh, smashed the stock of his rifle, and then pushed him from off the ledge of the precipice under which we discovered him. The second French light infantry were dislodged before twilight from the top of this mountain; but the sparkling flashes of small-arms continued after dark to wreath with a crown of fire the summits of the various rocks about Echalar. Thus, after a series of difficult marches, amongst a chaotic jumble of sterile mountains, the enemy were totally discomfited, with an enormous loss, by a series of the most extraordinary and brilliant efforts made during the Peninsular war. For three days the French had the vantage ground, owing to their superiority of numbers at a given point; but on the fourth day, the same divisions which had so heroically fought while falling back, sustained, with their backs to a hostile fortress, (whence the enemy sortied during the battle,) a most desperate assault made by the Duke of Dalmatia, over whom the Duke of Wellington gained a memorable victory, and ceased not in turn to pursue the French marshal, until he was glad to seek shelter from whence he came. The standards of Britain again waved aloft and flapped in the gentle breeze over the fertile fields of France.

THE BRITISH CAVALRY ON THE PENINSULA.

AFTER the affair of Toro, the French retreated rapidly; the line of the Douro having been turned, it was necessary to take up a new line, in which the natural difficulties of the country would assist them in checking Lord Wellington's advance. The French were unprepared for a retreat; Lord Wellington, on the contrary, felt confident in the success of his plans, and had everything ready to follow the enemy. The French retired with so much haste as to prevent our coming up with them, and Lord Wellington did not choose to separate his forces, by which means he might have pressed their rear: the route lay through a fine country, and the march was most agreeable. The writer was sent in with a flag of truce, and after riding seven or eight miles, he found the French outpost at Duennas. He approached that town without seeing anything of the enemy; no patrols appeared, and it was not till he arrived within a quarter of a mile of Duennas that he observed a single *chasseur à cheval*, posted upon a little round hill. The trumpeter (his sole attendant) sounded; and as it was evident that if he got round the hill on which the chasseur was posted, the view to the town would be uninterrupted, he advanced at a canter, and had already got so far as to see a small picket of chasseurs, and the piled arms of at *least* one hundred infantry, when the vidette, not approving of this peep behind the outposts, discharged his carbine. The danger was not great, as the chasseur had merely a bird's-eye view of us; but as he commenced loading we deemed it advisable to retire a little, to a position where we were concealed from his view. The cavalry officer of the picket shortly appeared, and, at the request of the flag, a staff-officer was sent for, who, when he arrived, received the letter which it was the object of the flag of truce to deliver. The staff-officer was a very fine young man, by name Prevost. He spoke English perfectly, and stated that he had a cousin holding a high rank in our service, to whom he begged a message might be sent, with a petition that his cousin would send him a horse, of which he was in great need. This, however, was not the business for which the flag was sent in; and as Charles Prevost was soon afterwards appointed to the imperial guard, he probably got a remount from the emperor. It appeared from the conversation of the two French officers that they had a great respect for the hussar brigade. They said that they had heard how anxious the Prince Regent was for the good appearance of the hussars; and they praised the prince for his consideration and proper military feeling in taking the horses out of gentlemen's carriages to mount his own regiment.

From what we saw in our peep behind the vidette, there can be little doubt that Count de Gagan, who commanded the rear-guard, was determined not to risk his dragoons in any partial encounters, or affairs of posts. The country in front of Duennas is open, yet he had withdrawn all his posts, and that one immediately in front of the town, and not above a quarter of a mile distant from it, which consisted chiefly of infantry. Nothing of importance occurred till we came into the neighbourhood of Burgos. The retreat was executed by the French without loss, and with great rapidity. They were very much favoured by circumstances. The weather was very fine, the roads good, the line through which they passed was not exhausted, and the crops of green corn furnished forage wherever the army halted, without fatigue to the men, or risk of foraging parties being cut off.

The French army collected in the neighbourhood of Burgos, and Lord Wellington halted his leading columns to enable the army to close up. About the 12th or 14th of June, Lord Wellington made a strong *reconnoissance*, and dislodged a French corps, which retired upon Burgos. Colonel Grant begged Lord Wellington to allow him to attack the retiring infantry with the hussars; but, in spite of the colonel's pressing solicitations to be allowed to charge, Lord Wellington would not permit it. This movement would probably have established the doctrine of the capability of dragoons, well led and ably conducted, being able to break squares of infantry. The writer was sent to reconnoitre the right of the French, taking with him a single well-mounted hussar. He found the French dragoons in occupation of a village with a large plain in front, whose margin was occupied by a line of videttes. That made it impossible to see into the village. Little information could be gained, and the writer retired about half a mile to a slight rise of ground, where he was enabled, with a telescope, to make out the rear of the village. While thus occupied, I directed the hussar to feed his horse,—which might have been done with perfect safety, although, by the carelessness of the man, it led to a ludicrous dilemma. While the horse was feeding by a nose-bag, the hussar standing by his side for a moment let go the collar rein while he tightened the girth of his own horse, when the beast galloped off. I was disturbed by the hussar's calling out, " Old Tom's loose!" It was a fearful piece of information, within half a mile of the enemy's picket. The horse was indeed concealed from the view of the French videttes by the fall of the ground; but if he galloped a hundred yards, it was all over. And a still more disagreeable circumstance occurred. On looking back, we saw Lord Wellington and his staff approaching at a gallop, and not above a mile distant. We felt aware that had we found an officer of light cavalry in such a situation, our *primâ facie* view would have been very unfavourable to his fitness for his office. The awkwardness of the situation, and the difficulty of explanation, was quite overpowering. The hussar was vainly attempting to catch Old Tom, who allowed him to approach within a few yards, when he went off with a kick and a squeak. We felt assured that the hussar could never do it; and observing that the old rogue had got to a green spot, where there was an abundant vegetation, from its being a well-head, I took off my sword, and stealing behind the horse, which was trying to drink, I was able to get hold of some of the horse-furniture; and the horse's fore-legs having sank into the soft ground nearly to the knees before he could disengage himself, he was secured by the head-stall. A moment sufficed to throw the nose-bag on the ground, and to slip the bit into Old Tom's mouth; when mounting, without fastening a buckle, I was scarcely in my seat when Lord Wellington rising the ascent from a little brook, was within fifty yards. All was right; and we shall be more cautious in feeding on the outposts.

Lord Wellington was of very few words—no unnecessary ones. "Have you found the right of the French?" "Yes, my lord." "Where?" "There." "Get your troop, and watch them." Away went the general on matters of more importance. We got the troop, and shoved back the line of videttes far enough to see a host of French dragoons, of which we sent notice. The videttes were supported, and throwing out a few skirmishers, we retired out of shot.

We had in the troop a Dutchman, for whom we had a great regard, but some people had taken up a notion that he wished to desert. He was a clever man; and we had soon an opportunity of making use of him, and at the same time of ascertaining his loyalty. The French withdrew their videttes, and were apparently retiring. We sent the Dutchman, Jaen Teer, to skirt the village, and ascertain what the enemy was doing. It was evidently better to obtain information in this way than with a single troop, unsupported, to follow the enemy into a large village composed of several streets. We saw Jaen Teer perform his duty admirably; and having attained a point whence he saw the whole operations of the French, he came back with the report that several squadrons were retiring through the wood, but that the enemy still retained a post outside of the village. As Jaen had thus been close to the enemy, while he was completely separated from his own people, there could be no doubt that, whatever were his intentions, he had no wish to desert. This was very satisfactory. Alas! poor Jaen was doomed to enjoy his fair fame but a short time. On the following morning he was reported sick. We found that, in preparing his mess the night before, he had used some onions which he had found growing in the field, although orders prohibiting the use of wild vegetables, and, above all, of that poisonous herb the wild onion, had been repeatedly read to the troops. He lived only two days.

On the following day a great part of the army, or perhaps the whole of it, moved to the left, and crossed the Ebro at St. Martin. The French army retired upon Vittoria. A gallant attack was made upon a division of French infantry by the light division, which drove the enemy from a strong position, walking them down.

The army was collected on the 20th, and we visited the outposts that evening, which were held by a brigade of Portuguese dragoons, closely supported by the 4th division. When we got to the picket, a flag of truce, as it turned out to be, had come to the outposts and driven in the videttes. The Portuguese had made a proper kettle of fish of it. (We beg to be excused so homely an expression. It is the most apt which occurs to us; and we do not mean to tell the story, which was abundantly ludicrous.)

On the 21st, the following day, the battle of Vittoria was fought. The field was a beautiful one, and probably the position was a pretty good one, although certainly too extensive for the army which occupied it. The chain of hills on the French left was strongly occupied, and capable of a good defence; but Lord Wellington, by turning the right of the enemy by a flank movement of General Graham's corps, threw them into confusion, and placed them in imminent danger of being altogether destroyed. It has been said that the French army was equal in force to the British;

but we doubt this, excepting in artillery, in which arm the French were probably superior. In cavalry, we were decidedly superior both in quality and quantity; and as above 25,000 men were detached under Generals Foy and Clausel, they were probably inferior to us in troops of the line.

We have seen in some French work that one of the reasons why Joseph fought at Vittoria, instead of retiring to the strong ground behind Salvatierra, was, that he wished for a field on which he might employ *sa belle cavalerie*. A worse reason could not have been given for maintaining his position at Vittoria, which was a place of consequence to him, both from its own importance, and as covering the road to Bilboa, as well as those into France. We chanced to meet a *curé* on the French side of the Pyrenees, at whose house General Merlin had been quartered shortly after the battle, who said that the general was furious, exclaiming against Joseph, and vowing that the *matériel* of three armies (that is to say, the armies of the south, the centre, and of Portugal) had been sacrificed to save fifty *putaines* and their baggage. This is a more likely reason, for Joseph thought more of *ses belle filles* than of *sa belle cavalerie*. Never was a general action in which cavalry was so little made use of. We do not recollect the charge of a single French squadron, nor of their being employed till the afternoon, when they behaved very steadily, and covered their infantry when it was in confusion.

It is more to be lamented that the British cavalry

was so little employed. Nothing could surpass the condition of the horses, and nothing had been neglected to put that arm on the most efficient footing. At the close of the action it is difficult to say what might not have been accomplished by a combined attack of the cavalry and artillery; and had the divisions been accompanied by a few dragoons during the battle, they would have been of great use in forcing the retreating columns to form, instead of their being allowed to run off in loose order, by which means they were enabled with ease to get away from our victorious infantry. It unfortunately happened that Sir S. Cotton, who had commanded the cavalry since the battle of Talavera, and who continued to do so to the end of the war, was absent in England, and no one had been appointed in his place. We believe that the gallant Baron Boch was the senior officer; but as he did not appear to take a lead in directing the movements of the body, it is probable that he was not authorized to act as commander of the cavalry.

The squadron to which the writer of these pages belonged was ordered to be ready to escort Lord Wellington on the morning of the 21st, and turned out two hours before daylight. The day was just breaking when Lord Wellington galloped past the squadron, accompanied by a single staff-officer, and went directly towards the enemy's videttes, which were posted along the river Zadora. The first shot fired that day was at his lordship. As the day cleared, Lord Wellington repaired to an eminence, from which the posts and most part of the French position could be seen. The covering squadron of course followed; and the writer had the satisfaction of sitting within a few yards of the great chief during the whole time he was directing the attack. It is difficult to describe the perfect coolness, nay, apparent unconcern, with which Lord Wellington gave the most important orders, directing the advance of a division as he perceived it could act with effect. In the early part of the morning, his eyes were continually directed to that part of the scene where he expected to see the head of Sir Thomas Graham's column appear, which corps was intended to turn the enemy's right, and prevent his retreat by the Bayonne road. Sir Thomas had found the roads worse than had been expected, which occasioned delay; and we believe that the attack was made before his corps appeared. Sir Rowland Hill had been warmly engaged for some time, and had driven the corps opposed to him from its position with considerable bloodshed.

The last order we heard was, that the light division, supported by the hussar brigade, should attack the round hill, which was covered with troops, and which, from the place we occupied, nearly blocked up our view of the valley of the Zadora. As we descended to the foot of the round hill, which the light division was to attack, (*i.e.* to carry,) we saw its summit bristling with bayonets. To the top was an ascent of probably three hundred yards.

We were behind the 52nd, which was formed in echellon, if we recollect rightly. As the hill became steeper, we gained upon the infantry, and before we had proceeded one hundred yards, we were close up to them. The writer was behind Capt. Curry's company; perhaps the reader was acquainted with Hunter Curry; if so, he will rejoice to be reminded of that gallant, honourable soldier, and warm-hearted friend; if otherwise, we must still beg to be allowed to offer our tribute of esteem to the memory of one whom we held dear. We have seen Curry in many situations—in all of them we recollect the perfect gentleman, the amiable and agreeable companion. Previously to the Peninsular war, when interesting subjects were rare, he used to give the mess a detail of the events at the camp on the Curragh of Kildare; and if he was attacked for telling an old story, he always managed to silence his adversary by some witty, but always good-humoured remark. As we ascended the hill, he leant upon the neck of the writer's horse, and nineteen years have not effaced the pleasing recollection of the kindly smile and beaming eye of our friend, who, elated by the prospect of again walking down the enemy, said, "If we do not find them at the top of the hill, we shall find them somewhere else." As we approached the crest of the hill, we marched with silence, in momentary expectation of a volley. The French had retired; the hussar brigade was halted and sent to the right, towards the high road; the 52nd proceeded in pursuit, overthrew the French, and forced them back in confusion; and the brave Curry received a mortal wound while in front of his company waving his cap on the point of his sword and cheering his men to fresh deeds of valour. After moving about for some time, the hussar brigade formed in line at a considerable distance in the rear. The Blues were in the act of dressing their line, when they were observed by the French batteries, which opened upon them, and the second shot killed one of the men.

When the retreat of the French was general, the hussar brigade was ordered to the front. In our movement to the front, we passed a fine brigade of Portuguese infantry formed in line, and proudly advancing through some corn-fields. An English officer, who saw the French retiring before the Valorosos, said, in their hearing, " The enemy takes them to be English." Immediately, the ensign advanced in front of the line, and waving the white banner of Braganza, shouted " Viva el principe!" It was pretty generally allowed, that under ordinary circumstances, the Portuguese infantry was little inferior to our own; thanks to the exertions of Marshal Beresford, and the gallant British officers he placed in the Portuguese ranks.

The hussar brigade was directed to the left of the town; the ground was flat, and apparently well suited to the operations of cavalry. In passing through it we found it intersected by deep gullies, so broad as to make it necessary to ride into them. The 15th hussars were in front, and passed a dozen or more of these cuts in their passage round the town, without meeting with any opposition. A few French infantry might be seen here and there. When we had nearly completed the circuit, a gun was brought up within two hundred yards; we saw it unlimbered and loaded, and were in momentary expectation of a discharge. Our advance, however, was so rapid, although two of the gullies intervened, that the French had not even time to give us one shot, but passed off at speed.

We now entered upon an uninterrupted plain of some extent—it was a scene of confusion. We passed through a crowd of broken infantry, who threw down their arms, although probably some resumed them, and got a shot at the hussars when they had passed on. The leading squadrons of the 15th charged some French chasseurs, upset them, and completely cleared the foreground. It was then we perceived heavy masses of French cavalry, who did not attempt to deploy; but Sir Colquhoun Grant discovered that he was accompanied by the single regiment which he had gallantly led into action. A staff officer had, most unwarrantably, stopped the other part of the brigade, and turned it through the town, and had not even given notice to Colonel Grant that he had done so. As soon as Colonel Grant discovered what had happened, he rallied the 15th, and formed line. But any further attack was out of the question; indeed, had the whole brigade been up, the French would have been an overmatch for it. But an attack would have been justifiable, and even advisable, as the British centre was coming up, and would soon have compromised the safety of the French dragoons. As it was, some skirmishing and cavalier sabreing occurred; when Captain Webber Smith's guns arrived, and as soon as he could clear away our men, he opened with canister shot upon the retiring dragoons, who abandoned the whole of the baggage of the French army, wagons, carriages, and packages of every description. The dragoons attempted to carry off some mules, but their loads were too heavy, and they were nearly all taken. In the ditches were seen mules struggling to shake off their cargoes, guns which had been abandoned by the artillerymen, and dying horses which had been struck by the grape-shot. One of the divisions of infantry came up to our right; it was preceded by Captain Norman Ramsay, with some guns. He was pressing forward with as much anxiety as if the success of the day depended on his personal exertions. As soon as he saw the column of French dragoons he unlimbered, and dismounting, laid one of the guns himself, and marked the effects of its fire, heedless of our friendly cheer, so completely was he engrossed in his own occupation. We feel convinced that no man in the army was more entitled to promotion than this officer, and it was deeply to be regretted that he did not share in the honours which were bestowed for the victory. His valour was allowed to pass unrewarded, in consequence of a mistake which had been very unintentionally made by a staff-officer. He was harshly dealt with. Norman Ramsay commanded the admiration of all his companions in arms, which, after all, is the most pleasing reward of merit.

After clearing the obstacles in the neighbourhood of Vittoria, the French dragoons formed, and retired in good order, protecting the broken infantry. Then was the time that an efficient attack might have been made by the British cavalry. No attempt of the sort was made. The army soon after was halted, and encamped in the advance of the town. We are decidedly of opinion, that the close of the battle of Vittoria was one of the finest opportunities ever offered to the cavalry of a successful army. The infantry had fully performed its duty. The arrangements of the commander-in-chief had been such, that the enemy could at no time have hoped for a successful termination to the battle. The divisions of the French army were defeated in succession: the whole of the guns, save two, had fallen into our hands, as well as the reserves of ammunition; consequently, the French infantry had nothing to depend upon but the cartridges remaining in the soldiers' pouches, which, in many of the divisions, must have been very small. The cavalry of the enemy was very inferior in number to ours; and lastly, the retreat of the French lay through an open country. Had the attack of cavalry been unsuccessful, which is a most improbable supposition, the enemy could not have profited by our failure. The infantry was coming up, and would have prevented the adverse cavalry from taking advantage of their success. But on the other hand, supposing the British horse to have driven the French dragoons out of the field, the infantry mob was at their mercy. Many thousands of them must have been made prisoners, and those who escaped would have only found safety in retiring from the high road; and in the hill country would have fallen a prey to the guerillas. Is it possible that any one can be so unreasonable as to blame the British cavalry for not taking advantage of these favourable circumstances? We answer yes. There are but too many who find it easy to censure the cavalry; asserting, that the infantry fought a hard battle, and gained a victory, while the dragoons would do nothing.

We recollect hearing of a major of brigade, who threatened to punish a guard for coming a file short—*i. e.*, to punish the thirty-nine files who did their duty, for the fault of the fortieth, which was absent. It is equally unfair to censure the British cavalry, who cannot be accused of remissness in the performance of the duty required of them, and who were most anxious to be employed, and on that occasion felt confident of success. By his own genius, and by the bravery of his infantry, Lord Wellington had gained a signal victory. He had freed the north of Spain of the French by one battle. The French were perfectly unprepared for such a disaster, as may be drawn from the state of the garrison of Pamplona, which had not two months' provisions; although, by economy, and by feeding upon horse-flesh, the place was enabled to hold out much longer. Napoleon was in want of soldiers, and Soult found some difficulty in getting together an army to carry supplies into Pamplona; which difficulty would have been augmented, had the victory of Vittoria been followed up, and a number of prisoners secured. The only book on the Peninsular war we have at hand is, Colonel Jones' "Account of the War in Spain and Portugal." Colonel Jones states the loss of the French at ten thousand. We should doubt its being so great. As the French had nearly all their artillery (one hundred and fifty-three pieces) in action, the attacking party necessarily must have suffered the greatest loss in killed and wounded; and we never heard of above two thousand prisoners.

So much blame has been attached to the late Sir Harry Burrard for not allowing Sir Arthur Wellesley to follow up the victory of Vimeira, and the censure having been even carried on to Sir Hew Dalrymple's account, for making the subsequent convention, that we must beg to be allowed to institute a comparison between the circumstances of the British army after these two victories. At Vimeira, Sir Arthur Wellesley, known only as the conqueror of Holkar, was at the head of a gallant army of *very* young soldiers. The French had a fine body of cavalry, which had taken little or no part in the action; and a fresh brigade of French infantry arrived from Lisbon just as Junot commenced his retreat. The British had a couple of hundred light dragoons at the beginning of the day, but they had been a good deal employed, and their gallant commander had been killed. At Vittoria, Lord Wellington was in a very different position. At Talavera, Busaco, Fuentes, and Salamanca, he had defeated the most eminent of the French marshals. "L'enfant gaté," in his hands, had no longer to boast of the caresses of fortune. The army of Portugal, which proposed to drive the English into the sea, was sent back without inflicting on our armies a third part of the loss it sustained itself. Marshal Marmont, who was considered the most skilful manœuvrer in the French army, was beaten at Salamanca, having been fairly out-manœuvred by the English general, who had, at this period, arrived at the highest point of military distinction. The British infantry felt themselves to be invincible. The cavalry was in beautiful order, and superior in number to the enemy. The French army had lost its guns and stores, and was dispirited by a series of defeats, and, conscious of its inability to check the British infantry, was in full retreat, and absolute disorder. We would ask, which of these two victories might have been followed up with the best prospect of success? It is an idle question, which admits but of one answer. Lord Wellington had accomplished the great object to which his efforts were directed, and he did not descend to what was comparatively of minor importance.

We wish to point out, that the cause of the cavalry doing so little was not any inherent defect in that body; but Lord Wellington having achieved a brilliant victory, did not choose to commence a cavalry fight; which, if it had terminated honourably to the French, would have been a small off-set to the defeat they had suffered.

* * * * *
* * * * *

THE retreat of the French, after the battle of Vittoria, was so rapid as to make it impossible to come up with them. A squadron of the German hussars, however, overtook and engaged their rear-guard, near Pamplona; the enemy employed against the hussars the only long gun he had remaining; the hussars forced back the enemy; and, as the gun was retiring on the high road, a carbine shot struck one of the horses, which becoming unruly, the gun was dragged from the causeway and upset. The hussars immediately took possession of it. The infantry was soon afterwards established on the Pyrenees; and while they were engaged in a most arduous service, the cavalry was cantoned in the rich plains of Aragon. It was not till the army had passed the Nive, that the cavalry could be of any service; about the middle of December, a considerable post was established at Hasparren, which town was the head-quarters of the fifth division and of the cavalry. The hussar brigade connected the infantry with Murillo's corps, which was on the right, and which again communicated with the Spaniards at St. Jean Pied de Port. At first there was great abundance of forage—hay of good quality, and straw; but the district was limited in extent, and forage soon became so scarce as to make it necessary to seek supplies on the flanks of the French posts, and even behind their videttes. This system of foraging gave rise to some very agreeable little affairs. Sometimes it was effected by placing videttes on the high ground in the rear, who were to apprise the foragers of approaching danger; while the foragers were, by stealth, to take the hay out of houses in the vicinity of the enemy's posts; at other times, the enemy's outposts were driven in by a small party, and before the French had time to rally and resume their ground, the foragers had loaded their horses and mules and got off: sometimes the enemy advanced so rapidly as to place their foragers in danger; a few shots were generally fired by the French, and a few mules were lost. On one or two occasions, a captain of the 7th hussars was wounded, and soon afterwards, strict orders were issued that this mode of foraging should be discontinued. We were very sorry for it; and the only remaining means to support the horses was by chopping at the gorge, the young shoots of which make a very palatable and wholesome food for horses doing moderate work; but as the hussars were a good deal on duty, and as it frequently happened that no corn was issued for several consecutive days, the horses lost both flesh and strength, and many became mangy.

Meanwhile, the adverse posts in the neighbourhood of Hasparren carried on their duty in the most peaceable manner, avoiding every species of hostility. A picket of the hussars was upon the high road, and two detached pickets on the flank were under the charge of the captain who commanded the main body on the high road. For a long time, no change of position was made by either party; each occupied a hill, and in the valley below, the videttes were placed within about three hundred yards of each other. The French, however, seemed desirous to occupy the neutral ground, and occasionally pushed forward their videttes. This having been observed, the captain of the picket received orders not to allow this to be done. On the following morning, he observed that the French vidette had been advanced above fifty yards, and he thought it most advisable to demand an interview with the French captain of chasseurs. A peasant was despatched, and returned with a message that the commandant would wait upon the British officer immediately, and in a few minutes the parties mèt on the neutral ground: the Briton stated the orders he had received, and explained, that, to avoid so *lache* a proceeding as to fire upon a vidette, he had solicited a meeting with the brave chasseur. The Frenchman expressed himself in the most flattering terms, and begged that the hussar might point out a situation which would be agreeable to him;—a thorn bush, about one hundred yards behind the spot the French vidette was posted upon, was mentioned as equally advantageous for the security of the French picket; while it would be such as the hussar was permitted by his orders to allow. The chasseur gave orders accordingly, the vidette was placed at the very spot which was recommended, and the Frenchman having expressed his satisfaction at the interview, produced a bottle of cognac: Two or three officers on each side now joined the party; a happy termination to the war was drunk; and the captain, whose name was (we think) Le Brun, said he trusted that it would not be the fate of war to bring into collision the parties who had met in so amicable a manner.

After the destruction of the French army at Leipsic, Napoleon found it necessary to demand contributions from his different lieutenants, to assist in repairing the grand army. During the winter, Soult was obliged to send away his division of dragoons, and was left with only chasseurs, to the number of two thousand, or perhaps two thousand five hundred; and it was therefore necessary for him to take such a line of retreat as should be the least suited to the operations of cavalry and artillery, in which arms we had so decided a superiority. Lord Wellington opened the campaign about the middle of February; and successively drove the enemy from St. Palais and Sauveterre, on the Gave d'Oleron. The French army was then collected at Orthes, and behind the Gave de Pau. The dragoons were daily engaged in skirmishes, and drove the poor chasseurs before them.

On the evening of the 25th we crossed the Gave de Pau at a ford, and as the enemy had a picket opposite to Berens, the retreat from which, towards Orthes, was by a road parallel to the river, this picket might have been cut off, simply by getting upon the high road, which was not five hundred yards from the ford by which we had passed the river: a troop of the hussars was trotting forward for this purpose, when it was halted; the picket of chasseurs was allowed to gallop past, and when the French had got a few hundred yards' start, the hussars were then ordered to follow them. A squadron of the fifteenth, under Captain Wodehouse, pushed in all the French pickets, cavalry and infantry, and was checked by a volley from a large body of the enemy. The flankers of the 15th were opposed to infantry as well as cavalry; and we must give an interesting anecdote which occurred. Ten rifled carbines per troop had been issued, and the men carrying these arms were always employed as skirmishers; one of the men, by name Fishlock, thus employed, had the stock of his carbine broken by a musket-shot. He went to his captain and begged to have another rifle, but as there was none to give him, he was directed to fall in: soon afterwards one of the skirmishers fell dead. As soon as this happened, Fishlock left the ranks, and galloping towards the spot, he disengaged the carbine from the dead man's grasp and joined the skirmishers.

The field at Orthes was chosen by Soult, as one on which cavalry could not be employed. A squadron of French chasseurs, under the command of the Captain Le Brun before mentioned, charged some of the British infantry skirmishers in the most reckless manner; but the chasseurs experienced a great loss, and were not able to render any service to their own army. When the French were finally driven from their position, the hussar brigade was ordered to pursue. A gallant charge was made by the 7th hussars, a great many prisoners were secured, the French were stopped on their retreat and brought up their guns; the pursuit was not urged as it might have been done, and the remains of the vanquished enemy were allowed to retire without molestation. The only charge of cavalry which was ordered was admirably executed by the 7th hussars. Had the cavalry been ordered to harass the retreat, it must have been very destructive to the enemy. After passing Orthes, the country became flat and highly cultivated; a great many cavalry affairs took place upon the high road, all of which were in the highest degree honourable to the British dragoons. The 10th hussars defeated a superior body of the enemy, and took a great number of prisoners. A day or two before the battle of Toulouse, the 18th hussars, under Colonel Vivian, attacked a brigade of French cavalry, and took nearly a hundred prisoners. At Plaisance, near Toulouse, a single squadron of the 15th hussars, under Captain Hancox, charged the French picket, which retired upon the regiment to which it belonged; the whole body was then charged and driven back,—a great many surrendered; but as they were enabled to escape by leaping over a broad ditch into the field, only an officer and twenty men were secured.

This sketch of the British cavalry has occupied so much more room than was intended, that we have gone over this campaign in a very cursory manner. The British cavalry was immensely superior both in number and in quality. We beg to add two anecdotes illustrative of the address of the soldiers; which we think necessary, as it is so frequently alleged that the British dragoons are not good upon out-post duty. A few days before the battle of Toulouse, it was desirable to ascertain whether the French were moving any force towards the town of Alby. A patrol was ordered to get upon the road from Toulouse to Alby, and to ascertain what was moving upon that road: this could only be accomplished by crossing the river L'Ers, which is nearly parallel to the Garonne; and on which the right of the French and our left flank rested. The villages on the other side, *i. e.* on the right bank of the L'Ers, were said to be occupied by small parties of gendarmes: it would therefore be necessary to have a patrol strong enough to set these gendarmes at defiance, while too large a party would be an incumbrance in case of a rapid retreat; or the want of an attempt on the part of the French to cut off the patrol.

The party sent on this duty consisted of an

officer, a serjeant, and six men, who, crossing the river at daylight, about half a mile in front of the outposts, proceeded towards a village upon the Alby road, which was distant about three miles from the bridge by which they had passed the river. The L'Ers, although narrow, is not fordable, and the patrol could not be interrupted. Several parties of gendarmes were seen turning out of the hamlets near the route of the patrol, and making towards the French line. The road, or rather lane, was deep, from the late rains, and having proceeded about two miles, the officer deemed it advisable to leave the serjeant and four of the men, and to proceed to the village on the Alby road, accompanied by the other two men. On his arrival there, he found the village in a very agitated state; the market-place was filled by the inhabitants, at least by the male part of them; and there appeared a great many well-dressed men, but no soldiers, nor any carrying arms.

M. le Maire was called for, and gave the information that a great many wagons had passed towards Alby, but they were filled only with sick and wounded soldiers. Another gentleman was questioned apart, and having given the same intelligence, the object of the patrol was fulfilled, and the departure of the officer was hastened by the information that a party of chasseurs was *crossing the bridge*, and would be in the town immediately. As the patrol left the market-place, eight or ten chasseurs entered at the other side, and pursued. As soon as the officer had joined the rest of his party, he formed the little band, and advanced to the charge. The chasseurs also halted, formed, and on the approach of the hussars, went about; to follow them far was impossible, or at least, it was exposing the party to the danger of being cut off. As the hussars halted, the chasseurs did the same, and commenced firing. The officer, having directed the serjeant to retire with four of the men, and to cross the bridge by which they had passed the river in their advance, remained with the two hussars who had accompanied him before.

The French, seeing their opponents so much weakened, dismounted to fire, which rendered the situation of these three unfortunates considerably perilous. One of the men went to the rear, and joined the serjeant, and the officer found himself supported by a single hussar, a little black fellow, named Churchyard, but a very intelligent and gallant soldier, and mounted on a blood mare: he was asked if he would also go away,—" No, I'll be d—d if I do, but I'll have a lick at the bloody chasseurs!" Putting spurs to his mare, he dashed at three chasseurs, who were loading, or preparing to fire; they were off in a moment, and by a repetition of these attacks, the chasseurs were not allowed to get a single fair shot, till time had been allowed the serjeant to carry off his party, who were joined by Churchyard and his officer as they crossed the bridge, and retired in safety: they had not reached their quarters ere the pickets were attacked by a squadron of chasseurs and driven back. The chasseurs having driven back our pickets, occupied a small village, and were seen to be straggling and drinking in the different houses: this was observed by Corporal Winterfield, a Prussian, belonging to the 15th; and when the chasseurs had completed their *reconnoissance* and retired, he followed them with the two men under his command, and keeping at a little distance, he saw some of the chasseurs falling in the rear; he gradually accelerated his pace, and when within one hundred yards, the three hussars put spurs to their horses, and each of them seizing on a chasseur, brought him off at speed before the eyes of the *chef d'escadron* and his host, who in vain attempted to catch them.

We venture to say that the conduct of these two men, Corporal Winterfield and Churchyard, could not have been surpassed. The squadron from which Winterfield was detached was entitled to share in this capture; but one and all begged that the produce of the three horses and their appointment, amounting probably to 60*l*. or 70*l*., might be left to those who had so gallantly won the prize. We could mention many instances of similar conduct, and we are sure that any officer in the service could do the same; but especially those who trusted in the ability of their soldiers, and let them be aware of the confidence placed in them. An Englishman is a straightforward creature, careless as to what is thought of him, and seldom affecting the acuteness which we see in foreigners; but let any officer frankly confide in his men, and tell them how much depends on their exertions, he will then learn, if he knew it not before, how much sterling good sense his countrymen possess, what sort of unflinching bravery may be elicited. At the battle of Toulouse, there was no opportunity of employing cavalry, and two days afterwards the general peace was proclaimed.

In every instance in which we have overwhelmed the French advance, it has always been by an open attack, such as the 13th at Campo Major, where, indeed, Colonel Head was drawn into a snare, when his victorious squadrons were not supported. In the passage of the Esla, a whole picket was taken; they allowed the 15th to gallop in upon them,—the picket was too weak to fight,—it was too late to run away. The following day the French chose to mistake the 10th hussars for Portuguese, although the hussar brigade had been lying most part of the preceding day almost in sight. A great many instances of the same kind occurred before the battle of Toulouse; in all of which the British were victorious, but not by stratagem. On the retreat to Corunna, and during the preceding few days, which formed the whole campaign, although the French cavalry was immensely superior in point of numbers, Lord Paget managed the British cavalry so well, as never to allow the French horse to be the slightest annoyance to our army, and also defeated them in many encounters. At Talavera, the French made little use of a host of cavalry, whilst the British cavalry, by a daring charge, rendered the most signal services. On the retreat to the lines, the French cavalry, outnumbering the British in the ratio of three to one, were kept at bay and defeated in numerous affairs. At Fuentes, 5000 French cavalry, in good condition, were detained by 1200 British, after their advance had been defeated. At Albuera, the defalcation of the Spaniards gave an opening to a brigade of hussars and lancers; but during the remainder of the day, the French were not able to make any use of their large body of cavalry. At Salamanca, the British cavalry rendered good service; and after that period, the French cavalry was in less force, and consequently never able to do anything of consequence.

We are quite at a loss to understand how the maligners of the British cavalry make out their case, and improve their own intelligence. It is not difficult to find fault with anything or anybody, as nothing and nobody is perfect. Now, we are far from pretending that the British cavalry is the one exception to human fallibility; but we do assert, that during that period of the Peninsular campaign in which the French cavalry always outnumbered the British in the ratio of two, three, four, or even five to one, nothing of consequence was achieved by the French; and when the numbers became equal, and, finally, when we were superior in number, the French cavalry became helpless, unless well supported by infantry. That the cavalry was not enough employed we willingly allow, but that must be attributed to a cause not affecting their merit, and one on which we do not choose to enter. We state these matters broadly. We are unable to enter the lists of logical discussion—the subject does not require it; and if we were challenged, we should answer in the words of an excellent lady, whose son's tutor sometimes corrected slight errors in her conversation:—"Now, don't contradict me, Mr. Brown, for that puts an end to all argument." In conclusion, we beg to offer a few remarks on the use of cavalry. They are, probably, commonplace, and not very interesting; but such as they are, we mean to wind up our sketch with them.

We consider that it would increase the efficiency of the British cavalry if all the heavy dragoons carried cuirasses. There are at present but ten regiments of heavy cavalry, independent of the household brigade, and we think that, probably, as great a force of heavy horse would be required in the event of a continental war. We are aware that many objections are made to the cuirass, and we acknowledge that some of them are well founded. The only material disadvantage, in our opinion, is the hardship to which the men are exposed in carrying the cuirass. We do not allude to the weight, for when the cuirass is well fitted to the shape, its weight is not oppressive. The difficulty the cuirassier has to contend with is, that cold and heat are each made more unbearable by the plates of cold iron attached to the body. This is the great objection, and the means we would employ to obviate this difficulty is to make the cuirass of solid leather instead of iron. It would be equally sword-proof, and little less effectual in turning a bullet; but whether it had that power or not, such an armour would give great confidence to the men, and that is the point to be attained. We feel convinced that the household brigade, as it is equipped, would set at defiance twice its number of any cavalry in Europe; and the dragoons of the line would be very little inferior to that fine body of men if equally clad in armour. We have frequently been told Englishmen do not require armour, but will fight as well without it. We do not mean to dispute the courage of our countrymen, though we do not admire the vain assertions we often hear of the heroism of Britons, coupled with the implication that all others are cowards; but we feel confident that a man of very ordinary courage *cuirassé* will be a match for the bravest man in Europe equipped as a dragoon, *i. e.*, without his shell. We do not know of any other alteration of moment, except giving all the cavalry good and efficient arms.

The second observation we would make is, that, on service, the same corps of cavalry and infantry should act together as much as possible. They would acquire mutual confidence, and there is an indescribable something beyond this. It is usually considered that good whist-players play best with those whom they have been accustomed to play with as partners; so the horse and foot soldier should know each other's game.

The third observation is, that the officers of

cavalry, instead of being restricted, should be encouraged as much as possible to acts of chivalry; that, by carrying off pickets, cutting lines of supply or communication, surprising posts, charging on the skirmishers which are covering the enemy's advance, the officer may acquire more address, and secure the confidence and admiration of the men. The objection we have always heard made to this principle is, that the loss of man and horse, especially the latter, would be too great; the effect would not be sufficient remuneration — in fact, that *le jeu ne vaut pas la chandelle;* but we think that the moral advantage would be sufficient recompence, and the mischief done to the enemy so much gain. The expense of cavalry on service, is the providing them with forage; compared to which, the value of the horse is nothing.

During the campaign of 1811, the royal dragoons had about 250 mules merely to carry corn from St. Joao de Pesquiera to their quarters. Government paid a dollar for each mule, and a dollar for each capatras, who conducted four or five mules. The amount for mule transport was—

250 mules	250 dollars
50 capatras	50
	300 dollars

which, at the rate of 6s. per dollar, amounted to 90l. per diem. At this time the regiment did not bring above 450 swords into the field, so that each of those cost government about 80l. per annum, merely for carrying corn forage from the

Douro. The corn had previously been purchased at a great price, shipped, landed at Oporto, reshipped into river-craft, and towed 140 or 150 miles against stream. We may have stated this matter somewhat incorrectly, as it has been done from memory; but we have no fear of contradiction in asserting that the expense of sending horses from England was trifling in comparison to the charge of supporting them in the field.

It would be very advantageous to have single squadrons of cavalry placed under the command of the general of division of infantry in battles. A single squadron, judiciously placed, may have the most beneficial effects. In case of discomfiture, a charge of cavalry may check the advance of the enemy, and allow time for the retiring party to form. On the other hand, when a corps of adverse infantry has been driven back, they may be advantageously attacked, and, at least, by being threatened, the enemy will be obliged to form, and consequently their retreat will be retarded.

When the line of posts and object to be attained has been pointed out to the officers of cavalry, they should be allowed to choose their ground, and should be responsible for the posting their pickets. In the same way, patrolling should be entrusted to the cavalry officers. Such is the case at present, when the duty is laborious, and little credit to be gained; but when matters are otherwise, then some staff-officer appears to take it into his own hands. We found this remark on the opinion of one of the most distinguished officers of our staff, now no more. The writer had the honour to be known to him; and having been applied to by another officer of the staff for a party to accompany him on a *reconnoissance*, the writer consulted the gallant officer above mentioned. He received for answer, "Give him no men; make the patrol yourself; you will do it just as well, and it is your business."

There is one evil which we shall take notice of, and which we should rejoice to see removed. We allude to the expense of living in a British cavalry regiment. This arises from the richness of appointments, the expense of the mess, and the frequency of quartering on inns instead of barracks. The writer joined a regiment on the 24th of September, (during the war.) He embarked for foreign service the beginning of January, having lived at an inn during the whole of the intervening period, with the exception of about three weeks. The mischief of this expensive living is very apparent. Three-fourths of the young men in the army are not able to enter the cavalry. In the British service, officers are employed in cavalry or infantry, as suits their taste and means of procuring the transfer. This is as it should be; for the principles of the service are intrinsically the same, and a good officer in one service will be equally so in the other. This is not the case on the Continent; and if the expense of our cavalry service was lessened, so as to make it attainable by a larger portion of our officers, it would be of great advantage, and would tend to place the British cavalry on that permanent station which it ought to hold, and which it will occupy when the elements of which it is composed are turned to proper account.

133

THE ACTION IN FRONT OF BAYONNE.*

ON the morning of the 9th of December, the right of the army, consisting of the 2nd, the 6th, and the Portuguese divisions, under Lieut.-General Sir Rowland Hill, crossed the Nive by the fords at Cambo and Ville Franche, and by a bridge of boats thrown across at Usteritz. The enemy made but a slight resistance to the passage of the river; and he was driven the same evening into the entrenched camp in front of Bayonne, with the exception of the left division, commanded by General Paris, which retired towards St. Jean Pied de Port. The 6th division was ordered to re-cross the Nive, in consequence of the attacks on the 10th, 11th, and 12th of December, on the left and centre of the army between the sea and the Nive.†

* Dec. 13, 1813.
† " The battles of the Nive equal those of the Pyrenees in obstinacy and duration. In the latter, the French marshal was the assailant; in the former, he was the assailed; and though both in this attack and defence he fought under the most favourable circumstances, in both he was signally de-

Marshal Soult, having failed in these attacks, moved the whole of his disposable force through Bayonne on the night of the 12th, in order to attack the right corps, which remained between the Nive and the Adour, and separated from the rest of the army by the former river. The bridge of boats constructed upon it below Usteritz, which formed the communication with the rest of the army, was carried away on the same night by the torrents from the Pyrenees, which, since they frequently caused a rise in the Nive of a couple of feet in a few hours, without any rain falling in the low country, rendered the communication by the

---

feated. In the Pyrenees, the passes were widely separated, the lateral communications indirect, the position extensive, and, consequently, vulnerable in many points. The shorter lines of Soult's position enabled him to mass troops together with rapidity, and the undulating surface effectually concealed his movements. Hence his attacks were made with overwhelming numbers, and although expected, they could not be distinctly ascertained until the head of his columns were in immediate contact with the pickets. At Bayonne, the situations of Wellington and Soult were exactly reversed. The allied general was obliged to operate on both sides of a dangerous river, with bad roads and long and inconvenient lines; while, at the same time, he had to secure St. Jean de Luz from any attempts that Soult might make to gain a point of such importance. The French marshal, on the contrary, had the advantage of a fortified camp, a fortress immediately beside him, excellent and short communications, with a permanent bridge across the Nive, by which he could concentrate on either bank of the river, and assail that wing of the allies which promised the best chance of success."— MAXWELL'S LIFE OF WELLINGTON.

fords higher up also very precarious. The bridge was quickly restored, so that but little interruption was caused by that event.

The corps of Sir Rowland Hill might, therefore, be considered as nearly isolated from the rest of the army; for, from the badness of the roads through the deep clay country on both sides of the Nive, no reinforcements could well be brought up before the enemy had full time to make his attacks in all their force. This corps was composed of the 2nd division, commanded by Lieut.-General Sir William Stewart, consisting of three brigades of British, and of one brigade of Portuguese infantry; of a Portuguese division, commanded by Marescal del Campo Le Cor, consisting of two brigades of infantry. If we take the battalions of British at 500 men each—a high estimate after the severe service they had been engaged in for the eight preceding months, during which had been fought the actions at Vittoria, the Pyrenees, and Nivelle— this gives 4500 men; and the Portuguese brigades may be taken at 2000 each, which will therefore amount to 6000 men.

The artillery attached to the corps consisted of one troop of British horse-artillery, having five 6-pounder guns and a howitzer, under Lieut.-Col. Hew Ross, and a brigade of Portuguese artillery of the same number 9-pounders, under Lieut.-Col. Tulloch.

The whole force may, therefore, be taken at 10,500 infantry, and twelve guns.

Besides these, there were two weak regiments of

cavalry, the 13th and 14th British, about 700 men, and a Spanish corps of infantry, of about 4000 men, under General Morillo; but this force was detached to occupy a position on the road to St. Jean Pied de Port, from which quarter the French, under General Paris, made demonstrations of attacking, at the same time, the rear of Sir Rowland Hill's position.

The centre of the position was not commanding, the rise from the valley being trifling. The chief advantages it afforded were from the three or four small houses called St. Pierre, situated at the point where the high road leading from Bayonne to St. Jean Pied de Port comes on the ridge, and from the ground to the left of the high road being hilly and broken, in many parts bristled with rocks and brushwood, with only one bad road or lane leading along it from the enemy's position; to the right of the high road the ground was also difficult, from thick hedges enclosing the fields; one hedge bordered the right of the road itself; another, parallel to our line, about one hundred yards in front of the guns, was so thick as to be almost impassable. The broken ground and these hedges greatly impeded the movements of troops, and at times were disadvantageous to us, but much more so to the enemy, whose attacking columns were, in consequence, obliged to move along, and confine themselves to the high road. This ground *was occupied by Major-General Barnes' British,* and Brigadier-General Ashworth's Portuguese brigades, and the artillery.

PENINSULAR SKETCHES. 137

From the above-stated obstacles, and the deep wet soil of the valley, no part of the ground admitted of the employment of cavalry.

The valley itself was large and open: seen into in every part from the position. The ground about the chateau, occupied by Major-General Pringle's brigade on the left, was wooded and strong, so that this flank was well secured; but the communication between it and the centre was such that no support could be easily brought from one to the other.

Major-General Byng's brigade occupied the right: one regiment was stationed on the hill beyond the mill-pond, a strong position, with a deep narrow valley in front, and houses along the road on the ridge leading to the rest of the army. The right seemed therefore secure. The other two regiments of Major-General Byng's brigade were posted in the valley near the head of the mill-pond. The two Portuguese brigades, commanded by Brigadier-Generals Da Costa and Buchan, remained in reserve near the high road behind St. Pierre. Lieutenant-General Sir Rowland Hill, with the head-quarters, during the early part of the action, took his station on a hill in rear of the centre of the position which commanded a view of the whole, and enabled him to order such movements as became requisite.

Such was the position in which the above-mentioned force had to sustain the attack of 30,000 veteran French troops—namely, seven divisions out of nine forming the French army, Soult having left only two divisions to maintain the intrenched camp beyond the Nive.

On the 12th of December, a large body of the enemy, under General Paris, made a demonstration on the road from St. Jean Pied de Port, as if intending to attack from that quarter. In consequence of which, Sir Rowland Hill ordered Major-General Barnes' brigade to march on Hasparran; but just before sunset, the bridge across the Nive at Bayonne was observed covered with troops marching into the town. The real point of attack being now evident, orders were sent to recal General Barnes, who was thus only enabled to come into the position above mentioned a little before daylight on the 13th. Orders were at the same time sent on the evening of the 12th to General Morillo, to cross the Nive at Cambo, and take up a position on the high road leading to St. Jean Pied de Port, so as to oppose General Paris, in case of his making an attack; and a staff-officer, Major Churchill, was despatched to order the 4th and 6th divisions to cross the Nive and join the right corps, and then to proceed to head quarters to apprize Lord Wellington of these movements.

On the 13th of December, the morning was clear, with sunshine, but for an hour after daylight a mist hung in the valley between the positions, and concealed the enemy's movements; heavy columns and the artillery could, however, be at times distinguished forming on the opposite heights, and about half-past eight o'clock he commenced driving in our advanced pickets.

The skirmishing soon became general throughout the valley, but more particularly pushing, on the part of the enemy, to our left of the high road, which, from the difficulty of the ground, had only been occupied by a detachment of Brigadier-General Ashworth's Portuguese brigade. This caused Lieutenant-General Sir William Stewart to withdraw from St. Pierre the 71st regiment, and two guns of the horse artillery, in order to occupy that part of the position, and thereby prevent the left centre being forced.

Major-General Barnes was thus left on the high road, with only the 50th and 92nd regiments, and the remainder of Brigadier-General Ashworth's Portuguese; in all, about 2500 men, and ten guns.

The enemy next pushed forward to the right of the high road, to take possession of a wood, which was occupied by some of the Caçadores of General Ashworth's brigade. This obliged General Barnes to detach half the 50th regiment to support the Caçadores, since the possession of the wood would have given the enemy considerable advantages for forming his attacking columns. The half of the 50th and the Caçadores remained in this wood until the close of the action, skirmishing with the enemy in front and with the left of his attacking columns.

At the same time that these attacks on the left and right of the high road, and on the road itself, were going on, the enemy were also driving in the pickets of Major-General Pringle's brigade on the left, and Byng's on the right of the position.

Notwithstanding the attempts on both sides of the high road to check the enemy, he kept steadily advancing along it. The skirmishing, which, during the half hour since the action commenced, had been gradually increasing, now extended along the whole front, and the valley presented an almost continued blaze and roar of musketry, which soon dissipated the mist, and on the high road was seen a dense column of infantry, covered in front and flanks with clouds of skirmishers. The artillery on both sides now opened. The enemy, however, soon gained the rise to our position, and commenced ascending it, driving before them, by their superior fire, the half of the 50th regiment and Caçadores remaining in front of St. Pierre, at the same time themselves suffering severely, particularly from our artillery.

The 92nd regiment, which had been kept in reserve at St. Pierre, were then ordered to attack; the enemy's column halted, and remained steady until all his skirmishers were driven in; it then broke, and retired, but was almost immediately replaced by a fresh column, which pushed forward, covered by skirmishers, as the first had been; and he at the same time brought four light guns down into the valley, near the bottom of his position, which opened and kept up a close fire that told severely. The enemy had at this time also brought more heavy guns into battery on the position; so that he now more than doubled us in the number of guns, and they were also of a larger calibre. The fire, both of artillery and musketry, at this period became and continued, until the repulse of the second attack, the heaviest that occurred during the day.

The 92nd remained on the ground they had gained, taking up a position across the high road, about two hundred yards in front of St. Pierre. In this position, from the large front which the enemy was enabled to bring against them, and the close fire of his light guns, they were obliged to give way, and retire to St. Pierre. The half of the 50th and the Portuguese were again left to check the enemy's advance, which they did well, considering the disparity of numbers.

The dense column of the enemy kept steadily moving up the high road, although the fire from Ross's guns was at times seen making a gap through it, and his light troops gained and began to line the hedge, about one hundred yards in front of St. Pierre. The Portuguese guns had limbered up, and were retiring, but General Barnes ordered them immediately to return to their ground, and resume their fire.

The hedge above mentioned was soon completely lined by the enemy's skirmishers; it was, however, too thick to admit their passing through it. His skirmishers to our left of the road were equally forward: the column itself only a little in the rear, and continuing to advance. All our skirmishers were driven in; and Ashworth's troops, drawn up in line, opened a running fire. The artillerymen were falling fast at their guns, as also the Portuguese in line, from the musketry in front, and the well-directed fire of the enemy's artillery; the shot passing through the Portuguese line, rattling on the houses, or tearing up the ground in front. The number of wounded crawling to the rear was considerable.

General Barnes was at this time wounded, and the French column had attained to within one hundred yards of the houses on the crest of the position. To one not aware that a regiment was at hand to charge, defeat seemed nearly certain. The 92nd, however, after retiring, had re-formed behind the houses, and at this moment, led by Colonel Cameron, suddenly appeared on the high road in close column, bayonets fixed, and the bagpipes playing in its front,—marching steadily down towards the column of the enemy, although at least four times its number. At the same time the skirmishers also again pushed forward on the flanks.

The French column halted,—perhaps wishing to deploy; this the broken ground on its right scarcely admitted, and on the left the hedge prevented it. They remained steady; and it appeared that the very rare event in modern warfare—personal conflict—would take place,—that bayonets would be used. But on the 92nd getting half-way down to the enemy, or within about fifty yards, the officer on horseback at the head of the column suddenly wheeled round, waving his sword, evidently giving the order to retire. Perhaps what was passing to his right might influence this determination, where, as will be afterwards detailed, the 71st regiment and Da Costa's Portuguese brigade were about this time re-taking their ground, and driving the enemy before them. However this may be, the column went about, and retired to their own position in fair order: nor in so doing did it suffer much loss, so many of our men had fallen, and so much exhausted were those that remained, whilst the enemy had always fresh troops to bring forward.

During this attack, General Barnes had his horse killed, and was afterwards himself shot through the body. His aides-de-camp, Captain Hamilton, was severely, and Lieutenant Hamilton slightly wounded; and his brigade-major, Wemyss, had three balls through his hat. General Ashworth and Lieutenant-Colonel Tulloch, of the Portuguese, were also wounded. Of three pipers with the 92nd regiment, two were killed. That regiment and Colonel Hew Ross's guns sustained the brunt of the attack; but the 50th and Caçadores, who had skirmished with the enemy during his advance, shewed great bravery in keeping the enemy in check, which gave time for the 92nd to re-form. The Portuguese line also kept up a galling fire on the enemy, when he appeared to be on the point of carrying the position.

It may be here remarked, that had this part of our position been carried, since the head of the 6th division had then arrived from across the Nive, the action would have been renewed on a new position, of which the hill where Sir Rowland Hill took his station would have been the principal feature.

The enemy soon afterwards made another attack along the high road, of a similar description to the two former, but not pushed with the same confidence and impetuosity. The troops in the centre were, as already stated, much exhausted, so that even a less resolute attack became now formidable. The 57th regiment was, however, in march from the right to St. Pierre, in order to be in readiness as a reserve.

In this last attack on the centre, after the skirmishers had been driven back, so much had we suffered, that neither general nor field-officer remained on the ground to give orders: seeing which, Lieutenant-Colonel Currie, aide-de-camp to Sir Rowland Hill, took the command, formed the 50th, and led them down to charge the enemy's column; but the latter scarcely attempted to maintain its ground,—probably influenced by the repulse of his left column; for at this moment, Buchan's Portuguese and the Buffs were re-taking the hill beyond the mill-pond, and rapidly driving back the enemy along its face.

The enemy, from this period of the day, about half-past eleven, merely skirmished to cover his retreat and carry off his wounded.

About this time the fourth division reached the ground; the 6th division having, as already stated, arrived a little earlier; and Lord Wellington also came on the position.

In narrating the operations on the centre, collateral attacks have been alluded to; it will be now necessary to give some detail of these.

About the time of the repulse of the enemy's first column by the 92nd regiment, the attack of another column to the left, on the ground occupied by the 71st and Portuguese, had been successful; for although these troops had kept the enemy for some time in check, he was enabled to bring upon them a large front and very superior fire, under which they at length gave way and retired—keeping up their fire and causing the enemy much loss. But they were finally driven completely back, and the enemy gained the crown of the position—the high ground to the left of St. Pierre, and from which that point could be turned. He was only, however, for a moment in possession of this commanding ground; for seeing the success of the enemy by his advancing fire, Da Costa's Portuguese brigade, which was in reserve to the left of the road behind St. Pierre, had been moved forward by Sir Rowland Hill in person to give support. This enabled the 71st to rally and attack the enemy, who was in turn driven back to the bottom of our position. This space, in its whole extent, was strewed with French and English mixed—shewing how obstinately it had been contested. In rallying the troops and endeavouring to restore the action at this point, Lieutenant-General Sir William Stewart had all his staff wounded, and Captain Le Marchant killed. General Le Cor, in bringing forward the Portuguese, was also wounded. The colonel commanding the 71st was, in consequence of what took place on this occasion, removed from the service.

This attack and that on the high road were the main attacks of the enemy. Those on the right and left flanks were probably only intended to occupy our troops and prevent their detaching assistance to the centre. On the right, however, part of Major-General Byng's brigade (the 3rd regiment) were driven back from the strong ground which they occupied,—the enemy having to attack,—across a deep valley and stream. On observing this, Brigadier-General Buchan's Portuguese brigade, which was in reserve behind St. Pierre, was moved to their assistance. In making this movement, the brigade was much exposed to, and suffered severely from, the enemy's artillery.

On General Buchan reaching the ground, the enemy had got possession of the greater part of the hill—viz., as far as the head of the mill-pond; but on being attacked, he gave way, was rapidly driven back and across the valley to his own position.

This, as has been already remarked, occurred about the time of the enemy's last attack on the centre.

A court of inquiry took place on the colonel commanding the Buffs in the above affair, which led to his resigning his commission.

The rest of General Byng's brigade had remained in their position, skirmishing in their front, during the whole morning, until, as has been stated, the 57th regiment was withdrawn to support the centre at the time of the last attack; the remainder of this brigade, the 31st and 66th forming a provisional battalion, were now moved forward to attack the enemy on a hill to the left of the mill-pond. The enemy were by this time, however, only skirmishing to gain time, and shewing a front to cover their retreat; so that the troops stationed on the hill gave way on the approach of this force. Major-General Byng ascended the hill about the time Lord Wellington reached the high ground occupied by the 71st, from which it could be seen, and probably from this cause is especially mentioned in the despatch.

On our extreme left, the position occupied by Major-General Pringle's brigade, the enemy made an attack early in the day. Success in this quarter would have been of great importance, since it would have endangered our communication with the rest of the army. He was repulsed, however, with considerable loss; and during the rest of the day merely kept skirmishing in front, making demonstrations as if again intending to attack.

In the rear of our position, on the high road to St. Jean Pied de Port, General Morillo's force was attacked by the French under General Paris. They occupied, however, a good position in a village on the high road, which they maintained, and there was no result from this attack.

Such are the details of this day's operations, so creditable to the right corps of the army, which, with 4500 British, 6000 Portuguese infantry, and twelve guns, in a position taken up on the occasion,—allowing, therefore, no opportunity of strengthening it, and affording in itself no great advantages,—repulsed the attacks of 30,000 veteran French infantry, supported by an artillery at least double the number of that of the allies.

The enemy, in retiring, after the last attack on the centre, endeavoured to withdraw the light guns which, in the early part of the action, he brought into the valley; our skirmishers were, however, pushing so close that a number of horses were killed, and he abandoned two of them. From the number of muskets left on the field the wounded must have been very great;—wounded men almost invariably get quit of everything that encumbers their retreat; but a musket is scarcely ever to be seen whole, as the first comer always snaps it across the small of the stock.

At the close of the action, the dead and wounded along the high road and on the ground adjoining it were lying thicker than perhaps, in an equal extent, on any field of battle which took place during the war, not excepting Waterloo, although the latter continued eight hours, whilst this was over in three. Lord Wellington, in riding over the ground, remarked that he had never observed so large a number of killed on so small a compass.

This was the last attack the French made from Bayonne, until we crossed the Adour in February, and completed the blockade. We were, however, so close that the troops were always under arms at their alarm-posts two hours before daylight; but notwithstanding this constant exposure, and during a winter in which there was a more than usual quantity of rain and frequently snow, very little sickness took place.

The loss of the enemy in the action may be estimated at full three times the amount which we sustained, for his troops were completely exposed to our fire during the movements across the valley to attack; also, from the greater number of men he brought into action, our shot must have comparatively told more. To judge also from the killed and wounded left on the ground, the French appear to have suffered at least in that proportion.

"TAKE THE HILL BEFORE DARK!"

THE evening of the 15th February, 1814, amidst the beautifully varied scenery of the Lower Pyrenees, was one of extreme loveliness; for though the early spring had not entirely obliterated all traces of winter, and the tops of some mountains were still clad in snow, yet the glowing sunset, with its ever-changing gold and purple, imparted to the magnificent display of mountain and forest, interspersed with fertile valleys, a richness and a colouring not to be described. But the peaceful serenity of nature was, that evening, strangely contrasted with the tumultuous violence of war—with the thunder of the cannon and of the volley—and with the mixture of hostile hosts, in the mortal strife of the charge.

The Duke of Wellington had, two or three days before, commenced his advance from the neighbourhood of Bayonne, after the temporary pause which an unusually severe winter had interposed in his splendid career of victory. In this advance, the right of the army, under Lord Hill, had most gallantly and most skilfully driven the enemy from position to position, allowing him no time to recover himself; and from the earliest dawn of the day mentioned, the troops had been moving by a mountain-road, the light infantry clearing the way. In their course, they had successively dislodged their active enemy from the numerous abattis he had thrown across the road, and from the strong ground which he everywhere found, and of which he knew so well how to take advantage. At one juncture, the duke in person had reconnoitred so closely that the French cavalry threatened a dash, when the grenadiers of the 39th regiment had the honour of covering his Grace. Late in the afternoon, Major-General Pringle's* brigade of the 2nd division, consisting then of the 28th and 39th regiments, with a couple of guns, had taken post upon a height to the left of the road. Immediately in their front was a deep precipitous ravine, which divided the height from a lofty hill close to the small town of Garris, on which a column of the enemy, 6000 strong, was in position. Both positions, together with the ravine between them, were rough forest ground; with portions, and particularly in the ravine, very thickly timbered. While the light infantry of the brigade, without pausing, had descended into the ravine, briskly driving in the enemy's light troops, the guns had, instantly, opened a vigorous and well-directed fire across

* Lieut-General Sir W. H. Pringle.

the ravine, and over the heads of the combatants below.

At the time that the glories of sunset had commenced, the arms of the brigade had been piled, to give the men a momentary rest. The officers and men were standing in small groups, anxiously watching the effect of the rapid discharges of the guns upon the enemy's columns, or listening to the continued rattling fire of the skirmishers, sharply engaged beneath, and who, though quite close, were concealed from view by the thick wood. Every now and then attention was attracted by wounded comrades, as they emerged from the dark hollow to regain the position. Among these was Captain Gale, commanding the light company of the 28th regiment, who was borne up mortally wounded.

The lateness of the hour precluded the idea that anything further could be effected that night. Wearied with their long and arduous day's work, the bystanders were looking forward to the repose of the bivouack, and were considering themselves rather as spectators than as actors in the deeply interesting scene, when an aide-de-camp, at full speed, quickly delivered an order from the duke, pointing to the enemy's position—" Take the hill before dark!"

The brigade fell in as by magic — the men needed no order. A proud smile played upon every countenance. Every one felt the high compliment paid to the brigade, in thus being allowed to take the bull by the horns. And the honour was enhanced by the promptness of the order, the perfect confidence it placed in the troops, and the total absence of all doubt of the success of the attack. And such was the high confidence which the troops, on their part, reposed in their illustrious chief, that his very giving the order was proof to them that they could execute it. They well knew that they would not be sacrificed in an unequal conflict, and that, if they needed it, they would be properly supported.

It falling accidentally to the good fortune of the 39th regiment to be principally and closely engaged that evening, its movements will now be exclusively followed. Its old and gallant friends of the 28th, how efficient soever were their services on the occasion, were directed upon a point of attack which did not happen to bring them in close contact with the enemy.

Excepting the influence which the character of commanding officers must necessarily have upon corps, there was little or no difference in the goodness of the regiments composing that army of brothers. All, governed by the same rules and animated by the same high sentiments and feelings, were equally anxious to do their duty; and although " Garris" does not yet beam, with other numerous recollections of glory, upon the colours of the 39th regiment, the honours of each may, in general, be estimated by its opportunities of earning them.

As soon as the 39th regiment had fallen in, its commanding officer, Colonel, now Lieutenant-

General the Hon. Sir Robert W. O'Callaghan, repeated the order to the regiment in the same concise but emphatic terms—" Take the hill before dark!" The effect was electrical. The men responded by the loud, deep, animating, truly British cheer. The words were then given—" Fix bayonets!"—" Shoulder arms!"—" Double quick!" and the next instant the regiment, in close column, plunged into the ravine.

For a few seconds, in the deep chasm, it must have been obscured from view; but though unseen, its course would be clearly noted by its continued enthusiastic cheering. It speedily cleared the bottom of the wild glen, and then steadily ascended the enemy's position, without firing a shot, under the heavy rolling volleys which he incessantly poured down from above. The sound of the balls bristling the trees on all sides had a singular effect. But during the ascent, which was exceedingly steep, the enemy's fire was a little too high to do much mischief, except to the mounted officers, all of whom were either hit themselves or had their horses shot under them.

Soon after commencing the ascent, Major-General Pringle, who had placed himself at the head of the regiment, was, to the regret of every one, very badly wounded, and obliged to be carried to the rear. As the regiment neared the summit, loaded with their heavy kits, the men suffered much from exhaustion, but with willing hearts kept steadily up the steep. Here Colonel the Hon. R. W. O'Callaghan and the Brigade-Major (Fancourt) both lost their horses; and shortly after, the Adjutant, now Major Henry Smyth, had his horse likewise shot under him.

At length, however, the summit was attained, and instantly carried. Misled by the nature of the ground, and perhaps by the shades of evening, the enemy no doubt took the attacking force to be far more numerous than it was, and very soon gave way, retreating, however, only to a short distance. The regiment lost no time in improving its advantage, by wheeling to its right to sweep the ridge of the position; and it was in the act of driving the enemy along the ridge, when, perceiving that at this point he was opposed only by a single battalion, he brought up his main force, to charge the advancing regiment in his turn. Hitherto the regiment had reserved its fire, but at this point, immediately before the enemy closed, it opened upon him with great effect. Among those who were seen to fall was a French drummer, a very fine fellow, who was coming boldly on in front, beating the charge. But the enemy, nothing daunted, still pressed on with great determination, until the bayonets, in many instances, were crossed. Personal encounters now ensued. Colonel the Hon. R. W. O'Callaghan, whose horse had been shot under him, and who was now fighting on foot at the head of the regiment, received one French bayonet at the breast, and another at the shin, at the same time. The late Lieutenant George Coleman nobly led the grenadiers. Lieutenant Evans, the brave commander of the 60th rifles, attached to the light companies of the brigade, personally grappled with a French captain, and they both fell to the ground together. Evans was a small man, and no match for his antagonist; but he kept up the unequal contest till a grenadier of the 39th, stepping forward to his assistance, the Frenchman was made prisoner. Among others, there were two privates of the regiment, of rather low stature, not well-looking, and so slovenly that everybody used to be down upon them. These two men distinguished themselves greatly. One of them was so badly wounded as never afterwards to be able to rejoin the regiment.

Wearied with his fruitless exertions, in a few minutes the enemy was compelled to retire in some confusion; but quickly rallying, and encouraged by his very superior force, he twice more returned to the charge, and was as often repelled. For about twenty minutes the regiment sustained the utmost efforts of the enemy to dislodge it from the height which it had stormed, The intervals between the bayonet attacks were filled up with active unremitting firing on both sides. Poor Colonel Fearon, commanding one of the Caçadore regiments, who, though without his men, had come up the height, was killed, while gallantly exerting himself to aid the common cause. In the confusion unavoidably attendant upon such a scene, two of the enemy's dragoons (possibly orderlies) remained quietly close to the regiment for a considerable time. The dress being then so much alike, they were mistaken for English, till, seizing their opportunity, they galloped off and rejoined their countrymen. English and French were sometimes mixed together. One Frenchman in particular was remarked, who, closely pursued by an officer, threw away his arms and kit, and with great celerity threaded his way through friends and foes, till he effected his escape. At last, the enemy beginning to waver, the regiment resumed its forward movement along the ridge; and another charge drove him in disorder completely off the hill, leaving many killed, as well as prisoners, behind him. The streaks of evening had for some time, one by one, been disappearing, the more distant mountains were no longer distinguishable, and the shades of night were now settling darkly upon the height; but the order was literally and fully executed. Brief space had been given; time pressed; there had not been a moment to lose, and not a moment was lost. The hill was taken before dark!

The enemy, not having anticipated so uncourteous an intrusion at so late an hour, had made extensive preparations for the comfort of his bivouack, in collecting large quantities of wood for his fires. Of this the regiment gladly availed itself, and that night its bivouack was far more brilliantly lighted than it usually was. Seated around the cheerful blaze, and while, with keen appetite, partaking of the simple supper which the havresack happened to supply, many a congratulation was exchanged between friends, and many an incident of the evening recounted. And there were few who did not, with grateful hearts, silently look up to Him who had given them the victory, and who had protected them in the execution of their duty. But, overcome with fatigue, it was not long before conversation began to flag; the various sounds of the bivouack gradually died away; and at length, trusting to the active look-out of the pickets, all, excepting those who had charge of prisoners, with their feet towards the fire, resigned themselves to comfortable repose.

The following morning, while the men were occupied in burying the dead in long trenches dug for the occasion, the late gallant and beloved Lieutenant-General Sir William Stewart, who commanded the second division under Lord Hill, paid a visit to the regiment upon the height. Not wishing, at such a time, that the regiment should fall in, he called for all the officers of it present; among whom was the late Major-General Sir Charles Bruce, then Lieutenant-Colonel, with his face bound up, and who, though severely wounded the preceding evening, refused to go to the rear.

Sir William warmly thanked the officers for their exertions in the action, and highly complimented the regiment. He had several times noticed its good conduct, and particularly at the pass of Maia. He had witnessed the attack of last evening; and though he did not then know that there was but one regiment opposed to the enemy at this point, yet when he saw the pertinacious manner in which with such force he three times returned to the charge, he could not but feel great anxiety for the result. And, in concluding, he

PENINSULAR SKETCHES. 159

kindly offered to recommend an officer, and a non-commissioned officer, for promotion.

The late excellent Captain Duncan Campbell, commanding the light infantry, obtained on this occasion a well-merited brevet majority.

His Grace the Duke of Wellington, Lord Hill, and many other distinguished officers, were eye-witnesses of the action, as must have been also the whole of the old 2nd division, and probably other troops.

The Duke of Wellington having to describe an extensive line of operations, could not be expected to descend much into detail. In adverting, however, to this attack, in his despatch, dated 20th February, 1814, after stating that, on the 15th, Lord Hill continued the pursuit of the enemy, who, under General Harispe, and reinforced by General Paris' division and other troops, "had retired to a strong position in front of Garris;" and that General Murillo's Spanish division had been ordered to turn the enemy's left, "while the second division under Sir William Stewart should attack in front;"—his Grace proceeds, "Those troops made a most gallant attack upon the enemy's position, which was remarkably strong, but which was carried without very considerable loss. Much of the day had elapsed before the attack could be commenced, and the action lasted till after dark, the enemy having made repeated attempts to regain the position, particularly in two attacks, which were most gallantly received, and repulsed by the 39th, under the command of the

Honourable Colonel O'Callaghan, in Major-General Pringle's brigade. The Major-General and Lieutenant-Colonel Bruce, of the 39th, were unfortunately wounded. We took ten officers and about 200 prisoners."

Such was the action of Garris, as imperfectly beheld in the intense excitement of such a scene of wild confusion, amid clouds of smoke and the long shadows of evening; and as imperfectly remembered through the vista of more than five and twenty years, unaided, too, by the recollection of others, no one being aware of the writer's intention of throwing these particulars together. But, such as it is, this little sketch may not be thought inappropriate, at a time when the bayonet is so much a subject of discussion.

A single bayonet may appear to be an insignificant weapon: its power consists in numbers, acting together as one machine in a closed compact line. There the unprotected left arm of the soldier is covered by his left hand man; and, without disturbing the close order so essential to military movements, which the use of the sword would do, it is calculated for thrusts, which are so much more quickly given than cuts with the sword. Cuts being also necessarily delivered upon the exterior of the person, frequently fail in disabling an adversary, whereas an inch or two of the bayonet would generally be mortal. The use of the bayonet in line is so simple, too, as to require little or no skill, which at a moment of great excitement is a valuable property. The firelock is perhaps heavier than it need be in the present improved state of the arts, but with its present length it is surely more convenient than a long pike. Had it been thought that the utility of the bayonet in the British service would ever have been questioned, the comparative ravages of the steel and the ball at Garris would have been ascertained. Some must have fallen by the bayonet, though probably only a small proportion. In the few cases where sufficient determination has been shown on both sides to allow of adverse bayonets meeting, irregularities in the ground, wavings in the line, or the two lines, on closing, happening to be inclined and not parallel to each other, have probably prevented more than a few files from coming into close conflict at any one point. These would use their bayonets; but the others, being obliged to conform to their line, and not being near enough to fight with the bayonet, would soon naturally resort to firing. But in the late war the enemy seldom awaited the onset of a British charge; and, in breaking, he, with his position, frequently lost many prisoners. And if, then, the British bayonet has thus been the means of taking many positions, and thousands of prisoners, it is not, perhaps, reasonable to quarrel with it, because it cannot be proved to have pierced many individuals. It is certain that, on the memorable evening alluded to, the brigade had no doubt of the power and efficiency of the bayonet; it had the very highest confidence in it, and marched to the attack fully determined to use it, should the enemy allow them; and the enemy knew that the brigade would do so.

The bayonet may or may not be the best weapon for infantry in close order and at close quarters. But the strongest evidence should be required of the superiority of a substitute, before we lay aside this truly national weapon; and, while it is retained, it is evidently wise and proper that the British soldier of the present day should be carefully taught zealously to value and to cherish it, as did universally his brethren of the war on many a hard-fought field.

REMINISCENCES OF BAYONNE.

THERE are few things that are more deeply felt by the old gallant soldiers of the Peninsular war than the total want of gratitude which seems to be entertained for their services; and, God knows, no army ever did more, or suffered more, for its country, than that army did. Yet, how stand they now?—as naught! Neglected and forgotten, without a riband on their breast, or one thing to distinguish them from the military tyro of the day, excepting, indeed, scars and premature old age. In thinking over all this, I have felt very doubtful whether anything connected with the Peninsula would not be "like a tale that is told," and afford but little interest in these days. However, as still a few of my old comrades are left to me, I have ventured, in this short paper, to remind them of some trifling anecdotes which may cause them to look back with a smile and a sigh to those happy days, when we were young and light-hearted, with bright hopes and prospects before us—now, alas! all fled for ever.

On the night of the 22nd of February, 1814, the first division got under arms, and marched upon the Adour. Our advanced guard consisted of three light companies of the first brigade and a brigade of artillery. Our route lay through a deep, gloomy pine forest, over a bad cross country road.

Alexander and myself were smoking our cigars, and laughing and talking, when an officer of rank rode up, evidently much out of temper, and expressed great anger at finding us, as he said, "making so much noise," where silence was of so much consequence; "and actually smoking!" exclaimed he. Our cigars were, of course, instantly thrown away, and Colonel Alexander made no reply. He merely pointed to the guns, which were marching with flambeaux at the horses' heads; and the rumbling that the said guns made was enough to have aroused "the seven sleepers."

By daylight the next morning we had established a battery of eighteen-pounders on the left bank of the river,* which was very shortly

* The Adour, like the Gave, is a name common to many rivers in the Pyrenees, both simply meaning water in some of those primeval languages, the remains of which are still widely preserved in the appellations of rivers and mountains. The greater and noted stream, into which the others are received, has its sources in the county of Bigorre, under the Pics du Midi and d'Espade, two of the highest mountains in the chain. It passes by Campan, Bagneras, Montgaillard, and Tarbes, and begins to be navigable near Granade, a small town in the little county of Marsan. Having been joined by the Douze, on its right below Tartas, it inclines

engaged with a corvette; and the enemy likewise dropped some gun-boats down the river. The latter gentry we amused with some rockets, but the effect was not such as to give me a very exalted opinion of that weapon. The rockets* went skipping about the river like mad things, and dancing quadrilles in every direction but the right one. Some of them came back to ourselves, but happily without doing any mischief. The only one that took effect—and this seemed quite an accident—stuck in the bow of one of the boats, and sank her. The French soldiers, at that period wholly unaccustomed to this arm, were so frightened, that they jumped overboard with all their accoutre-

---

to the south-west from its junction, passes Acqs, and then holds an almost southerly course to meet the Gave de Pau, which brings with its own waters those of the Gave d'Oleron, into which the Gave de Mauleon has been received. The Adour is then joined by the Bidouse, and lastly by the Nive. —ED.

* " There was a prejudice in the army against this weapon, which had hitherto not been used in the field. The opinion seems to have been, that if it had been an efficient means of destruction it would sooner have been borrowed from the East Indian nations. Lord Wellington, however, was willing that they should be tried; and some experiments that were made at Font-Arabia gave reason for supposing that they might be found useful on the Adour. The direction of this new arm was assigned to Sir Augustus Fraser, but the trial was to be made under all the disadvantages of inexperience; for the corps was composed of men hastily brought together, and entirely ignorant of the arm they were to use; and the rockets themselves were equipped in five different ways, and consequently liable to as many failures."—SOUTHEY.

ments, and were drowned. The practice from our battery was not good at first, from the want of platforms; but this was soon rectified, and the corvette got a most handsome pommeling, and was glad at last to sheer off with the loss of her captain, and more than half her crew killed and wounded. One of our shots cut her flag-staff in two, and the tri-colour flag was seen floating down the stream. An artilleryman, stripping off his clothes, swam in, and brought it out, and it was soon seen waving on our battery as a trophy. Captain M——n, of the artillery, was walking about that evening a most ridiculous figure. A shot had shaved off the skirts of his coat, and being rather Dutch-built, he looked just like a fat cock-pheasant, whose tail had been shot away by a bungling sportsman. Whilst this was going on, Sir John Hope was passing the troops across the river; but as we had only two or three small boats, this was a slow and tedious operation; and the extraordinary thing was, that the French garrison from Bayonne never attempted to molest us until the evening, when a strong column of about four thousand men were seen advancing on the opposite bank of the river. At this time we had only succeeded in passing over two light companies of the second brigade.

When the enemy's column came within long range of the battery on the left bank of the river, it opened its fire on them, and with some effect; but they soon sheltered themselves behind the sand hills, and continued their advance against the small force opposed to them; and, as we could render them no assistance from our side of the river, we considered them as *enfans perdus*. On came the French, with their drums beating, and in the full confidence of making an easy prey of the two companies. They were destined, however, to a severe disappointment. Our party was, I believe, commanded by Lieutenant-Colonel Cotton,* who very judiciously fell back to a favourable piece of ground, where his flanks were secure, and awaited the attack. Sir John Hope had sent over some rockets to their assistance; and as soon as the French came close enough, the rockets were fired, and, most fortunately, at the first discharge, three went smack into the very centre of them. Instantly the drums ceased, and the large column burst and fled in irretrievable confusion. The ground was very favourable for light troops, and they were followed for a considerable distance, and suffered severely. Our loss was only five men killed and wounded.

On the morning of the 24th we observed a small fleet of *chasse-marées*, commanded by Captain O'Reilly, and destined to form our bridge, rapidly approaching the bar, which is, perhaps, as dangerous a one as exists; and, excepting at spring-tides, only to be crossed by very small craft. Of the first boats that attempted it, two were swamped, when Captain Elliot and all hands perished! Still the rest came cheering on

* Now Lieut.-Gen. Sir Willoughby Cotton, G.C.B., &c.

through the surf;—for what dangers or difficulties ever stopped our noble seamen!

It was a fearful sight;* and although accustomed (as I was at that time) to view death in its most ghastly forms, still it was impossible to look upon this scene unmoved; and I could have burst into tears of joy when I saw the remainder of the gallant little fleet riding safely and triumphantly in the deep waters of the Adour, loudly cheered by the army. No time was now lost in forming the bridge; and, as everything had been previously prepared at St. Jean de Luz, it took less time than might have been expected. The boats were secured, fore and aft, with double anchors, their gunwales sawed away midships, and the bridge laid.† Two

---

* "When the water rose again, the crews were promised rewards in proportion to their respective daring, and the whole flotilla approached in close order; but with it came black clouds and a driving gale, which covered the whole line of coast with a rough tumbling sea, dashing and foaming, without an interval of dark water to mark the entrance of the river. The men-of-war's boats first drew near this terrible line of surge; and Mr. Bloye, of the Lyra, having the chief pilot with him, heroically led into it, but in an instant his barge was engulphed, and he and all with him were drowned. The Lyra's boat, thus swallowed up, the following vessels swerved in their course, and shooting up to the right and left, kept hovering undecided on the edge of the tormented waters. Suddenly, Lieutenant Cheyne, of the Woodlark, pulled a-head, and striking the right line, with courage and fortune combined, safely passed the bar."—NAPIER.

† " It consisted of six-and-twenty *chasse-marées*, lashed to each other, and moored by the bow and stern to resist the current that changed at ebb and flow. Heavy guns were

strong booms were fastened across the river, and five gun-boats placed between them and the bridge, to protect it from any attempt which the French might make to destroy it: behind was another boom, to act as a sort of breakwater. As soon as the whole of the first division, with the guns, stores, &c., had crossed, the officers' baggage was allowed to pass over. We officers of the light infantry, who had been shoved to the front, could not leave our companies for a moment. But as soon as our baggage had arrived on the right bank of the river, we were anxious to hear about it; and very shortly, Captain G—e's old servant, Kettle, was seen advancing with a rueful visage and dejected air.

occasionally substituted for anchors; and cables were strained by capstans across the centre of the decks, with strong oak planks laid transversely, and sufficiently secured to form a platform, at the same time pliant and substantial, calculated to rise or fall with the tide, and strong enough to support the weight of artillery. Immense stone piers had been erected by the French to contract the channel of the stream, and, by an artificial current, prevent the sand from accumulating on the bar. These, from their breadth, formed an admirable causeway, while they lessened the space of water to be bridged to an extent of two hundred and seventy yards. It was supposed by French engineers impracticable to secure pontoons so as to resist the ocean swells and mountain floods to which the Adour was so constantly exposed; but a fortunate shifting of a sand-bank formed an excellent breakwater; while a boom was laid above the bridge to arrest fire-ships or floating timbers, which it might have been expected the enemy would employ for its destruction.—MAXWELL'S LIFE OF WELLINGTON.

"What is the matter?" said G——e.

"Why, sir, Garcia has drowned the mule."

"What mule?"

"Zarifa, if you please, sir."

"Zarifa! why, the very best animal I have. D——n that young Portuguese vagabond, I'll be the death of him! Don't let him come near me, or, by Heavens, I will put my sword through him!"

Now, the poor old boy had lived with Captain G——e many years, and was quite aware that his first burst of rage was like the first spurt of a bottle of soda-water, and would pass away as soon. A kinder-hearted man never lived; and when Kettle was satisfied that the froth of his master's passion had in some degree subsided, he said—

"The mule is not dead, sir."

"Not dead?— Why, you told me she was drowned."

"No, sir, if you please, I meant to say that she was *nearly* drowned; but you would not give me time to speak."

G——e looked him hard in the face, with a doubtful expression of countenance; but Kettle never moved a muscle.

"Is the mule much hurt?" said G——e.

"No, sir, I think she is as well as ever, and she has eaten a good supper of chopped straw and furze—but the baggage is very wet."

Poor dear G——e was so happy to find that his favourite mule was safe, that the minor misfortune of the wet baggage was little thought of; and I have no doubt but that old Kettle's judicious diplomacy saved Master Garcia from a skinful of sore bones.

We remained quiet until the 27th, when we advanced in earnest to invest Bayonne closely. It was a sharp affair, but completely successful, and the garrison were driven within their walls. Our advanced post on the Bordeaux road was at the little village of St. Etienne, within pistol-shot of their advanced work. The light companies were directed to take a large old building on the banks of the river, which had formerly been a convent. In passing over some flat ground, between the mill in front of the village of Beaucout and the convent, we were under a heavy fire from the French batteries. One shot struck down two men near me: one was killed, but the other ran laughing up to us, with his knapsack hanging from one shoulder, and shirt, stockings, brushes, &c., streaming behind him. The shot which had killed his comrade had ripped open his knapsack. The French did not attempt to defend the building, but retired within their works. One company was now sent forward to establish our outpost, at a short distance in the front, which was done after a slight skirmish. The other two companies were lying under a bank, tolerably well protected from the enemy's fire. I have often heard of men being knocked down, or hurt, by the wind of a shot, but I have always felt doubtful upon this subject; and a circumstance occurred here which tended very much to confirm these doubts. Observing one of our non-commissioned officers to have had the top of his cap shot away, I went up to him, and found him sitting under the bank scratching his head, and looking with great disgust at the fragments of his cap.

"Never mind about your cap, man," said I, "there will be more hats than heads presently, when you can fit yourself with another." He looked up at me with a most comic expression of countenance, and evidently had some good joke in his head to which he did not think it respectful to give utterance. He assured me that he felt no inconvenience whatever from the shot; although it was one of very large calibre, and must have passed within half an inch of the top of his head. In the evening we took possession of the convent: the only inhabitants were an old Spaniard, whom we instantly christened "The Monk," and his family. The next morning we were, us usual, under arms an hour before daylight. As I had been very ill for some time, and the morning was wet and raw, Alexander persuaded me to lie quiet, as, in case of an attack, I could be with the company in a moment; but his kindness had well nigh cost me my life. Finding that I could not sleep, and was anxious and restless, I turned out and joined the rest. Shortly after daylight, our old monk was showing us a large room, which appeared to have been in former days the refectory of the convent, when suddenly the French commenced a furious cannonade, and three or four shots came into the room, sending the bricks and mortar flying about our ears, and kicking up such a dust that we could scarcely see our way out. The room that Alexander and myself had slept in was a complete wreck, and the beds upon which we had been lying knocked all to pieces. When the firing ceased, we discovered the monk in a cellar, crouching in a corner. The fight had quite unsettled the poor old man's mind, and he never recovered his reason afterwards.

I never remember to have lived better than we did here. The peasantry soon found out that they were well paid for everything; and eggs, butter, poultry, and all that we could desire, were to be had in abundance, and at moderate prices. There was a bugler in one of the companies, who, as he was a remarkably clever, intelligent fellow, was occasionally employed to assist our servants, and one day that he was wanted he was nowhere to be found: every hole and cranny were searched without effect. He was an excellent soldier, and liked by his officers and comrades; the suspicion, therefore, that he had deserted was never entertained for a moment by any one; and conjecture was at a stand still. At last, some one in passing through a dark passage struck against something hard, which he found to be a shoe with a foot in it! It appeared that the company, coming in from the advance, had thrown down their great coats in a corner which Mr. Bugler Page had chosen for his dormitory. Lights were brought, and he was literally dug out from under about a hundred wet greatcoats; the wonder was, that he was not smothered. It was ever afterwards a standing joke against him; and we often heard his comrades badgering him, and begging to know "if he wanted ever a greatcoat." We soon converted the rambling old building into a very respectable infantry post; and I think that it would have been more than "Johnny Crapaud" could have managed had he tried to turn us out of it.

While all this was going on, and we were cutting a trench across the flat in front, the duty was very severe; and the soldiers hearing that it was the general's intention to send some men to assist us from the battalion companies, a deputation from the three companies came to Alexander. The spokesman said that they hoped his honour would tell the general that they felt very grateful to him for his kindness, but that they had nothing to complain of, were quite satisfied, and that they would sooner work till they dropped down dead than have any d—d Buffers* amongst them! This elegant speech was duly delivered. Being strong enough for the defence of the post, and not having a man on the sick-list, the general very wisely left us to ourselves. This caused as much satisfaction to the officers as to the men. We lived together in the most perfect harmony and good fellowship, and a happier or merrier set than we were never wore the green feather. Our commanding officer, too, was beloved and respected by every one. He had the happy art of instilling into those under his orders the same zeal and love for the profession which he himself ever displayed. We had the most unbounded confidence in him as an officer, and well has he proved since that our opinion of

* Soldiers belonging to battalion companies.

him was a just one. A better or more gallant soldier does not breathe.

About this time Mr. S—d—n came to see our part of the army; and, as he was a very old friend of mine, he frequently dined with us at the convent. The first day he visited us, Alexander was telling a story after dinner, in which we were all much interested, when S—d—n heard a loud crash and clatter over his head. "What is that?"

"Oh, only a shot," replied Alexander, proceeding with his story. The same thing happened two or three times, and S—d—n looked a little astonished, but said nothing. Now, we knew that it was impossible for any shot to hit the room in which we were sitting, but that was kept a profound secret from S—d—n. I must, however, do him the justice to say, that this never made the slightest difference in his coming to see us, nor did it appear to have any effect upon his appetite. He seemed to enjoy the good things before him as much as any of us, although he must have thought that the next thing that went into his stomach might very possibly be a 24-pound shot! He was a most entertaining companion; and it was always considered a sort of jubilee when he came to see us,—for what with his ready wit, good humour, and funny stories, he kept us in a constant roar of laughter; and he seemed as much at ease in the old convent, as if he had been presiding at the head of his own hospitable board at Castle S—d—n. Whenever he came to visit us, and found that it was my turn to be at the advanced post, he always went on picket with me, although he had lost his leg very early in life from an accident; and as our orders were not to defend the post if seriously attacked, but to fall back gradually, he could not even venture to take off his cork-leg at night, and his horse was always saddled and ready for him to mount at a moment's notice.

I cannot recollect that we ever lost any men within the convent walls; but we were so close to the French works, and their practice was so good, that we occasionally lost some of our advanced sentries from their fire. One day, poor G——e and myself were amusing ourselves in the garden in front of the picket-house, by playing at the very intellectual game of "pitch and hustle," when our sentry at the bottom of the walk called us up to him, and pointed out a French sentry who had just been posted immediately on the other side of the hedge, and quite within our lines. Colonel Alexander, who happened to be at the advance, went up to him and told him that he must go off. The man replied, that he dared not leave his post, but that when the relief came, he would tell "Monsieur le Caporal" what the colonel said. Alexander desired him to beckon up some one from his picket, and a non-commissioned officer came directly, who said that he would send the officer. Alexander told the officer that he had no wish to hurt the sentry, but that if he was not withdrawn in a quarter of an hour he would be shot. The French officer was a very reasonable and gentleman-like young man; and after many bows, and the exchange of a pinch of snuff, he went back to his party, taking the sentry with him.

On our return to the picket-house, we found that one of our sentries was badly wounded, and wished to see us. We found him lying covered with a blanket. He begged hard that Alexander would order his comrades to blow his brains out, as there was no chance of his recovery. The lower part of his body was completely smashed, and his left hip torn away; yet, notwithstanding the severity of the wound, he lingered in great agony for as much as twenty minutes afterwards. The poor fellow was a great favourite in the company; and we found, the next morning, that the soldiers had placed a rough stone at the head of the grave, with a cannon-shot, and these lines:—

> "On sentry I fell a sacrifice,
> In cold blood to French cowardice;
> Above my head a cannon-shot you see,
> Resembling that as was the death of me."

A few nights afterwards, some deserters gave information that the French intended to sortie that night; and in going round the advanced sentries, I came upon a good old soldier, who was quite a character in his way; and on my telling him that he must be particularly vigilant, and give immediate notice of any unusual sounds that he might hear, he said,—

"I do not think that the French will come arter us, sir."

"Why so, Swinney?" asked I.

"Why, sir, the last time as we had a brush with

them, we sarved them up a sarce they did not much relish."

I then inquired who had made the verses.

" Oh, sir, that 'ere was Probyn; a wonderful scollard that man, sir."

Probyn's fame was now perfectly established with his comrades, as the greatest literary character and poet of the age.

The French did not attack that night, but the garrison was certainly under arms. About one o'clock in the morning there was a violent barking of dogs; and an officer who had crept forward as far as he dared to venture, reported that, by laying his ear to the ground, he could distinctly hear the tread of a large body of troops in the direction of the dockyard.

Behind the convent there was a solitary lane, leading to the village of Beaucout, which was very little frequented, the usual route from the camp being across the heights. One of our surgeons, in passing that way without his sword, was assailed by a gang of savage dogs, belonging to no one, which were in the habit of scratching up those bodies that were slightly buried, and had become very ferocious, The doctor being sleek and plump, they no doubt thought that he was in sufficient good condition to afford them an excellent dinner. Most fortunately for him, some soldiers, who were accidentally returning that way, came to his rescue, and the discomfited doctor hopped into the camp with only a bite in his leg, but with his trowsers dangling in shreds about his person,—no trifling loss at that period, when both money and cloth were scarce articles. On the morning of the 14th of April, before daylight, the French garrison made a desperate sortie. But of this I can give no account, having been ordered to England, on my promotion, a short time before it took place, and I left my old battalion with sincere regret. But when it was again ordered on service, before the battle of Waterloo, I was fortunate enough to effect an exchange into it, and was immediately posted to my old company. At Waterloo we lost our green feathers; and when I next joined the company in England, I found them with unwieldy bear-skin caps on their heads. As for myself, being remarkably short, and my cap a very high one, there was nearly as much to be seen above my face as below it; and I looked, for all the world,

Like Tommy Noddy,
All head and no body!

When we were metamorphosed into a grenadier regiment, the light companies requested to be allowed to retain the feather under which they had fought so long: but this was not granted.

* * * * *
* * * * *

BEING at Pau in the course of the last summer, I† could not resist the pleasure of visiting

† An officer of the British Guards.

Bayonne and its immediate neighbourhood; interesting ground in many respects to *all* military men, but, perhaps, in a higher degree so to those who may happen to belong to corps which, in the beginning of the year 1814, formed part of the division charged with the blockade of its citadel.* The details of the *sortie* made by the garrison on the morning of the 14th of April are so well known, that it would be unnecessary to repeat them. At the same time, a short description of a morning's walk over the position occupied by our troops, but more particularly of the burial-ground of those officers of the first battalion Coldstream-guards, who fell in the *sortie*, may not be without interest.

Crossing the Adour by the Pontoon Bridge, (constructed provisionally until the old wooden one is either repaired or replaced by a stone one,) you enter the Fauxbourg of St. Esprit, and ascend the hill on the Bourdeaux road. As you leave the

---

* A very singular occurrence at this time was remarked. The left wing had just secured themselves in their new positions, when an immense flight of eagles was seen hovering in the air. They remained about Bayonne for several days, occasionally alighting on the sand-hills, and finally turned their aërial course in the direction of Orthez. "It is not improbable that they were the same flight of birds, which, for months after the battle of Vittoria, were seen constantly frequenting that scene of action, sometimes in such numbers as to make it alarming, if not dangerous, to roam singly over the field."—BATTY'S CAMPAIGN.

PENINSULAR SKETCHES. 181

Fauxbourg, you first get a sight of the glacis of the citadel, which stands on the left, immediately above you. On the right, upon a prominent point of ground, is seen a small outwork, thrown up by the French to command the Adour, and threaten the church of St. Etienne. Moving forward, you arrive at the point of junction of the Bourdeaux and Toulouse roads. This was an important point of the British position. The Jews' cemetery fills up the angle. At this point, turning towards Bayonne, the church of St. Etienne is to your left, the citadel immediately in front, and on the right is the line of picket-houses and gardens occupied by the brigade of guards. A deep lane running from the Bourdeaux road, opposite the entrance-gate of the Jews' cemetery, in rear of the picket-houses, conducts you to the Chateau Basterreche and Boncou. This chateau, standing in a grove of trees, and overlooking the deep ground which separates this part of the position, may be said to have formed the key-post of this portion of the cordon of pickets, for the position at this point takes a sudden turn at nearly right angles, and is prolonged to the Convent of St. Bernhard, situated near the right bank of the Adour.

The distance separating the several picket stations of the guards, from the advanced works thrown up by the French in front of the north and west faces of the citadel, is very trifling. A minute's walk from the Jews' cemetery down the Toulouse road, brings you to the churchyard of

St. Etienne, the death-scene of the lamented Major-General Hay. A plain stone slab, placed at the north-east angle of the church, by the officers of the 1st, or Royal Scots, marks the spot where his remains lie buried. Few vestiges of the havoc made by the fire of the citadel remain. The Chateau Basterreche (behind which the late Lord Hopetoun, then Sir John Hope, was wounded) and the Convent of St. Bernard are still in ruins. It was in the above-mentioned lane that many of the guards lost their lives, for the French, having broken through the chain of pickets at the Chateau Basterreche, came down the lane upon the rear of the other posts, and, covered by the darkness, were enabled to deal their destructive volleys for a time with impunity. Thus, unseen or mistaken for British, a party of French felled, at pistol-shot distance, the gallant Lord Hopetoun and his accompanying staff, who, unconscious of the enemy's being in possession of the lane, were galloping up the road from Boncou.

It is not my object, however, to recur to the events of that night; but I may add, that it is impossible for any one to walk over this interesting ground without feeling the deepest regret, not to say indignation, that so many gallant fellows should have been sacrificed on the eve of a general peace, to the mortified spirit of a revengeful soldier of Napoleon's; for it seems to be clearly ascertained, that the commandant of the citadel too easily listened to the reproaches of a lieutenant-general, who was then in the town, that he had been culpably inactive during the two months that the British had blockaded the fortress. The sortie was the result of these taunts, coupled, perhaps, with the conviction that the opportunity must shortly pass away. Some slight excuse has been offered for the Frenchman's conduct, as far as regards the charge of duplicity, in attacking the British lines after he had been informed of the fact of Napoleon's abdication, and the entry of the allies into Paris. It has been sought to justify the sortie by the assertion that the commandant had a perfect right to consider the blockading force as an enemy so long as it continued to maintain its hostile position, especially as it was understood that the British general had refused to confirm his own impression of the truth of the reported news from Paris, by retiring from his line of investment, and thus virtually raising the blockade. Be this as it may — let " Bayonne" be henceforth a watchword in our service, to awaken wariness and caution in the presence of an enemy.

It is near the Chateau Basterreche that the stranger must inquire the way to the burial-ground of the British officers. A footpath, somewhat intricate, conducts to it through a cottage yard and garden, standing on the right of the road leading to Boncou. The spot itself is sufficiently marked by the poplars and cypress flourishing within its walls. The choice of the ground was determined by the simple occurrence of a round shot having lodged in the stem of a tree standing in or near the camp of the Coldstream-guards. At the foot of this tree the bodies of the six officers of the first battalion of that regiment who fell in the sortie were deposited. The ground was subsequently bought by subscription, and the purchase duly registered at Bayonne. It was reserved, however, for a friend and comrade of the killed, one who had himself shared the dangers of that morning, and had been wounded in the sortie, to become the guardian of the sacred spot, and the liberal instrument of recording their names on the simple but handsome stone monument which decorates the upper end of the cemetery. A low stone wall surrounds the spot, which is entered by means of rough projecting stones fixed in it as steps. A tablet inserted in the walls at this place introduces the stranger to the object of his curiosity. The inscription is as follows:—

> "Burial-ground of the British Officers, especially of the Coldstream-guards, who fell in action near to this spot, on the 14th April, 1814, the night of the sortie from the Citadel of Bayonne."
>
> "Tombeaux des Officiers Anglais tués au champ de bataille près de ces lieux, dans la nuit de la sortie de la Citadelle de Bayonne, le 14 Avril, 1814."

Opposite to the entrance, on the north side, stands the monument executed by the order of Vigors Harvey, Esq. It bears the following inscription:—

"Sacred to the memory
Of the under-mentioned British Officers,
Who gallantly fell at the sortie made by the garrison
From the Citadel of Bayonne, on the 14th April, 1814.

COLDSTREAM-GUARDS.
Lieut.-Colonels.
G. Collier, Sir H. Sullivan, Bart., M.P.
Captains.
Hon. W. G. Crofton and Wm. Burroughs, Adjt.
Ensigns.
F. Vachell and W. Pitt.

FIRST REGIMENT OF GUARDS.
Ensign.
W. Vane.

THIRD REGIMENT OF GUARDS.
Captains.
C. White, J. B. Shiffner.
Lieutenant.
F. Holbourne, Adjt.

SIXTIETH REGIMENT.
Lieutenant.
J. Hamilton.

This tablet was placed to the memory of the above-mentioned Officers by their friend and companion at the sortie, J. V. Harvey, formerly Captain in the Coldstream - guards, and since H.M. Consul at Bayonne — 1830."

The friends of the three officers of the 3rd regiment here named cannot but feel gratified to find their names recorded on the tablet, although, in point of fact, they do not lie in the ground, having been buried on the other side of the adjacent hill, near the camp of their regiment. It is also worthy of honourable mention, that the British government have authorized Mr. Harvey to expend annually a small sum for the purpose of keeping the place in order.

A NIGHT IN THE PENINSULAR WAR.*

THE war which was waged in Spain and Portugal for several years previously to the downfall of Napoleon, afforded innumerable instances of adventures as interesting and surprising as any that are found recorded.

A great many, if related, would seem to be intended for the pages of romance, and are now told at the firesides of the small towns and villages of France oftener than in England. This is owing to the fact of individual French officers finding themselves in dangerous situations more frequently than the British, as they had the disadvantage of being in an enemy's country, where, if they lost their way, or from any cause were separated from their compatriots, they had to oppose dexterity to treachery, and boldness to revenge. The following pages relate the adventures, and, perhaps, escapes of a British officer attached to the medical staff of the army during the above period; and although they do not equal in intensity several of those

* By James Byron Bradley, M.D.

which have been recorded, may yet be read with interest by many who still indulge in reminiscences of Spain and Portugal.

It was, I think, in November of 1812, that I was attached to a hospital at Castello Branco, a town in the province of Beira, in Portugal. I had been for a considerable time in a state of great debility from sickness, having suffered from dysentery, ophthalmia, and intermittent. Headquarters were at this time in Spain, and the only medical officers in Castello Branco were Mr. Maclean, surgeon to the forces, Mr. Kearney, hospital-assistant, and myself. I was ordered to attend sick and wounded troops who were to be conveyed down to Abrantes. There might be fifty or sixty; some in wains drawn by bullocks, others upon mules, and a few were able to walk. The only authority over the troops, besides my own, was that of a serjeant—a drunken, worthless fellow. At six o'clock in the afternoon we set out, and when we had proceeded as far as the extremity of the town, Mr. Kearney, who, if he be alive, and should chance to read this, will recollect the circumstance, looked out of his window, and said, "Bradley, I am just sitting down to dinner, (that is to say, soup made with ration-beef and tomatos,) you had better come up and take a basin of it." The weather was very cold, and I was not sufficiently recovered to eat anything but soup; I therefore gladly took his offer, and ordered the serjeant to proceed with the troops. In about half an hour I bade adieu to my friend, remounted my horse, and left Castello Branco, with the wish that I might never see it again, having suffered there much from sickness and much from vexations.

At a short distance from this end of the town the road has two turnings, one to Sarnadas, and the other I know not whither. The one to Sarnadas I ought to have remembered, as I had travelled it in my journey from that place to Castello Branco. Unfortunately, my servant, Juan Rodriquez, a boy sixteen years old, and who was well acquainted with the country, had gone on with the troops, and I took the road to the left. Having pursued it for some time, I began to wonder that I did not come up with the cavalcade. It did not occur to me that I ought to retrace my steps, and I continued until darkness overtook me. At length I was convinced that I had mistaken the route, and recollecting that I had passed a building, I rode back a considerable distance to make some inquiry. I could not determine from its appearance whether or not it was an inhabited place; however, I knocked and knocked again, and no one answering, I concluded that it was not a dwelling. I considered what to do, whether to return to the point where the road divided, or to resume the route which I had just retraced. I decided upon the latter. I walked my mare three or four miles, and went off the road into a field on the left, there being no hedge or wall to prevent me. I made my way to a tree, and there let the mare graze. Waiting some time, I thought I was not quite safe, as if any prowlers were to pass they would perceive me, and might be induced to offer violence for the purpose of robbing me. I, therefore, went further from the road, and took my station under another tree; with what purpose I can scarcely say, as I could not expect that it would be daylight for several hours. I was now exceedingly hungry, and my mare evidently as hungry as myself, from the avidity with which she ate what the field afforded. I felt the symptoms of the cold stage of an ague coming on, and consequently felt no longer hungry. I began to jump and move about, in the hope that the exertion might arrest the paroxysm. It did so in part. I became warm, and soon felt a gentle moisture over the body, the ague-fit having gone through its three stages. The paroxysm was not severe, and, therefore, the debility which supervened not so great as it otherwise would have been.

Seeing that it was doing nothing to remain where I was, I left the field, and pursued my way along the road. I went a foot-pace for two or three miles, and found myself at the foot of a hill. I continued, and when arrived at the summit, perceived on the right, forty or fifty yards from the road, a large building resembling an English barn. By the light of a large fire on the ground, close to the building, I observed five or six Portuguese soldiers. I called aloud, and it appeared strange that I could not attract their attention. At length one of them left his party, and came slowly towards me. When within two or three yards he drew his sabre, and demanded what I wanted. I saw that he was a Portuguese dragoon, and his appearance and bearing were such as to create some alarm. Being entirely alone, enveloped in total darkness, and having, in common with many British officers, a very unfavourable opinion of the Portuguese lower orders, I judged it prudent to ensure my own safety by letting him see at once how dangerous it would be to attempt anything hostile. I asked him the way to Sarnadas, and assumed a somewhat authoritative tone and manner, keeping him in front of me. He could not tell me, but I learned that he and his companions were in charge of stores for the army, which were deposited in the barn-like building. There was something extremely forbidding in the appearance of this man. He was a tall, brawny fellow, with a complexion so swarthy as to appear black, with enormous whiskers and mustachios. I said, " I am the commander of a regiment of English, which are at the foot of the hill, and our route is to Sarnadas." I thought it advisable to say a regiment of troops, as the number would deter him from meditating any attack on me; and that I was the commander of them, thinking, perhaps justly, that if he and his party might be disposed to attempt anything against a humbler individual, they would hesitate to do so against one whose presence they would know was so necessary to the regiment; and that whilst the commander of it was absent, it would remain at the foot of the hill until his return.

He had put several questions to me before I told

him that I was accompanied, which were calculated to excite some suspicion—such as, if I were alone, if I had the means of paying a guide, &c. I thought it prudent to get away from him as soon as possible, and turned my horse round with that intention. In turning round, I fancied that his long sword was uplifted. It was a moment of great alarm; but, knowing that it was not a time to show any fear, I immediately turned my horse's head towards him again, spoke to him in a commanding tone respecting the stores which he had in charge, and during this time kept backing my horse, so as to have the dragoon in front, until I had gotten to the brink of the hill which I had just ridden up. When there, I suddenly turned round, called out "Viva Senhor!" and sending the spurs into the animal's sides, galloped down the hill as fast as she could go.

To retrace the road I had already passed was useless; I therefore resolved to traverse the country to the left, where a narrow opening seemed to lead somewhere. In a short time I found myself in paths which scarcely admitted my horse to pass, and, withal, entangled with briers. The path every now and then was so steep as to be almost precipitous, so that I was frequently in danger of losing my seat. I came at last to a deep gulley, which I did not perceive at first, but fortunately my horse could see better than myself, or otherwise I should have been killed. Of course there was no alternative but to turn back, and having wandered through paths sometimes narrow, and at other times the reverse, I found myself upon the bank of a broad river. I tried in vain to recollect what branch of the Tagus it could be. I dismounted and sat upon a large stone, and being very sleepy, dosed for some time. I regretted that I had not come to one of those little chapels which are seen in all parts of Portugal. Every officer who served in the Peninsular war will remember these little chapels, or shrines, more properly speaking, which are scattered over the face of the country. They are about five yards in length, by four broad, and have in them only an altar and crucifix. There devout peasants, and peasants not devout, resort occasionally; the former, to pray for the forgiveness of sins already committed; the latter, of those they may commit. The door of these little buildings is always left open, and one of them would have been a comfortable asylum for the night; but I did not meet with one until six o'clock in the morning, when I no longer wanted it.

My anxiety for the arrival of morning was intense, and putting up a fervent prayer to Him who grants his protection to all of his creatures who humbly implore it, I remounted my patient and hungry steed, and proceeded by a path which I was certain must lead to a point different from any at which I had already been. In about an hour I found myself in a broad highway, and, continuing at a footpace, observed on the left, at the distance of a small field, a large fire. I concluded that there must be somebody near it, and called as loud as I could. Several minutes elapsed before an old man came towards me. A low hedge, not very usual in Portugal, separated him from me. I asked permission to approach the fire, which he refused; I requested him to give me something to eat, which he also refused; and then begged for something for the poor mare; this was also denied. I spoke to him of his unfeelingness, represented that the English were in his country for the purpose of expelling a ruthless enemy, and that they deserved at the hands of his countrymen sympathy and assistance. My arguments had no effect, and having my sword in my hand, I should very probably, from the irritability which long sickness had produced, have inflicted a cut upon his face or his arm; but as I had, during our parlance, seen two or three other men near the fire, discretion had the mastery over anger. I left him, after applying to him two or three opprobrious epithets well known in Portugal, and expressive of contempt and hatred, if the latter feeling may be considered compatible with the former.

I pursued my solitary route along the road, which continued level and broad, and, at the distance of two or three miles, heard the barking of dogs. As I proceeded, the barking increased, the noise of the horse's feet upon the hard ground inciting the watchfulness of the dogs. On the right, among some hills, I perceived the reflection of a fire, and from this and the barking, I knew that a camp of Spanish muleteers must be there. During the Peninsular war, Spanish muleteers were constantly seen on the roads between head-quarters and Lisbon. They were employed to carry provisions, chiefly flour, biscuits, &c., to the different depôts where our commissaries were stationed. Each company consisted of a few Spaniards, with twenty or thirty mules; the latter carrying the stores, not in panniers, but in sacks. The appearance of these muleteers will be well remembered by the British officers, and by many of the privates; they and their mules recalled to our minds those youthful and innocent days which we spent at our own homes, where, surrounded by those most dear to us, we read the exploits of Don Quixote de la Mancha, and laughed at the rogueries of Lazarillo de Tormes. The Spaniards habited in their dark brown close jackets; a coarse red worsted sash or belt round the waist, and the Spanish sombrero on the head to shield them from the sun: the mules with gaudy trappings, two or three of the foremost having bells about their necks; and the conductors themselves seated carelessly, singing ancient ballads, which spoke of war and of love, and of the deeds of chivalry performed by noble Spaniards during their long contention with their paynim invaders. A certain wildness characterized the airs of the stanzas, and the burthen of the songs had a strain of melancholy, which, mingling with the tinkling of the bells, created reflections that carried us back to the days when the genius and fiery spirit of the Moors were opposed to the obstinate and steady resistance of the Spaniards.

There existed between the Spanish and the Portuguese a mutual dislike: the latter hating the Spanish, and these affecting to despise the other; so that it not unfrequently happened that broils took place when they met, which occasionally ended in bloodshed. On this account the muleteers generally encamped during the night, and, being often molested by the Portuguese, were obliged to be always upon the alert: hence, they were accompanied with dogs, which acted as pickets, and whenever these gave the alarm, the muleteers discharged some muskets, which they constantly carried with them, to warn the prowlers of danger if they ventured to approach. Consequently, I had not gone much further, before two shots were fired, one immediately after the other, and I judged that they had been directed towards the point where I was; nevertheless, I proceeded, but in a few minutes two more came whistling so close that I felt the imprudence of remaining on horseback, and directly dismounted, and had the precaution to place the mare between the shots and myself, that, if the firing were repeated, *she* would be killed or wounded. I turned the animal's head and retraced my steps, leading, or rather driving her, and taking care to have her constantly interposed between me and the camp. Several other discharges took place, but I was evidently getting more and more remote from them. At the distance of a mile or two I turned up a narrow bye-way on the right, which seemed to be interminable, and which, at length, entered what appeared to be a wood, or small forest. The path was about two yards broad, and presented a gentle acclivity, with brushwood on each side. On a sudden the mare stopped, every limb trembled,—she pawed the ground with her right fore foot, then flung it repeatedly outwards with great violence. The whole of the night had, until now, been very cloudy; the clouds had dispersed, so that I was enabled to see the cause of this physical phenomenon. The mare had trodden upon an enormous snake, which had instantaneously entwined itself round her leg up to the knee.

There is a singular and useful operation of the human understanding which enables it to correct, with surprising quickness, the first suggestion of the mind in moments of real or apparent danger,—singular as well as useful,—because, on other occasions, the second corrective idea is the result of reflection, short or long, according to the object or objects which the first comprehends. My first impulse was to draw my sabre and cut the serpent through and through, but I immediately recollected that I should most likely cut some of the tendons of the mare's leg, and thereby lame her so effectually as to prevent my further progress. Instead of that, as I was again mounted, and as the snake was twisted round the right leg of the horse, which accident gave me more power, I whipped it with all my force, and in a very short time the reptile loosened its coils, and darting under the brushwood, I heard it trail its long loathsome body away. I patted my poor steed, which, from hunger and fatigue, might have claimed sisterhood to Rosinante, and wended my way onwards. The path continued in a direct line through the wood, an opening presenting itself every now and then on the right and left. Going slowly along, I thought I heard footsteps, and stopping to listen, was convinced that some one was at some distance behind me. The place was a forest, and one that offered every incitement to rapine and murder; I therefore turned down an opening on the right, keeping sufficiently near to the road that I might see what passed. I dismounted, and waited with breathless anxiety the approach of the individual who was evidently nearing the point not far from which I stood. Whilst here, my trepidation was increased by the apprehension that another snake might visit me; and this fear was strengthened by the recollection of a circumstance which had happened to me some months before, when doing duty at the sick camp of Rocio, close to Abrantes. Four medical officers and I had a marquée on the banks of the Tagus, very near to the camp; and Staff-Surgeon Bell, who had the medical superintendence of the sick, inhabited a quinta, or small country-house, at some distance from our marquée. I, in common with the others, had to communicate with him professionally on the cases under my care, and I was in the habit of going to his quinta by a short cut, through a vineyard, instead of traversing the field by a path that led directly to his residence. On one occasion, I was crossing this vineyard, and the vines being very thick and close, there was no path. I thought that I trod on a thick rope, but, instantaneously, a snake, more than a yard long, and very thick, wrapped itself round my leg. The sensation I experienced was one of extreme terror. I felt my heart beat with such violence, that it seemed to knock forcibly against the ribs. I stood motionless, but in a few seconds the reptile disengaged itself, and crept rustling away. I staggered back to the marquée, and one of my colleagues, Mr. Lonsdale, who, unfortunately for his kindred and humanity, found his grave in Portugal, ran to me, and seeing me pale as death, poured some wine down my throat, which served to revive me.

At last the cause of my expectation and alarm made its appearance. A donkey, or *boura*, as it is called in that country, passed, laden with sticks for firewood; and it was clear that he must have a driver. I saw that there was now little to fear, yet I thought it advisable to know what sort of owner the boura had, and therefore remained until an old man walked past. I waited to see whether one or more persons accompanied him; when I felt assured that he was alone, I did not hesitate to venture out, as he was old and unarmed. I hallooed, and the old man, turning round, was evidently alarmed at the sight of me. Indeed, my appearance was anything but prepossessing. Fancy a decrepit old man in the midst of a forest, and in the night, being suddenly accosted in a loud tone by a person with a visage rendered swarthy by the sun, his whiskers and mustachios not clipped for months, a huge black-leather cocked hat upon his head, and a sabre in his hand. I perceived that I was the cause of much greater alarm to him than he was to me, and I endeavoured to calm his fears by telling him that I was an English officer who had lost his way,—that I had been wandering about all the night,—and that I would reward him if he could direct me.

I found great difficulty in understanding his dialect, as it is here, as in all countries of Europe when very remote from the capital, that the peasantry and the majority of the middle orders speak a *patois*, or dialect, which a foreigner, who speaks the language of the country as it is written, or as it is spoken in the chief cities, finds it almost impossible to comprehend. I could gain no information respecting the way to Sarnadas, nor, indeed, of anything else. I was very anxious to know the hour, and how soon it would be daylight. He made several attempts to tell me; but finding I could not understand him, he betook himself to the following method of informing me. He took out his snuff-box, which was large and round, and looking at me for a moment, pointed with his hand toward the east, then pointed to his box, around the circle of which he drew the end of his index finger; then placing the palm of his hand upon the lid of the box, so as completely to cover it, he let it remain for a moment, then moved it a very little downwards, so as to leave uncovered a small segment of the circle. Previously to shifting his hand, so as to expose a portion of the circumference of the box, he threw up his chin very rapidly three or four times. From all these signs it was easy to gather that he wished to indicate the sun, and to give me to understand that it was still dark, but that, in a very short time, it would appear above the horizon. I nodded in token of satisfaction, that conveyed to him that he had made himself intelligible, and motioned that we should go on, which we did; but it was obvious that my new acquaintance did not feel quite at his ease, as every now and then he looked at me suspiciously, and two or three times attempted to lag; however, he became more assured, and in a short time, as he had foretold, the rays of the sun, to my inexpressible joy, fell upon the hills, and grey morn appeared. Now it was that I met with one of those little chapels of which I have already made mention, and of which I should gladly have made use some hours before. To my utter astonishment, the turrets of the large monasteries of Castello Branco presented themselves to my view, so that, after wandering from six in the evening until six in the morning, during which I must have traversed a great extent of country, I found myself not far from the place at which I had started.

My "Viva Senhor" to my old companion was heard with apparent delight; and turning down a narrow road, which, it was plain, must lead to the town, I bent my steps to Kearney's billet, and knocking at the door, that gentleman looked out of his window, and I remember his telling me that he had a presentiment I had missed my way. He gave me a good breakfast, and my mare a good feed; and after he had performed his professional duties at the convent of Sant Antonio, which we had converted into an hospital, during which I and my mare had some time to rest, he mounted his horse, in order to accompany me, that I might not commit the same error again. At the distance of five or six miles from Castello Branco, we shook hands, and I have never seen or heard of him since, although a period of thirty years has expired.

I expected fully to find the troops at Sarnadas, which was seven miles further, and was disappointed and chagrined on hearing that they had gone on to Villa Velha. This I learned from an aid-de-camp whom I met on the road, and who was proceeding to head-quarters, which were at this time, I think, at Fuentes d'Onor. Accordingly, I did not turn up the path that leads to Sarnadas, and which stands on the right, at some distance from the high road. Villa Velha is several miles beyond this village, supposing that you are journeying towards Lisbon. It was evening before I arrived at the foot of a steep mountain, upon which Villa Velha is situated, and meeting with two goatherds, I was led to fear, from their answers, that the troops had not rested there, but had proceeded to Nisa.

I remember seeing the carriage of a cannon that remained in the valley where I stood, and under which I determined to bivouack during the night, as I was so exhausted by sickness and fatigue as to preclude any effort to mount the hill, and the poor mare suffered so much from a sore upon her back, that I considered it cruel to torment her any longer. I beckoned to a peasant whom I saw, and offered him a crusado novo (three shillings) if he would go up to the village and bring me word if the party were there. In due time he returned for his money, accompanied by the serjeant, with whose assistance I got up the hill, and my reappearance gave unbounded delight to two individuals; the one, my servant, Juan Rodriguez, who had been wringing his hands, and bewailing the fate of his poor master, whom he supposed to have been robbed and murdered; the other, a beautiful dog, which had been given to me by a monk at Castello Branco, and which I had named Branco. My mare was also welcomed by her foal, which had started with us, and which accompanied us down to Abrantes.

In the morning we pursued our route, the mare being led, on account of the sore upon her back, and myself being mounted upon one of the mules. I took care to keep up with the cavalcade over which I had charge, and at noon arrived at Nisa, where the Juiz de Paz billeted me upon an apothecary, in whose house I had once been lodged before. His wife prided herself on having been born in Lisbon, and on speaking the best Portuguese. I was soon visited by a priest whom I had known before, and who loaded me with caresses, and covered my cheeks with kisses. These latter were the severer ordeal to pass through, as they were impregnated with the effluvia of snuff, cigars, and garlic; and the day after, at the moment of bidding adieu to the boticario, at the door of his botica, I made all haste, before the priest should make his appearance, in order to avoid his salutations and his squeezings, and had got my foot in the stirrup, and was just vaulting into the saddle, when I was suddenly pulled back, and was immediately in the arms of the priest. After some minutes of intense suffering, I escaped, and leaving Nisa, continued my journey; and in three or four days, we all arrived at the place of our destination, Abrantes.

The fatigue which I underwent, and the anxiety which I suffered during the night, the painful passages of which I have endeavoured to describe, naturally suggest to me thoughts at this distant period, when reflection has been quickened by the vicissitudes of accident, and the understanding ripened by the maturity of experience. How often does it happen that the occurrences of life assume an aspect that engenders dread, and yet pass away without trouble or grief. The dangers of the night were perhaps but apparent, except when exposed to the firing from the muleteers' camp. He who passes his life in the constant anticipation of evil, and gives way, with timidity, to the creations of fear, will have much to endure, and but little to enjoy. Prudence and regularity point out the error of losing sight of those whom it was my business to accompany; and half an hour spent in eating soup, was the occasion of a whole night of anguish and distress. He who listens to the persuasions of indulgence, and deviates from that which he knows to be his duty, must expect to bear the mortifications which indulgence begets, and yield, with submission, to the blame of neglect.

RECOLLECTIONS OF THE LATE WAR IN SPAIN AND PORTUGAL.*

On the 17th March, 1811, the fourth division of the grand army, under the orders of General Sir Lowry Cole, entered Thomar, a city in Portugal, which had been evacuated only two days before by the French. As our regiment was truly Irish, and this day the one dedicated to Ireland's national saint, our music struck up *Patrick's day*, which awakened our recollections in no common manner. Though drenched and cold with the wet of the preceding night, which we had spent in the fields without any covering except our blanket, we moved cheerily through the muddy streets, and the most tired and dejected were for a time enlivened by the sounds of this favourite quick step. The approach of this day, bringing with it so many recollections of home, had for

* By J. Emerson.

some time become a subject of general interest, though, from the scarcity of both money and liquors, there was little chance of our being enabled to *drown our shamrock*. Still, hopes had remained of a change of fortune, and amidst our numerous privations we hailed the return of *Patrick's day* with an enthusiasm, of which those who have never experienced such a feeling in a foreign land can have no proper conception.

We were quartered in the ruins of the religious houses, which, in this city, had been numerous and splendid. In the evening, a few countrymen arrived with mules loaded with *Pellejos*, or skins of *Aquardiente*, a kind of brandy made in the country, which is brought to market in the skins of animals, the hairy side being turned in, and the seams on the outside besmeared with tar. This was a most seasonable supply, and found a ready sale with those who had money; and they sharing freely with their less fortunate companions, many a bumper was tossed off to *Ould Ireland*, and *Patrick's day in the morning* resounded through the corridors and cells of the cloisters from a thousand hoarse voices.

On the following day we strolled through the city, every part of which presented evident marks of the devastations of the enemy. The convents and churches standing were without either door or windows, and fragments of their altars were lying about half burnt or broken; and a mutilated image of the Virgin, or some saint, frequently met our eyes among the filth and rubbish in the courtyards. As in many other places, we here witnessed the extreme carelessness of the enemy in the interment of their dead. On looking into several of the ruinous houses, dead bodies were seen piled in corners, or strewed upon the floors; and on opening some closets and chests in search of something useful, they were found filled with dead in different stages of putrefaction, one glance of which commonly deterred further search in that quarter.

Having arranged matters for our further progress, on the 19th we left Thomar for the purpose of forming a junction with the second division of our army. The country through which we passed on this day exhibited a fearful scene of desolation from the excesses of the enemy, by whom it had been occupied the preceding winter. Neither man nor beast was to be seen, though, from the ruins of houses and olive plantations, it had evidently been inhabited until lately. Of the many stone and wooden crosses set up near the roads not one was standing. From the size and strength of the former, their demolition must have been a work of labour, and could have answered no possible purpose, but must have incensed the inhabitants still further against the French, who were never mentioned without visible horror and execrations.

In the evening we passed the river Tagus by a bridge of boats, and halted for the night on a rising ground nearly two miles from where we had crossed. Our places of halting were always called by the name of encampments, but they little deserved that name, as, from the difficulty of transporting equipage, not more than six or eight tents appeared in an encampment of as many thousand men. When obliged by fatigue to lie down, we wrapped our blankets about our bodies, placing our knapsack for a pillow. When in the neighbourhood of an enemy, no one was permitted to take off his belt till clear daylight, before which time we always stood to our arms for about an hour.

After crossing the Tagus, the country assumed a different aspect, as it had not been visited by the French the preceding winter, and suffered comparatively little from the contending armies. We again saw human faces besides our own; and though long used to scenes of desolation and misery, none were more truly so than the country near Thomar.

Arriving at Portalegre, a large walled town with towers on its ramparts, but dismantled, we halted for one day, and were served out with a kind of shoes made in the country. They were very clumsy, and of a dirty buff colour; and as many amongst us were without stockings, their rough seams soon made their wearers hobble like so many cripples. The religious houses here were numerous and magnificent. In one I observed a large and richly adorned figure of the Virgin, differing from any I had yet seen. In one hand she held a large silver heart, and in the other a gilt spear, with which she appeared to pierce it. In the same church were also numerous images of saints adorned in a manner nearly as splendid, a certain proof that the French had not lately visited this place. We here learned that the enemy were in force at Campo-Mayor, for which place we immediately set forward. Near Arronches, a small town half-way between Portalegre and Campo-Mayor, we joined the second division, and soon after were met by Marshal Beresford, with some regiments of British and Portuguese cavalry, and he immediately took the command of the whole forces.

About two miles from Campo-Mayor, we halted under cover of a wood, and the 13th dragoons were sent forward to endeavour to learn the state of the enemy in that town. They soon discovered that they had evacuated the place, and were making a precipitate retreat towards Badajoz. But the dragoons, in their ardour of pursuit, forgetting their great disparity of numbers, made a vigorous charge, drove in their rear-guard, killed a number, and took several men and horses prisoners with very little loss. On the report of this action we were ordered forward with all possible dispatch, and ran near three miles at *double quick*, but were late, the French having made good their retreat, which they could not have done had the dragoons who were with us in the wood been sent forward in time. The prisoners taken in this affair were intoxicated, having plundered the inhabitants of the town before its evacuation. In the evening, our division entered Campo-Mayor, which had been but a short time before taken from the Portuguese militia. The breach made in its walls during the siege was not yet repaired, and scarcely a house remained which did not bear evident marks of the effects of the enemy's shot and shells.

We were quartered in the shattered dwelling-houses, the greater part of which were without inhabitants; and, as was customary on similar occasions, we commenced a diligent search for victuals or articles of value. Where I remained the boarded floors were raised, and the ceilings torn down without effect, when at length some hams were discovered in a draw-well in a corner of a kitchen. A few silver spoons, also found in the same recess, were quickly bartered for wine; and a fire being now made with the furniture, our fatigues were, for a time, forgotten in the noise and luxury of the feast. We halted here for a few days, during which many of the inhabitants who had been secreted in the woods or mountains returned to their desolate homes. They appeared to be in great poverty, and exulted in the defeat of the common enemy, hailing us with their *vivas*. In a day or two, confidence was so far established that a kind of market was held; but wine, with preserved fruits, were the only articles offered for sale. We here left the second division, and passing through a desolated and dreary country, entered Elvas. This city stands on a rising ground, is strongly fortified, and entered by drawbridges. Without the walls are two forts; the largest is called La Lippe, and stands on a high and steep hill, above half a mile from the walls of the city. The water that supplies the inhabitants is conveyed by an aqueduct near three miles in length. In our advance thither, that portion of it extending from the brow of a hill, across a valley to the ramparts of the city, had a most striking and romantic appearance. This fortress, and the country in its immediate vicinity, having been free from the presence of the French for some years, the effects of the war, which had desolated the greater part of the kingdom, were scarcely visible. The religious houses were numerous and splendid; processions of different religious orders frequently passed through the streets; the shops were open, and the working classes engaged at their different callings; so that the crowds of military, and their warlike equipages, were the only things denoting that war was really at no great distance. Halting several days, we again set forward and passed Jurumanha, a small fortress on a height adjoining a little town of the same name, on the river Guadiana, which at this place forms the great boundary between the kingdoms of Spain and Portugal. In the evening our brigade, the 13th dragoons, and some Portuguese cavalry, crossed the river on a float. The two other brigades, some German artillery and riflemen composing the division, remained on the opposite bank till the following day. We took up our ground for the night in front of a large farm-house, about two miles from the river, with orders not to take off our belts, but to be ready at a moment's call. Guards were placed, and pickets sent out, as usual; and while many sunk to rest on their grassy couch, a few of us slipped to the rear, and entered a garden of unripe beans behind the farm-house, now occupied by our chief officers. Having in some degree satisfied our wants with the beans, and talked over our probable route, we gradually dropped asleep. The night being fine, we had slept some time, when the report of a musket close by aroused our attention. This was followed by a rapid succession of others, many of which were more distant. In a moment all was uproar, and we sprang from our lairs to grasp our arms, while the shouts and hallooings of, "The French are among us," resounded from men of several nations. The noises from every quarter, the clashing of arms as they were taken from their piles, and the cries and shrieks of the women, added not a little to the bustle and confusion, while shots continued to be heard almost without intermission. Presently the firing became less frequent, and after a short time gradually ceased. The distant call of a bugle, which had been heard at intervals, also dying away, all was again silent except the calls of the sentinels, and the hum of the people in our camp.

The cause of the alarm not having as yet been discovered, we remained under arms till morning, passing our time in vague surmises as to the origin of all this confusion, which was afterwards understood to have arisen from the following cause. A strong detachment of the enemy's cavalry, under the guidance of a Spanish spy, succeeded in surprising and taking prisoners a patrol of Portuguese dragoons, who were forward about two miles on the road to Badajoz. The French advanced, and when challenged, answered as Portuguese, by which stratagem they also captured a detachment of the 13th dragoons, under the orders of Major M——, who had just alighted from patrolling, and were feeding their horses. Emboldened by their successes, they proceeded towards the farm-house occupied by our general, near which, one of their horses treading on a German soldier, who was asleep, he uttered a loud cry. On this, the dragoon attempted to cut him down, but missing his aim, the German renewed his shouts, and the enemy retreated with precipitation. The shots heard chiefly proceeded from our sentinels at the outposts, who had been alarmed by the sounds of the bugle, and the trampling of the enemy's horses as they retreated. It did not appear that any person had been killed in this rencontre, but a few of the dragoons who escaped during the confusion were severely wounded.

On this day the remainder of our division crossed the river; and on the following day we set out for Olivenza, a small fortified town, then held by the French, to which we laid siege. We were stationed near a grove of olive-trees, with orders not to injure them; but when it was afterwards discovered that the owner was in the service of the enemy, the trees were cut down for firing, for which purpose this wood excels all others. Batteries were raised, and no sooner did our cannon open on the town than they sent out a flag of truce, with proposals to capitulate; but their terms not being accepted, the firing was renewed, and in a few hours they surrendered prisoners of war. The garrison amounted to only about 360 effective men. In their passage through our lines, a few of them were disburdened by us of their knapsacks, but they were destitute of anything of value, the Frenchmen secreting money, trinkets, or the like, in a kind of belt worn next the skin. The contents of a Frenchman's knapsack was, to us, always an object of attention. In it we were almost certain of finding some plunder taken from the inhabitants, as shirts, shoes, stockings, and even needles and thread. Still, if alarmed or pressed on a retreat, he was almost certain of instantly relinquishing his burden; while, under similar circumstances, we rarely threw off ours, however trifling might be its contents.

About the 18th of April, we moved for the village of St. Martha, where we encamped for several days. Our brigade again setting out, we retraced our steps, crossing the Guadiana at Jurumanah, and passing Elvas and Campo-Mayor, halted at Montijo, a small town in the Spanish province of Estremadura. The French had but lately abandoned this town, and the inhabitants were loud in their complaints of the cruelties and oppressions they had imposed upon them; yet such was their jealousy of us heretical strangers, that neither gratitude nor goodwill was evinced towards us for their deliverance. Their behaviour was exactly similar to that experienced in every other part of Spain; they were haughty, distant, and suspicious. When we were quartered in their houses, they continued equally reserved, though the only favour ever obtained from them was leave to lie on their floors, and we usually removed without exchanging a kind look or salutation. On the slightest dispute, or alleged offence, they hastened to inflict summary vengeance with their favourite weapon, the knife; and if on duty with their soldiers, it was evident, from their sullen looks, that they were far from regarding us as friends.

The conduct and feelings of the Portuguese towards us were very different. The populace were ever on the alert to hail our approach, and receive us as deliverers, testifying their joy by loud and repeated cries of "Long live the English!" often, from their miserable state, the only evidence of friendship or goodwill they had to bestow. Both nations, however, appeared virtually sunk in the grossest ignorance, and equally the slaves of religious bigotry and superstition, of which some amongst us took advantage on the least relaxation from our perilous duties. It was discovered that none of our army were regarded as Christians, except those who gave out that they came from Ireland, all of whom they believed to be good Roman Catholics. Such a declaration was commonly followed on their part by some kind office; but suspicions occasionally arising, it became necessary to give ocular proof of our sincerity, by crossing ourselves, conformably to the rites of the Romish church. In this great test, mistakes were sometimes committed by those not really Roman Catholics using the left hand; which blunder not only exposed the deception, but was also considered an act of gross impiety. On those discoveries, the inhabitants always appeared greatly agitated, exclaiming, with many significant gestures, "They are not Christians!" By degrees this irreverend error was in a great measure corrected; and as far as regarded this pious manœuvre, many incorrigible heretics became truly " good Christians." We afterwards proceeded to improve on their notions of piety, asserting that our regiment was a select body of the faithful, the true church militant, the especial servants of a great convent in Ireland, raised to war against those infidels, the French. To remove all doubts of the truth of this statement, we referred to the rude figure of a castle* on our breast-plate, as the mansion of our revered patrons, which usually removed all scruples on this subject. It was likewise observed, that the common people were partial to certain names, especially to that of Antonio, the name of a highly honoured Saint, in this sainted country; and soon the number of those who hailed each other by that name exceeded all the other names in our regiment.

The agriculture of those countries appeared miserably defective; the most common implements

* The badge of the 27th, or Enniskillen Regiment.

of tillage were either unknown, or of the rudest description; and the soil, though sandy, or of a loose mould, was so imperfectly cultivated, that the surface seemed merely scratched. Their ploughs were without iron, or any other metal, having only one handle, and so truly simple, as to resemble a branch lopped off a tree, with the end for turning over the earth pointed with a hatchet or knife. We often witnessed men going out to labour, carrying the plough under the arm, and driving before them the bullock or cow, to which one of those sorry instruments was to be attached. Their harrows were entirely of wood; we never observed either spade, shovel, gripe, or any implements likely to answer for similar purposes. In a few places in the northern parts of Spain, when the earth was heavy, they turned it over with a kind of hoe; and in one instance, a number of men were seen raising a rich loamy ground, with iron prongs fastened on a pole, about three feet in length. Those persons stuck down their forks together into the earth, and turned over the sod with the like union of strength. They were followed by women, who, with wooden mallets, broke the large lumps or clods thus cast over. The process of separating their grain from the straw was performed in an equally primitive manner, being trodden out by the feet of cattle. Bullocks, cows, or mules, are indiscriminately taken for this purpose; the work is completed by their drawing over the spread grain a massy board, the under side of which is closely set with sharp flints. In some districts,

Indian corn is the chief grain grown: after a few ears have been extracted to loosen the pods, the others are pressed out by women rubbing two heads vigorously against each other.

They are equally deficient in the most common necessaries of household use. In all our wanderings in either kingdom, we never saw an iron pot, pan, bellows, spinning-wheel, or check-reel. Their substitutes for the former, were small earthen pots called penellas, which they set at the sides of the fire, turning them about occasionally to the heat. In using their olive oil, they had a brass pan called a caldera. Their bread is all baked at public ovens, of which there are several in each village. Instead of bellows, they blow with their mouths through a long reed. In spinning flax, they use their distaff; and for a reel, they have a straight stick with a knob at each end. Their looms are as simple as can be well imagined, and the linen cloth all wrought by females. The houses of the working classes in both kingdoms are mostly tiled, and those in Portugal without chimneys, the smoke being left to find its way through the roof. Firing is scarce and dear, and consists chiefly of small fagots.

Throughout the country towns and villages of Portugal, especially in the northern provinces, the common people were sunk in the most abject poverty. In their miserable hovels were rarely any beds, the people lying on mats, without any covering except the filthy rags they wore during the day. Their chief food was coarse bread, made of rye or

Indian meal, kidney beans, pickled olive-berries, dried figs or grapes, and sometimes a few potatoes. If in their power to procure it, they used a portion of olive oil at each meal. We frequently observed them pour some of this oil into a caldera, and cutting down turnip-tops, kidney-beans, and a few slices of potatoes, stir all together, and after heating the compound some time on the fire, sit down to this frugal meal as cheerful as the wealthy to the most luxurious feast.

The condition of the peasantry in Spain was evidently much better, their houses were generally clean and whitewashed; many of them lay on beds raised off their floors, and their persons were usually free from that disgusting filth so common among the poorer Portuguese, for whom Nature appeared to have done much, their rulers nothing.

Though those nations were so very contiguous, of the same faith, and at this period engaged in one common warfare, against an enemy whom they mutually detested, yet their soldiers maintained the most inveterate animosity towards each other. Even when serving in the field, it was evident from their looks that their rooted hostility was not forgotten for one moment. They studiously avoided one another, and if they accidentally met, they were sure to exchange opprobrious names, and sometimes it required all the influence of their officers to restrain the animosity that raged between them. On any dispute arising between us and the Spaniards, the Portuguese always espoused our cause; if any difference occurred with us and the

Portuguese, the Spaniards looked on with indifference, taking no interest in our squabbles.

At this season, the country in the vicinity of Montijo was teeming with luxuriant crops of wheat, barley, and beans; the latter were so far advanced as to be nearly ripe. Indeed, the Spanish peasantry rarely left their homes, neglected the cultivation of their lands, and troubled not themselves with the issue of the contest, waiting coldly to see who would be the victors. We several times witnessed them employed in the avocations of the field, between the contending armies, and only moving aside when the hostile columns were about to close and renew their bloody warfare.

While at Montijo, we were served with goats' flesh, unsavoury both in its taste and smell; and to remedy its rankness, the beans near the town were made a constant auxiliary. For several days their owners paid but little attention; but, perceiving it was likely there would be no end to our visits while the beans lasted, they lost all patience, and took their measures accordingly. A number of them watched together in the fields with long poles, and on our approach they pointed to fields more distant, as much as to say, take some from them, rather than all from us; and if we neglected this hint, they endeavoured to drive us off. Yet, on the provost-marshal, or his gang, taking any of us prisoners, they immediately changed the object of their resentment, and if the guard was not deemed too strong, applied their poles earnestly to release the offenders. This, we learned, was owing to their clergy advising them not to make a complaint against the soldiers for the value of a few beans, as it would occasion them to receive stripes as their Saviour had suffered—yet to preserve their property from ravage.

* * * * *
* * * * *

About the 5th of May we left Montijo, and the other corps composing our division, which had been quartered in the neighbouring villages, also moving at this time, the whole proceeded towards Badajoz, for the purpose of besieging that fortress, then held by the French. We were stationed on the right or south bank of the river Guadiana, opposite Badajoz, to attack St. Christoval, a strong fort communicating with Badajoz, by a massy bridge of twenty-eight arches.

A strong detachment of the enemy still remaining without their works, it was determined to drive them off. To effect this, skirmishers were sent forward, who commenced a smart firing, while we advanced in line to their support. During this service, the city and fort kept up a constant fire of shot and shells, and a large shot striking the ground in front of a section, cast up such a mass of earth and sand as completely to overwhelm the whole. We concluded that they were killed, but were soon agreeably surprised to see them getting up, shaking the earth from their clothes, and resuming their places in the ranks. Having accomplished the object of our attack, we placed a strong guard on the ground gained, while the greater part of those who had been engaged retired to the camp about one mile and a half in the rear. On this night, which was very dark, I was on picket close to the enemy's works: our officer (a Frenchman) kept us stepping slowly backward and forwards the whole night, in rear of a chain of our sentinels, some of whom were not more than thirty paces from the palisadoes of Fort St. Christoval. The silence of this tedious night was only broken by the solemn tones of the city clock, and the voices of their sentinels. We could hear distinctly the "*qui vive*," as they challenged on the ramparts, and every quarter of an hour their cautionary call, "*Sentinel, gardez-vous*,"—Ho! sentinel, take care of yourself. On the first streak of daylight, we retired under shelter of a rising ground, but were greatly annoyed by the shot and shells from the garrison. If a shell dropped beside us, our only resource was to fall flat on the earth, and remain in that state till after the explosion. Watching those shells from the time the dull report of the mortar announced they had left the enemy's works, till they burst or fell, furnished us with ample matter for speculation, and even of mirth, at the desperate runnings on seeing them come near. On this day, a detachment of Portuguese infantry of the regiment of Elvas, who had joined us the day before, were stationed in advance, and the shells falling freely about them, their officer, a portly citizen, commenced a precipitate retreat. When observed, he was running at a furious rate, and at his heels the men. Coming near, we cheered; on which a serjeant, evidently ashamed, turned about, and rallying the greater number of the fugitives, came over to us; but his officer continued his route, taking a final leave of the glorious but perilous laurels of the tented field. The Portuguese, however, when under British officers, often evinced the utmost bravery, though their ranks were recruited by compulsory conscriptions. We often witnessed their levies arrive guarded by cavalry, and fastened together by ropes, in the manner convicts are sent off for transportation. These recruits were as dirty and ragged as can be well imagined; barefooted and covered with large broad-brimmed hats, and at first sight they appeared as so many miserable old men; but when clothed, we were often surprised to see them, as it were, metamorphosed into a body of athletic young fellows.

Two evenings after, I was ordered on a covering party—that is, a body of men who are to protect those about to cast up intrenchments, raise batteries, carry gabions, fascines, or any other work connected with the service. At dusk we moved from our camp in the utmost silence, and arriving in the vicinity of St. Christoval, we lay down flat beneath a rising ground, a little in rear of the place where intrenchments were about to be cast up. Then with a slow and silent pace came an engineer heading the working party, with picks, spades, and shovels; these were followed by others carrying gabions, which they laid down in rows a little in advance of where we were couched. The engineer now pointed out the intended works, afterwards called the grand battery, and the massy picks struck the earth; but never shall I forget the terrific noises that followed the breaking of that ground. For a time our ears and senses were alike astounded by the conflicting peals of the artillery and musketry, which, bursting at once on the stillness of the night, gave such an appalling shock to us who were inactive spectators, as the oldest veterans had never experienced in their numerous conflicts. Occasionally, the atmosphere was partially illuminated by the comet-like fusees of the bombs in their passage towards us; in a few instances they burst in the air within view, thus affording us a momentary respite from the dread of their effects.

In the meantime, gabions continued to be brought up from the rear, and placed close to each other, six deep. Their carriage was truly a perilous service; the men were without shelter of any kind, and as they advanced with their unwieldy burthens, many were killed or wounded under the eyes of their comrades. Every minute we heard from the works going forward the cries of "*I'm wounded!*" while the men who still remained unhurt, toiled on with a furious assidulty, in order to get under cover. The shot continued to fly over us with a fearful noise; and owing either to the distance they had come, different degrees of velocity, or causes to us unknown, they seemed to emit a variety of sounds, some of which at another time might have been accounted musical.

In this state of awful inactivity we lay listening till near daylight; and though the firing of the artillery of the garrison continued without intermission, yet some of us dropped into a kind of sleep, from which many were destined never to awaken in this world. At daybreak a large shell alighted on the brow of the hillock above where we lay, and giving a few rapid rolls towards us, burst between the legs of a serjeant, tearing off his thigh, and killing or wounding seventeen others. On the noise of this explosion I started up, and the first object that met my half-opened eyes was a German soldier, whose knapsack was on fire, shouting lustily to get it off his back. It appeared that the fusee of the shell having caught his cartridge box, it blew up, setting his knapsack in a blaze, and in his terror and confusion he was unable of himself to get rid of his fiery burden.

During this day the enemy slackened their fire; and as the workers were by this time nearly sheltered, little loss was for a time sustained. The chief annoyance was their shells; wherever a group of us sought shelter, shells were almost certain of falling immediately after; and although their near approach was announced by the smoke of their fusee, and a kind of whistling noise, we were kept in a state of perpetual agitation to elude them. In several instances I observed the shells, after their fall, roll about, sometimes like enormous foot-balls, and passing over the bodies of several who had fallen flat, exploded without doing the least injury.

At twilight, the party we had been anxiously expecting from the camp for our relief, appeared; on which the enemy opened a most tremendous fire of grape and musketry, and though they came into the trenches at *double-quick*, several were killed and wounded. We retired in a like hasty manner, and also suffered some loss.

From our camp we could perceive that, of the two other brigades of our division, which, under General Stewart, were stationed on the opposite side of the city, where the firing of cannon and musketry was constantly heard, our only communication was by a ford, several miles up the river. At this period, cannon and military stores were arriving daily from Elvas; they were forwarded on large cars, drawn by bullocks, and called by us *Shea*-cars, from the term used by the drivers when goading the animals forward. Our provisions were forwarded on mules, which travelled in troops; and, besides the muleteers, each troop was under the direction of a leader, called the *Capitras*.

On the evening of the 9th of May, I was one of a picket of eighty men at Major Ward's battery, then erecting on the right of the great road leading to St. Christoval. The night passed over without any event that could be deemed remarkable in our situation. We had, as it were, the same annoyance by shot and shells as on a former night—the same painful scenes to witness of killed and wounded, and similar hairbreadth escapes, watchings, and alarms. At daybreak, the sentinel, at the outer end of the bastion, reported that the French were coming out of St. Christoval in considerable numbers, and the next minute, that they were outside the palisadoes; and in his third report, that they had set out at *double-quick* towards our grand battery, where the next moment resounded the firing of musketry. We immediately set forward in that direction, but no sooner were clear of the trenches, than the fort opened its fire, and in crossing the road leading to the bridge, we suffered severely, the grape-shot literally pouring upon us. Before our arrival, the enemy had been repulsed, and were now assailed in their turn. We were ordered to advance, and sprang over the rampart with alacrity. The French had by this time got under cover of their guns, which now commenced a most destructive fire; and our gallant leader, Captain Smyth, having fallen, and the enemy moving into the fort, the bugles sounded a recal, and we retired into the trenches, now half-filled with the dying and the dead. Those of the French smelled strongly of brandy, of which they were reported to have had a double allowance that morning. Before the firing had entirely ceased, the light companies of our brigade from the camp appeared on the road near the bridge; and at the same time their esteemed commander, Major Birmingham, was observed to fall from his horse, being struck on the thigh by a grape-shot. These troops, perceiving that the enemy were not only repulsed, but also moving along the bridge into the city, from which many of them had come that morning, retired to the camp. Major Birmingham died on the following day, regretted by every man in our regiment, by whom he was regarded as a brave officer and common friend. On returning to our former station, we had to cross the road near the bridge, where so many had fallen on our advance, on which the fort again opened its guns, but not with such destructive effect as before. Amongst the dead was recognised our fugleman, with his head and shoulder besmeared with blood and brains; and some observing that he was alive, gave him a push with their feet, on which he moved his eyes, and we hurried him into the trenches. It was soon discovered that he was not even wounded, and that the blood and brains must have been those of the person who covered him in the ranks, and whose head had been struck off by a cannon-shot, and dashed against *his* with a force by which he had been knocked down and stupified. For some time he was unconscious of his situation, and at length complained greatly of his head, which we bound up, and he remained lying in the trenches till our relief arrived. He did not recover the effect of this shock for several days, though as brave a man as any in the regiment. On counting our files, it was found that of the eighty men who set forward to oppose the sortie made by the enemy, exactly forty were enabled to resume their stand in the ranks. Our total loss in this affair amounted to near 400 men. On the same day an officer of the engineers got on the bastion to view the enemy's fortifications, to which our guns were about to be opposed. He remained standing with a spy-glass for about ten minutes, had turned round, stooped a little, ready to jump down, when a cannon-shot carried away his head. His glass dropping from his hand as his body fell into the trenches, we had a hard struggle for his instrument while the shot were flying over our heads: so callous had we become by custom to every sense of danger, that death had lost the greater part of his grim and grisly terrors.

On the 12th, I was again on duty at the grand battery, which was yet uncompleted, and without cannon. The great ramparts of earth cast up prevented our receiving much injury, either by round or grape shot, yet our situation was even more perilous and irksome than an any former occasion. By this time the besieged had arrived at such fatal precision, as to the due distance of throwing their shells, that they mostly either fell on the gabions, or dropped into the trenches, thus rendered as unsafe as any other place within range of their guns. We retaliated briskly, by taking aim at those exposed when loading their cannon at the embrasures; and in this deliberate work of death we were pretty successful, as was evident from the irregular discharge from those parts exposed to the effects of our unceasing shot. On this day a large shell dropped into the trenches, near a Serjeant Fullen, who, to evade its effects, caught it up like a large putting-stone, and, to the terror and astonishment of many, threw it over the bastion, where it exploded without doing the smallest mischief. The other occurrences and casualties at this time were so very similar to those already mentioned, that I omit their relation.

Here, as on other occasions when mingled with the Portuguese soldiers, we had frequent dealings with them for their rations of rum, which they reserved in horns, and being very abstemious from liquors, were always willing to dispose of. If provisions were scarce, they would only exchange their rum for bread; if plenty, they would have money; but as we sometimes had neither, stratagem was resorted to in their place. Their common salutations, when holding out their horns, was *Compra ruma?* "Will you buy rum?"—our answer, *Si Senhor, provemos primeiro,* "Let's try it first." Taking a hasty mouthful, and passing it to another, we exclaimed, "*Ah nao esta bom ruma!* "It's not good rum!" And in this manner their horns were often nearly emptied in these trials; on which discovery, their owners would exclaim, in great agitation, *Ah, ladrao! bebe todo!* "Ah, thief! you have drunk it all!" When higgling, and not likely to agree in those bargains, they would put the horn to their mouths, and giving a great stagger, declare that they would get drunk and fight like the *Inglezes.*

On the morning of the 14th, the grand battery, consisting of brass twenty-four pounders, and some howitzers, opened on Fort St. Christoval; but, though a spirited fire was kept up, it was soon evident that they must be silenced by that of the enemy, who being in a great measure disengaged on that quarter, poured a terrible and overwhelming fire upon them. By the following morning, our fire was considerably abated, several of the cannon being dismounted, and the muzzles of others so beaten by the large shot struck against them as to be unserviceable, and by noon only one gun was enabled to reply to the furious and unremitting cannonade of St. Christoval. Major Ward's battery was still without cannon, hence unable to take any part in the severe and conflicting events going forward. Fortunately, on this evening an express arrived from Marshal Beresford, to raise the siege, and hasten to join him in the direction of Albuera,* as Marshal Soult was advancing from Seville with a powerful army to the relief of Badajoz. At twilight, our outposts were withdrawn, and every article brought off that was serviceable; and pressing forward with cheerful alacrity, we entered Elvas by eleven o'clock the

* "The village of Albuera is a street of mean houses, with a church, situated on a little river, from which it is named. This village is traversed by the high road leading from Seville to Badajoz, which, about two hundred yards to the right, crosses the river by a handsome bridge of stone. Immediately to the left of Albuera, and just below the rough and rising ground on which it stands, there is another bridge of unhewn stone, old, narrow, and incommodious. The river, in summer, is not knee-deep. Its banks, to the left of the old bridge, and directly in front of the village, are very abrupt and difficult; but to the right of the main bridge the passage of the stream is easy for all arms."—SHERER.

same night. Heartily tired of the dangerous and harassing service we had left, we rejoiced at decamping from a place that had been marked by a succession of the most perilous services, and conceived that any change must be for the better, compared with our state for the last eight days. Indeed, there is no duty so truly harassing to a soldier as a protracted siege, and certainly none to which he feels so marked an aversion. A general action or assault brings matters to a speedier issue, and valour and military gallantry have there a more extended field; and, except a disastrous retreat, there is no situation which damps the spirit and ardour of an army so much as a tedious siege.

We halted only a few hours at Elvas, and continuing our route, crossed the Guadiana at Jurumanha, and during our march, heard at intervals the deep rolling sounds of artillery in the direction of Albuera. Late on this evening we entered Olivenza, where we halted till about two o'clock next morning, and on setting out, met some of those who had been wounded early in the action we had heard the preceding day. Their accounts were vague and contradictory as to the probable issue of the contest they had left. In our progress we passed numerous groups of wounded, seated on mules or asses, and many straggling slowly forward on foot, or lying by the road, some of whom were already dead. Their numbers increased as we advanced, and fully testified that the battle had been one of the most sanguinary kind. Such scenes as these were really ill calculated to excite a thirst for military fame, and the "pride and pomp of glorious war," yet they did not in the least damp our ardour to step out, for though generally young in years, we were veterans in warfare, and as well inured to the warlike sounds of the cannon as to that of the bugle or drum.

About six o'clock, A.M., we came in sight of our troops on the field of battle at Albuera:* the French were discerned near a wood, about a mile and a half in their front. We now advanced in subdivisions, at double distance, to make our numbers appear as formidable as possible, and arriving on the field, piled our arms, and were permitted to move about. With awful astonishment, we gazed on the terrific scene before us; a total suspension took place of that noisy gaiety so characteristic of Irish soldiers; the most obdurate or risible countenances sunk at once into a pensive sadness, and for some time speech was supplanted by an exchange of sorrowful looks, and significant nods. Before us lay the appalling sight of upwards of 6000 men, dead, and mostly stark-naked, having, as we were informed, been stripped by the Spaniards, during the night;

* "The position chosen by the allied leaders was an undulating ridge, having the Albuera river in its front, and the Arroya in its rear. The extreme extent might be four miles. A rivulet, called the Ferdia, unites itself, immediately above the village, with the Albuera; and the intermediate surface, and the whole country beyond the larger stream, are thickly but dispersedly covered with ilex trees, a species of wood sufficient to conceal the formation, but not interrupt the movements, of an army."—MAXWELL'S LIFE OF WELLINGTON.

their bodies disfigured with dirt and clotted blood, and torn with the deadly gashes inflicted by the bullet, bayonet, sword, or lance, that had terminated their mortal existence. Those who had been killed outright, appeared merely in the pallid sleep of death, while others, whose wounds had been less suddenly fatal, from the agonies of their last struggle, exhibited a fearful distortion of features. Near our arms was a small stream almost choked with bodies of the dead, and from the deep traces of blood on its miry margin, it was evident that many of them had crawled thither to allay their last thirst. The waters of this oozing stream were so deeply tinged, that it seemed actually to run blood. A few perches distant was a draw-well, about which were collected several hundreds of those severely wounded, who had crept or been carried thither. They were sitting, or lying, in the puddle, and each time the bucket reached the surface with its scanty supply, there was a clamorous and heart-rending confusion; the cries for water resounding in at least ten languages, while a kindness of feeling was visible in the manner this beverage was passed to each other.

Turning from this painful scene of tumultuous misery, we again strolled amongst the mangled dead. The bodies were seldom scattered about, as witnessed after former battles, but lying in rows or heaps; in several places whole subdivisions or sections appeared to have been prostrated by one tremendous charge or volley.

We here found the Fusileer and Portuguese

brigades of our division, whom we had not seen since we went to Badajoz, where they had also been employed. They had arrived on the ground just before the action commenced, in which the former brigade was nearly annihilated. When we separated from them at Olivenza, the Fusileers amounted to at least 2250 men, and on their muster this day, only about 350 stood in their ranks.* Before their going to Badajoz, 29 men of our regiment had been detached to this brigade, to assist as artificers during the siege of that fortress; of these only one now remained fit for service. The loss in several other British regiments was reported to have been equally severe; those of the 3rd, 31st, 48th, 57th, and 66th, were particularly mentioned, and the field before us presented ample proofs that those reports were but too true. All the survivors with whom we conversed were

* "That such continued and desperate fighting must cause an enormous loss may be easily imagined. Besides 2000 Spaniards, and 500 Germans and Portuguese, placed *hors de combat*, the British casualties amounted to 4407—an enormous loss, when it is remembered that little more than 6500 English soldiers were actually on the battle ground. Houghton died, cheering his men on—and Myers and Duckwork, at the heads of their respective regiments. Stewart, Cole, Inglis, Blakeney, and Hawkeshaw, were wounded. Few regiments could muster in the evening a third of the number with which they went into action; and the loss sustained by the 57th—known afterwards by the *soubriquet* of 'Die-hards'—stands without a parallel. Its strength, when led into fire, was about 570 bayonets; and its casualties at two in the afternoon were, 23 officers, and nearly 400 rank and file."—MAXWELL'S LIFE OF WELLINGTON.

heartless and discontented. They complained bitterly that the army had been sacrificed by a series of blunders, especially in placing the Spaniards on the key of the position, and in not crediting that the Lancers, who had for a time been mistaken for Spaniards, were really French. In our inquiries amongst the Fusileers, the following particulars were collected on the spot; but before proceeding to their relation, I shall notice the numbers of the contending armies, and relative situations to the bloody field.

The combined army was under the orders of Marshal Beresford, and amounted to nearly 28,000 men, forming in round numbers about the following proportion: 12,000 Spaniards, 8,000 Portuguese, some German artillery and riflemen, and the remainder British. Marshal Soult commanded the French forces, consisting of at least 25,000 veteran troops, about 4000 of whom were cavalry, a species of force in which we were very defective. The enemy occupied exactly the same position as noticed on our advance thither; and our army the same ground as at this time. About half a mile in our front was a river, from which the ground towards us rose in a gentle swell, free from ditches or wood, except a few dwarfish shrubs. Near the extremity of our line on the right, the ground was more elevated, rising into a few knolls; and rather in front, on the left, was the ruinous village of Albuera, on the great road, leading to a bridge over the river. The only living creatures seen in Albuera at this time, was an old man and a cat.

About eight o'clock on the morning of the 16th, the enemy began to move from the wood seen in front, which till that time had concealed their numbers. Soon after, several columns advanced towards the river, one of which immediately crossed on the right, and commenced a vigorous attack on the Spaniards, while others attempted to pass at fords and at the bridge. The Spaniards, consisting of the united corps of Generals Blake, Castonos, and Ballasteros, defended themselves with the utmost bravery, but were at length driven from their position, leaving behind them ample and indubitable proofs of the obstinate valour by which it had been maintained. From this post the enemy's artillery was now enabled to rake the field, and scattered death throughout our line. Before even attempting its recovery, it became necessary to change our front, and while executing this manœuvre, a large body of French lancers, which had for some time been hovering about, dashed between the open divisions, and in the confusion that ensued, a dreadful havoc was made before they could be expelled. Favoured by a tremendous shower of rain and hail, which had fallen early in the action, those lancers passed the river unobserved, and on the storm abating, they were seen in front within musket-shot of our lines, and reports were made that they were French, but not credited. From their being thus allowed to move quietly about, they evidently perceived that they were mistaken for friends, and kept in a compact body, waiting an opportunity to pounce upon us. At length, while our divisions were detached, in the act of deploying into line, they advanced in squadrons at full gallop, shouting in Spanish, "Vivan los Ingleses," "Vivan los amigos de España," and the next moment they were in our ranks, which were so completely surprised, that whole companies were destroyed without firing one shot.

The defeat of the enemy, the recovery of the heights that had been so fatally lost,* and the

* " In a few minutes more the remnant of the British must have abandoned the hill or perished. The French reserve was on its march to assist the front column of the enemy, while with the allies all was in confusion; and as if the slaughter required increase, a Spanish and English regiment were firing in mutual error upon each other. Six guns were in possession of the French, and their lancers, riding furiously over the field, threatened the feeble remnant of the British still in line, and speared the wounded without mercy. At this fearful moment the boundless gallantry of British officers displayed itself: Colonel Arbuthnot, under the double musketry, rushed between the mistaken regiments, and stopped the firing; Cole pushed up the hill, scattered the lancers, recovered the guns, and passed the right of the skeleton of Houghton's brigade, at the same instant that Abercrombie appeared upon its left. Leaving the broken regiments in its rear, the fusileer brigade came forward with imposing gallantry, and boldly confronted the French, now reinforced by a part of its reserve, and who were, as they believed, coming forward to annihilate the "feeble few" that had still survived the murderous contest. From the daring attitude of the fresh regiments, Soult perceived, too late, that the battle was not yet won; and, under a tremendous fire of artillery, he endeavoured to break up his close formation and open out his front. For a moment the storm of grape

other events of this memorable action being so well known, I omit their relation, and shall only observe, that my narrators gave their commander little credit for what has been since termed one of the most brilliant victories of the Peninsular war.

poured from Ruty's well-served artillery, staggered the fusileers, but it was only for a moment. Though Soult rushed into the thickest of the fire, and encouraged and animated his men,—though the cavalry gathered on their flank and threatened it with destruction,—on went those noble regiments; volley after volley falling into the crowded ranks of their enemy, and cheer after cheer pealing to heaven, in answer to the clamorous outcry of the French, as the boldest urged the others forward. Nothing could check the fusileers; they kept gradually advancing, while the incessant rolling of their musketry slaughtered the crowded sections of the French, and each moment embarrassed more and more Soult's efforts to open out his encumbered line. The enemy's reserve coming forward to support their comrades, was forced to the very edge of the plateau, and increased the crowd without remedying the disorder. The English volleys rolled on faster and more deadly than ever—a horrid carnage, making all attempts to hold the hill vain, and thus uselessly increased an unavailing slaughter. Unable to bear the withering fire, the shattered columns of the French were no longer able to sustain themselves,—the mass were driven over the ridge,—and trampling each other down, the shattered column sought refuge at the bottom of the hill. On that bloody height stood the conquerors. From 1500 muskets a parting volley fell upon the routed column as it hurried down the height. Where was the remainder of the proud array of England, which on the morning had exceeded 6000 combatants?—stretched coldly in the sleep of death, or bleeding on the battle ground!"—VICTORIES OF THE BRITISH ARMIES.

Their complaints were loud and general, and always ended with some expression of deep regret for the absence of him whom we looked up to with unlimited confidence, whose presence gave us additional courage, and under whom we deemed ourselves invincible and certain of success,—need I add, that person was WELLINGTON.

From the heavy rain that had fallen the preceding day, and the trampling of men and horses, the field of battle was at this time a perfect puddle, without one dry or green spot on which we could repose or be seated. Wearied and chilled after our forced march, and wading through the sloughs, we kindled fires, and as fuel could not be had, the muskets lying about were thrown on promiscuously for that purpose. These arms made truly a crack fire, for several being charged immediately exploded, the balls whistling through the mud and casting it up in our faces. Alarmed at those salutes, we for some time examined if the guns were discharged, but tired of those researches, several again exploded, happily without doing any mischief.

On this night our situation was, if possible, more gloomy and uncomfortable than any we had yet experienced, war on every hand presenting one of his most horrid and terrific forms, while at the same time we laboured under the greatest privations. Neither provisions nor liquors could be had at any price, and the surrounding country was so wild and depopulated, as to bid defiance to all attempts to better our state, even by marauding. The only place of rest, if such it could be called, was sitting on our knapsacks in the mud, into which many occasionally dropped, overcome with sleep and fatigue, and remained for a time as insensible as the gory corpse on the field. During those heavy and lengthened hours, when about to fall into the mire, I several times started up and gazed on this strange and appalling scene. The ghastly lines of the dead were faintly visible through the gloom, while the deep snoring of those lying about, or who still maintained their balance on their seats, nearly drowned the calls of the sentinels and the low moanings of the mutilated soldiers who still continued to feel. The dull monotony of those sounds were at times broken by others in strict unison with such a time and place. From about midnight, the howling of wolves was heard in the direction of the river; they had probably left their dens in the adjacent wood to feast on this field of carnage. Their howls seemed at times as if answered by the calls and croakings of the birds of prey which kept hovering about. I even thought that they seemed to say, "Why remain you here, after having laid out for us such a grand and rich repast?" The thoughts of home, the friends I had there left, and the fabulous legends of infancy, passed over my memory in quick review; I paused, and found that the most horrid of those "tales of terror," all the ideal terrors of romance, were surpassed by the horrid realities before me. I several times endeavoured to collect my bewildered thoughts in contrasting my former and present state, but recoiled with horror from the task, and found that truth was indeed strange, "stranger than fiction."

RECOLLECTIONS OF THE PENINSULA.*

The evening before leaving Lisbon, we buried one of our officers, who died in the morning, having been only ill of cholera ten hours. It was a weary tribute to his memory performing the Dead March from the Rocio Square to Buenos Ayres, particularly as we had to get ready for our long pedestrian jaunt that was to commence the next day. I should not have introduced such an occurrence, had it not been to shew that, before Asiatic cholera came into fashion, its European prototype could perform its business occasionally in an off-hand sort of way; in this instance, it left the word promotion at immeasurable distance, for this poor fellow had been a subaltern at the siege of Gibraltar, and was no more when we buried him.

From some supposed difficulty in the routes in the north of Portugal, the division of Sir John Hope, with our small handful of cavalry, was to

* By Lieutenant-Colonel Wilkie.

march by Abrantes and the banks of the Tagus, having in charge the whole upholstery of the army,—the remainder of the troops moved by different routes and by single regiments. Nothing could be more pleasant than the march from Lisbon to Coimbra. The month of October, as to weather, was very similar to what we had in England last September—beautiful and clear. We halted on the march occasionally near running streams of clear water, which abound in Portugal; the distances were moderate, and good quarters awaited us at night. Our route was by the Tagus as far as Villa Franca, from thence to Olla; and from that place we took a cross-road that brought us back to our former line of march at Las Caldas. The epigram on the Highland roads of Marshal Wade—

" Had you seen these roads before they were made"—

would scarcely involve a *bull* applied to a Portuguese cross-road; for, in point of fact, there can be little difference between a road " that was never made" and one that was never repaired; the tracks of cart-wheels alone gave evidence that people had travelled that way. In many places the softer materials had been washed away, leaving only the bare rock, and these leaps were often above two feet in height; *the few carriages* we had were obliged to be hoisted up or lowered down by ropes. I can imagine that when the Portuguese cars travel by such roads, that they must do the same thing as at the *portages* of the rapids in North America,

—unload at the bottom and carry up the cargo piecemeal. At Caldas, we had no longer ambition to indulge in the sulphur bath; but some very good port wine, with the factory seal, afforded full compensation.

The next stage brought us in front of the princely convent of Alcobaça. This has been already described by various travellers, but a few words may not here appear intrusive, particularly as speaking of things that have been; for the conventual property was confiscated to the benefit of the state in the days of Don Pedro, the monks dispersed, and I have not yet heard if any part of the edifice has been restored after the destruction to which it was doomed by Massena. From the roof of the convent, it was said, that all within the horizon was the property of the establishment, which would give a vast idea of its wealth; but a large portion of this view, particularly towards the east, was little more than barren and unproductive hills,—still there was sufficiency of riches to enable these jolly friars to live on the fat of the land, and bestow their hospitality with open hand. The building that gave lodging and employment to these worthy cenobites was of great extent, standing on an elevated platform, that on the north touched on the village of the same name; the largest portion of the edifice belonged to the convent itself, which contained a spacious entrance-hall, two splendid apartments for the entertainment of guests, numerous sleeping-apartments, and dormitories; infinitude of corridors, leading no one could guess where, and a wilderness of different passages, apartments, &c. There was nothing to distinguish the refectory from that of other convents, except, perhaps, the good things that were served up in it; but the kitchen was the real wonder of the place—an immense apartment with a lofty arched roof. It appeared to me large enough to have contained the whole population of the adjoining village. There were rows of stoves, variety of ovens and hot hearths; but what distinguished it from all other kitchens was, having a rivulet running through its centre. A portion of the water was diverted by pipes to the purposes of cookery and cleanliness, but the main body of the stream passed through a succession of wooden boxes or reservoirs, in which were swimming many varieties of river fish, looking as if they said, Come, cook me! Every sort of *comestible* might be seen in heaps; and this was no vain show, for, in a short time after our arrival, a dinner was served up in one of the large apartments I have alluded to, for all the officers, which would not have disgraced the board of a prince. There were all varieties of fish, flesh, and fowl, pastry and sweetmeats. Behind each officer was stationed one of the lay-brothers, or a novice, to look after his wants, change plates, &c., while the abbot, assisted by the elder monks, superintended the whole arrangements, directing fresh bottles of wine to be placed on the table as those there became empty, with all the *petits soins* of the most accomplished hosts. Dish after dish succeeded each other in endless succession, and the feast was crowned by an ample dessert. It was a sight that would have warmed the heart of Dalgetty, and probably have tempted him to become a Benedictine monk. For where in the world could he have expected to meet with such an excellent supply of "*provant?*"

When the whole ceremony of dinner, dessert, &c., was over, the abbot invited his guests to view the wonders of the place. In this visit were included the wives of two officers who were quartered in the village;—this was a most special favour, the head of the monastery declaring, most solemnly, that they were the two first women who had been within the convent walls! I have already given an idea of the convent itself: the church, which joined it, had little in its heavy or gloomy structure that was striking; and the only thing remarkable in it was the chapel and tomb of Pedro and Ines. The library, on the contrary, which joined it on the south, was light and cheerful, and the shelves well furnished. Among masses of theological learning were several modern works, and a few of these of rather doubtful character, connected with the sanctity of the place. Taken altogether, the convent of Alcobaça might be pronounced to have been perfect for all religious purposes, and something more. I have been in the convent of St. Martin's, near Monreale, in Sicily, which had the character of being the first establishment of Benedictines in Europe, as regarded splendour and comfort; but it would bear no comparison with Alcobaça.

While the *lion* hunt was going on, one of our youths who little delighted in that species of chase, remained in the dinner apartment, gazing out of the window, and enjoying the *dolce far niente*, when the brother of the convent who acted as purveyor entered the apartment to ask at what hour the English officers would like to sup, when he was told that the English officers never ate supper. I have related, in speaking of South America, some anecdotes of this *poco curante*. When we landed at Mondego, all the officers and men carried, or were supposed to carry, three days' provisions with them. We all observed this hero's havresack to have a very attenuated appearance, and question was made what he had got in it. This he appeared shy of affording, but he was soon hustled, and the contents of his bag displayed. His provision for three days proved to be, one sea-biscuit and a dirty pack of cards. At Alcobaça he did not get so easily off, for as soon as the rest of the officers learned how they had been cheated of their supper, they were all open-mouthed against the offender, for presuming to pronounce on the state of appetites of twenty-five people. It was pointed out to him, that not only he had inflicted an injury on the gastronomy of his comrades, but the evil would be reflected on all the poor fellows that were to follow in our track, who could never know the reason why they were sent supperless to bed. In the morning, chocolate, coffee, &c., were handed about, and a kind farewell given by this excellent brotherhood on our departure. Similar instances of kindness and hospitality afforded to British officers by these worthy monks, drew upon them the ire of Massena.

During the time that his head-quarters were at Santarem, the convent was sacked, the wine drank, and the place set on fire. There was little inflammable matter about the church, and probably it escaped, or at least it has been repaired; but the property of the monastery was seized on by the government of Don Pedro; and although I have made many inquiries, I have never been able to learn what became of our kind and hospitable entertainers, or whether the convent has been in any degree restored.

Our route was by Alpedriz, Leiria, and Pombal, the last named place being quite new to us. With exception of the principal thoroughfare, the town had a dull and sombre appearance — scarcely a sign of life about the great old-fashioned houses. Within doors, the lofty apartments, gilt mouldings, immense mirrors in old-fashioned frames, with the sofas and chairs covered with tapestry, brought one back to the age of Louis-Quatorze. The whole place contrasted strongly with our next halting place, Coimbra, which, seen on approaching from the south, offers a very pleasant and cheerful prospect. It is situated on a hill of some elevation, at the base of which large masses of building connected with the university give it the appearance of a fortified place. This contrasts very well with the upper part of the town, which is of lighter structure and shade; seen under the influence of a bright sun, and with the clear and (then) tranquil Mondego in the foreground it affords a very agreeable picture. Here we remained for two days, and were much amused with the speculations, in this seat of learning, on our future destination and prospects.

November had now arrived, and it might be expected that our promenade over the hills would not be exempt from moisture. As we passed the Busaco range, and descended to Mortuaga, the mists hung heavy on the hills; and the next day, between the latter place and Viseu, the rain came down in a fashion I have never seen exceeded on the coast of Africa. From Viseu to Celerico the road for a certain distance is well marked out, until it arrives at the foot of some hills, where it is lost amidst numberless tracks. This chain, which takes its rise at the north end of the Sierra de Alcoba, runs in a direction nearly south-east to its termination at Garda; and although of no great elevation from the plain immediately at its foot, is sufficiently bleak and rugged. As we gained the summit, the rain, which had rather abated in the morning, resumed its downfal in earnest. It was of that quality which Panurge describes, when he says, "L'eau est entrée en mes souliers par le collet." Peering about amidst this deluge, I saw, near the road, a few miserable sheep and goats guarded by what appeared a bundle of straw, but, in fact, a man in a thatch. A coarse piece of sacking is cut out to form a surtout, with a pointed cape like a friar's cowl; and into this are sewed pieces of straw overlaying each other in the fashion of thatch, so that a man has only to turn his back to the wind to be perfectly sheltered from the heaviest rain. Had I been leaving Portugal I should have liked to have brought one of these as a specimen for the Arcadians of Salisbury Plain.

At Celerico and Pinhel we were hospitably received in our billets, the people sharing the little they had with us, and trying to promote our amusement in the evening by getting up little dances, and furnishing some refreshments. I should not have dwelt so long on a road so every way hackneyed had it not been to let military readers form a comparison between what occurred to us as the first visiters, and what they experienced themselves at a later period.

Considering the state of the weather, we arrived at a small village, about gun-shot distance from the glacis of Almeida, in tolerably good condition, and here we bade farewell to the rain. Following the well-beaten track across the bridge over the Coa at *Barba del porco,* and passing the rivulet below the fort of Concepcion that separates the two countries, we supped that night at St. Felices, as Sterne would say, " so incontestably in Spain," that the Inquisition might have proceeded against us if we had allowed them. We had now gained the great plateau, the most elevated table-land of that extent in Europe, which comprises the Castiles and Leon, and henceforth moved on level ground to Salamanca. Before we gained the last village, previously to entering that city, I had seen near the road a quantity of fine mushrooms, with which I filled a handkerchief. On arriving at my billet, and unfolding the treasure, my Spanish host shook his head with many marks of disgust; and although I had little doubt that what I had picked up were of the right sort, yet I asked if they were wholesome; to which he always replied, "Mucho malo." I had nearly sacrificed the mess, when I thought of asking him if nobody in Spain ate such things. "Oh, yes," he said, "they eat them in Salamanca," where, it appeared, that he himself had carried them for sale. This was but a slight example of the ignorance, or rather the prejudice, of these people. This man continued to ask me all sorts of foolish questions about the army, and how long we thought it would be before we got to the kingdom of France. As the mushrooms were stewing, he asked me if there were any olive-trees in England, to which I answered "No," and that we had no grapes for the purpose of making wine. He shook his head with much solemnity at this, as much as to say, "How can you live? No wonder, poor wretches, that you are glad to pick up a Spanish fungus to keep you from starving!" Yet was this man one of the best specimens I have seen of the finest peasantry in Europe, as far as external appearance goes. *On an average* the men are about five feet nine inches in height; seldom you meet with any much under; and persons of six feet, and upwards, are equally rare. With the upright carriage of a well drilled grenadier, they have that ease of carriage and freedom from restraint which, in this country, are supposed to be the attributes of high breeding; while, in point of shape and figure, four out of six might serve as models for a statuary, These personal advantages are set off by the national dress, which, however much the materials may be deteriorated by wear, always fits well, and has a picturesque effect. See the man, however, in his gala dress, and hear him speak in his own fine and sonorous language, which he generally does correctly, and free from provincial accent, you will set him down at once as the head and model for all his class throughout the world. This fair temple is, however, deceptive in appearance, as it is the abode of ignorance, cruelty, and indomitable pride. These defects and vices stood directly in the way of any attempts to organize the masses, and form them into regular armies, which failed in every instance during the long struggle that existed in Spain.

A walk of a few miles in the country will soon make a person understand the value of the French saying as a comparison of what is impossible or difficult, "building castles in Spain." The word *chateau* in the proverb means a country-seat, and these are altogether invisible in this part of the Peninsula. There is not even such a thing to be seen throughout the country as a farm-house, and one is quite at a loss to imagine in what way the land is cultivated. The half of a man's time must be consumed in passing to and fro from his *pueblo*, or village, where he resides, and the place where his labour is bestowed.

The approach to Salamanca from the west gives a very favourable view of the city and university, with the Tormes and its fine ancient bridge in the foreground of the picture. We marched in with all the honours of war. The officers were billeted on the inhabitants, and the men quartered in the deserted colleges. Although belonging to different brigades, the 42nd regiment and ours were the first two that arrived in Salamanca. The men had hardly taken off their packs when they were ordered to stand to their arms. A report had arrived, which, if true, would have soon sent us to the right-about—namely, that a French army of 70,000 men had entered Valladolid, only forty miles distant. It turned out in the sequel that it was a patrol of French cavalry that had entered Valladolid, and ordered rations for that number of troops—a sort of means of creating a false alarm. This little occurrence may serve to show how insulated our little army was at Salamanca. In place of meeting native armies, and other support of the same nature, which had been promised, we could never even place dependence on any of the various reports that reached us, and knew as little of what was actually passing at Madrid as at Constantinople. It was very clear that, unless attacked by a superior force, we must remain where we were until our artillery joined us, and it was left to ourselves how best to dispose of the time. The city had not yet been visited by the enemy, and some of the agreeable means of filling up our leisure were at hand. The markets were well supplied with meat and vegetables; droves of turkeys were every day driven into the town, and it was the pig harvest. Immense quantities of pork, fattened on cork-acorns, were constantly exposed in the market, and the roasters of chestnuts were busy at every corner of the streets. There was under the corridor of the Plaza a pastry-cook's shop, which had abundant custom. Here they boasted of their cakes being made with *manteca de vacca*, a very necessary distinction to mark the word butter, as, in Spanish, *manteca* signifies every kind of grease—hog's lard, pomatum, &c., as well as the produce of the cow. The square itself is a handsome mass of building. There are only two entrances for carriages in the middle of the opposite sides, and a communication for foot passengers with the market at one of the angles. On occasions of great festivals, this plaza is converted into an amphitheatre for that barbarous amusement of the Spaniards, the bull-fight, which can only hold its place amongst a people pretending to any degree of civilization, by administering to that innate love of cruelty which forms so large an ingredient in the character of the Spaniard. A recent instance of this depraved taste has been exhibited on the young queen assuming her premature authority. The highest compliment the Madrilenos could pay her was an invitation to a bull-feast—a special and appropriate amusement for a young girl of thirteen, the torment and death of a poor animal, and the interesting spectacle of horses gored by the beast in its excited rage moving about the arena with their bowels trailing on the ground!

The corridor of the plaza, which is somewhat similar in construction to the Palais Royal at Paris, but infinitely inferior in the display of its shops, was, at the time I speak of, the rendezvous of all the *quidnuncs* of the army, where a considerable quantity of news was manufactured; of real events passing within a hundred miles of us, we were as much in the dark as if we had been in the South Sea Islands. It was at this daily parade of newsmongers that I met the late Sir Robert Ker Porter, who had come out to Spain as an amateur, in the same way in which he subsequently attended the movements of the Russian army during the campaign of Moscow. His conversation, in which were equally blended instruction and amusement, shortened very frequently to me what would have been otherwise tedious hours of expectation and suspense. The pleasure of his company, which was altogether unexpected, will always make me look back to my sojourn at Salamanca with satisfaction. It may perhaps also serve as an excuse for introducing the circumstance here, as I could not let the occasion pass by without offering this feeble tribute of regret and esteem to the memory of my earliest and best of friends.

The weather was clear, with a slight frost, a great inducement to taking exercise; but the immediate vicinity of Salamanca, like that of all other Spanish towns, is quite devoid of interest; some pleasant walks, however, were discovered along the banks of the Tormes, not, however, possessing sufficient attraction to make the repetition very desirable. Among other means of banishing *ennui*, was paying visits to such of the convents as were accessible to strangers. Much delusion exists about the female inhabitants of convents; persons dream of beautiful creatures shut up in these dismal abodes, pining away their existence. Whatever they may be when they enter the conventual state, I cannot pretend to say, but in all the convents that I have seen in different countries, I cannot tax my memory with having seen a single pretty girl. The life they lead of vigils, fastings, restraints of all kinds, and being deprived of proper air and exercise, are sufficient of themselves to cause beauty to fade rapidly, independently of the emotions of the mind. All the nuns I have ever seen, bore evident marks of premature old age. The convent that we used to visit at Salamanca was similar to the rest in this way; with the exception of certain pairs of dark eyes, there were no other remains of even good looks. These nymphs were very well inclined to be chatty, and there was a good deal of King Ferdinand's Spanish murdered in endeavouring to make ourselves understood. There was, however, no mistake in music; they were quite delighted with having the band brought up for their entertainment, which was done frequently. At last, one of these ancient virgins begged that the band would play what they used when they went into battle. It would have been idle to persuade them that people had other things to think of; so the next day the drums were ordered to accompany the band, and treat the sisterhood to the *réveillée*, which, if not enough to raise the dead, was sufficient to start the heaviest sleeper, when performed in the streets of a town.

All this noise, concentrated in so small a space, may be easily conceived; by substituting a narrow convent parlour for the caverns of Tartarus, the celebrated lines of the Italian poet might have been made applicable to the occasion:—

> "Trema il *augusto parlatorio*
> E l'acr *chiaro* a quel rumor rimbomba."

I was not present on this occasion, but was told that, at the first crash of the drums, the frightened nuns, who had not time to give regular screams, made a sort of squeak, and ran into the convent like a parcel of rabbits; presently, however, they returned cautiously, one by one, to the parlour, and being convinced that the house had not actually fallen about their ears, took courage gradually, became reconciled to the noise, and finally were so delighted with it, that they requested its frequent repetition.

While we thus endeavoured to

> "Lose and neglect the creeping hours of time,"

the elements for our destruction were gathering fast round our heads; large masses of French troops had passed the Pyrenees, and Napoleon was on his way to Madrid. Every morning the first question of the Spaniards was, when our guns would arrive; as they thought that as soon as that was accomplished, we had nothing to do but to march on the capital. The delays that had taken place on the road, had so prolonged the difficult and critical march of Sir John Hope's division, that we began to despair of ever seeing it again; and even when the guns did arrive, it was quite indispensable that the animals should have some rest. When all that was accomplished, it would have been then too late to retreat on Lisbon; we should have had the whole of the French army from Madrid close on our heels, been encumbered with a ponderous artillery, and without cavalry to support it, we should have run the risk of being intercepted by the fourth French corps, then in Estramadura, and would ultimately have been obliged to abandon Lisbon, and lose that pivot of future operations.

DOLORES.

AN INCIDENT IN THE PENINSULAR WAR.

> "Pero no me compadezcas,
> No llores me dulce amiga;
> Que todo la muerte acaba,
> Y no tadarà la mia."

AFTER the long and severe retreat from Burgos, in the autumn of 1812, the regiment in which I held a company was cantoned in the province of Beira, near the Serra d'Estrella.

The tide of war, which had rushed like an impetuous and overwhelming torrent through other parts of the Peninsula, had passed over this more fortunate district with a quieter stream. It is true, indeed, that hostile armies had marched through it, and that troops of different nations had been quartered in its towns and villages; but still the dreadful ravages that had laid waste other parts of the country with fire and sword, had been but lightly felt here, and the peasantry were a kind-hearted, happy, and contented race of people. My company and another were quartered in the little village of Oliveira, which is situated in a lovely valley, through which winds a rapid mountain-stream. The country is perhaps as romantic and beautiful as any that is to be found in Portugal. It is mountainous, and well wooded by nature with the fir and the ilex. The sides of the hills are cultivated with the vine and olive, and Indian corn, and in the neighbourhood of the streams are well-irrigated meadows. In the distance is the magnificent range of the Estrella mountains, on whose lofty summits snow may be seen nearly the whole year through. The country abounds with game; and it was my custom, as soon as I had dismissed the company after morning parade, to sally forth with my two pointers in quest of woodcocks.

On my road to my favourite covers, I had to pass the farm belonging to old Pedro Vanzella, whose garden was the neatest in the village, and which was under the especial superintendence of his eldest daughter, Dolores. Dolores was one of the most beautiful girls I have ever seen. She was rather below the common height, but perfectly formed; and with the large dark eye and raven locks of her country, she had a much fairer complexion than is usually found in Portuguese beauty. Her smile was the sweetest thing imaginable, and her countenance beamed with intelligence. I invariably found her in the garden waiting for me with some little present of oranges or sweetmeats; and, from her manner, it was evident that she not only wished to become acquainted with me, but to make me her friend, while to the other officers in the village she was shy and reserved. Dolores was the merriest little creature that ever lived; and I have often found myself beguiled of an hour's shooting by laughing and talking with her over the wall of her father's garden, or by listening to her singing some of the beautiful modinhas peculiar to Portugal, which she executed with great taste and pathos. I was for some time at a loss to account for her conduct, for the vainest man that ever lived could not for one moment have mistaken the innocence and modesty of her manner.

The mystery was at last cleared up. I found that Dolores, and a young man in my company, named Seymour, had become attached to each other, and that a wedding was in contemplation; and she naturally enough wished to make a friend of her future husband's captain. Seymour was a remarkably handsome young man, and a good soldier: he was civil to every one, obedient to his officers, and attentive to his duty; but at times there was something peculiarly repulsive in his countenance; and I had observed that, when speaking, he would never look you fairly in the face. He was the son of a yeoman in Devonshire, and had had the advantage of a good education. Before he enlisted he had been clerk to a lawyer in Exeter; but why he exchanged the pen for the musket I could never learn. As soon as Dolores found that I was in possession of her secret, she threw off all reserve, and would talk openly to me of her attachment to Seymour and her future prospects. It was impossible to know the sweet gentle girl as well as I did, and not to feel a sincere interest in her welfare. I now passed much of my time in her company, and she would listen with the deepest interest, with her large beautiful eyes fixed in my face, while I told her stories and gave her descriptions of England, where she expected to spend the rest of her life. She would then tell me all her plans and prospects of future happiness. Her father was to give her a considerable sum of money on the day of her marriage; and as Seymour was enlisted for a limited period, their scheme was, as soon as he could leave the army, to purchase a small farm in Devonshire with her money, where Dolores looked forward to passing the remainder of her days as the happy wife of the man of her heart. One day Dolores and myself had arranged that I should ride over to the neighbouring village of Ranhados the following morning, to speak to the commanding officer upon the subject of her marriage. We were seated under an orange-tree in her own garden, and were both of us in the highest spirits. I had been laughing at her vain endeavours to pronounce some long English words after me, and she had been equally amused at my attempts to twist my Spanish into tolerable Portuguese. Alas! at that very moment even her happy hours were numbered. Long after I had left her, I could distinguish her joyous song ringing through the valley; it was the last song I ever heard Dolores sing. I returned home that evening in high glee, with tired pointers and a well-filled game-bag, and found the grim old pay-serjeant of the company waiting at the door of my quarters to speak to me, and learnt from him that there were rumours amongst Seymour's comrades that he was already married, and that his wife was living somewhere in Ireland. I immediately sent for him, and he did not deny the fact, but seemed rather surprised at the indignant manner in which I upbraided him for his conduct towards Dolores. He told me that he and his wife had separated by mutual consent, in consequence of her misconduct; that she was living in Cork with her family, and that there was no chance of their ever meeting again. The difficulty now was, how to tell the poor girl of Seymour's villany. I watched an opportunity the next morning, when Dolores was in her garden, to tell her mother what I had heard; and she undertook the painful task of breaking it to her daughter. For the next two or three days I went often by her garden, but Dolores had deserted it. At last I made an effort, and went to see her, and I was not deceived in my apprehensions. She received me in her usual kind and affectionate manner, but her sweet smile was gone for ever: she was deadly pale, and I could observe traces of recent tears upon her cheeks, which had been hastily brushed away. I saw at a glance that the blow had struck home. Her mother told me that Seymour had made various attempts to speak to her; but Dolores was firm and resolute in her determination never to see him again, or to hold any communication with him. She was never heard to complain, or to allude to the cause of her grief; but she kept her sorrows locked up in her own bosom.

In a few days we received our route for Oporto; and on the morning that we marched, the road was crowded with the inhabitants of the village, who had collected there to take leave of us; and many a wish was breathed, and many a prayer offered up to their saints by the kind-hearted peasantry for the success and welfare of their friends, *los Colorados*.* The band struck up a lively march, and Oliveira was soon left far behind us.

After I had been about six weeks at Oporto, I was sent back to Viseu, together with three or four other officers, to bring some sick and wounded to the battalion that had been left there in hospital. On reaching Viseu, I found that the detachment which I was to take charge of, would not be sufficiently recovered to march for at least a fortnight; and as I had now plenty of time on my hands, I used to amuse myself by riding round the different villages in which the battalion had been quartered. I need scarcely say that the first village I rode to was Oliveira, and the first house that I went to was Pedro Vanzella's. Dolores was there, and, on my entering the room, two bright spots lit up her pale face, which, in the same instant, resumed its

---

* A name given by the Spaniards to the English soldiers, from the colour of their uniforms.

ashy paleness. I could hardly believe it possible that the poor melancholy and emaciated girl before me was really the same light-hearted merry Dolores who had been sitting under the orange-tree with me, singing and laughing, only two short months before. Grief and blighted hopes had, indeed, done their work most rapidly. She was evidently in the last stage of a consumption. She extended her hand, and attempted to rise and receive me; but the exertion was too much for her, and brought on a severe fit of coughing, and her mother gently replaced her in her chair. Her old father stood with his arms folded, the picture of manly grief; and Maria, a beautiful child ten years old, who used formerly to run bounding towards me like a young kid, now turned away, and, burying her face in her hands, cried as if her little heart was breaking. The poor child, young as she was, knew but too well that her affectionate sister and kind playmate was dying. The only person who seemed quite unmoved was Dolores herself. She was perfectly collected, and talked quietly and calmly. She asked after all those whom she had known in the regiment; and although I was the only officer that she had been acquainted with in the village, still she remembered their names, and inquired about them. Her old mother, Joaquina, had been busily employed in spreading the table with the best that the house afforded; but though my ride had been a long one, and I had fasted for some hours, the sight of the poor broken-hearted girl had completely taken away every inclination to eat, and the repast was removed untouched. The day was at last fixed for my leaving Viseu, and the evening before, I rode over to Oliveira to pay Dolores a final visit. I was careful to drop no hint that could lead her to suppose I was come to see her for the last time; but the poor girl certainly suspected it, for she did what I had never known her do before. She held my hand in hers the whole time that I was with her; and when at last I did take leave of her, she was much affected, and I suspect that she was as well aware as I was myself that we were saying farewell to each other for ever. I found her father at the door holding my horse himself. He did not speak,—the old man's heart was too full,—but he wrung my hand kindly and affectionately.

It may seem strange that I should have formed this sort of friendship for a poor Portuguese girl; but Dolores was a superior creature. She had a very refined mind, with a strong natural understanding, and her father, who was a man of some property, had given her the best education that the neighbouring convent at Viseu could afford. She was, in fact, as well educated as half the noblemen's daughters in the country, and she was, moreover, one of the most gentle and affectionate little beings that I have ever met with. On reaching Viseu I went straight to my own quarters, feeling too much depressed in spirits to mix with my merry comrades; and I made our early march the next morning an excuse for not joining their party at dinner. A few easy marches brought us to Lamego. There I embarked the detachment, and proceeded down the Douro towards Oporto, where I rejoined the battalion late on the second evening.

I could never observe that Seymour showed any symptoms of remorse for his conduct; his voice was as loud, and his laugh as frequent, as that of any of his comrades. But it is impossible that his conscience could have slept when standing, in the stillness of night, a solitary sentry on out-post. He never returned to England, but was killed afterwards at the passage of the Nive.

In the river in Cumberland, in which I usually follow my favourite amusement of fishing, there is a spot which so nearly resembles an old haunt of mine near Oliveira, that I generally find myself, when fishing in that neighbourhood, passing rapidly over some of the best pools and streams in the river, in order to eat my luncheon at my favourite waterfall. Here the Irthing comes tumbling over a perpendicular rock, sixteen feet high, into a deep basin; and then pursues its course down the narrow valley, dashing and foaming over rocks and shallows. The banks are steep and precipitous, and the oak, the ash, and the mystic rowan-tree,* of the north, grow there naturally. Here, then, old scenes and recollections will rise before me, and the friends and companions of my youth. Of these, some have filled an early grave

* There is a superstition in the north of England, that any person bearing a sprig of the rowan-tree (or mountain ash) is safe from the spells of bogles, fairies, and witches.

in the wilds of the Pyrenees; and others lie mouldering on the bloody field of Waterloo. The poor Portuguese girl, too, will appear to my mind's eye as I last saw her in her father's cottage. Dolores and her sorrows are, most likely, long since forgotten in her native village, whilst her English friend still thinks of her in a far distant land.

I have sat thus at sweet Croma Lynn, forgetful of sport and heedless of time, till roused from my reverie by my little rough terrier, Rock, shoving his cold black nose against my hand, and looking wistfully in my face to entice me to resume my walk. I am now an old soldier, and as much attached to my profession as ever, but yet, "*Flumina amem sylvasque inglorius.*"

JOURNEY TO HEAD-QUARTERS NEAR BURGOS.

In the year 1812, I joined at Lisbon, after a passage of some weeks from England, and got the accustomed leave of about a week to recruit and prepare myself to join the army, then before Burgos; during this period, I was quartered in the Convent of St. Vicente, which being one of the largest, and placed upon one of the highest, hills in Lisbon, my room being in the upper story, I had a most superb view of the city and surrounding country. There were not many friars in the convent, as part of it was given up for the accommodation of the troops. I once dined with them, and an excellent mess they had. Many of them were rich: they had a library and billiard-table; the latter more used than the former: most of them had a *chère amie* in the town.

It was generally customary for officers at Lisbon to make a party to go to head-quarters; accordingly, four of us arranged it so that we should meet at Sacaven, two leagues from Lisbon. A surgeon and myself who were quartered in the convent, were up by four o'clock, so that we might have our mules properly loaded, that no accident should happen, as servants and all were strangers to the country. I had only one animal for baggage, and a horse for riding, so that I was soon ready; the doctor had two, and he could not divide his baggage properly between them, for as soon as the second was nearly loaded, down came the load of the first. At last, after about two hours' hard work, he reported himself ready, and started, but had not got to the gate of the yard, when down came all his baggage: there was no alternative but to pack again; at last he made a second attempt: mine was so well loaded, that it got across the street, when down it came in the mud. These disasters occurred frequently, but our servants having all the trouble, they soon contrived to get it properly arranged, and we got on without more difficulties on that head.

On this day I got rid of *all my money;* rather unfortunate on the first day's march, with between two and three hundred miles before me; but when the sum is taken into consideration, it is not so wonderful, as I departed from Lisbon with no more than a half-testoon, ($7\frac{1}{2}d.$,) which I gave to a boy for holding my horse, and showing me the residence of the Juiz de Fora, or chief magistrate. Here a fresh difficulty arose. Not one of our party could make him understand what we wanted; a knowledge of the Portuguese language was a part of our education that had been neglected. I was the only one that could speak anything besides our mother tongue; I had Italian and French pretty fluently. I first tried Italian, the old Juiz only shook his head; by the by, he was a cobbler—French, just as bad—English, nothing but a shake of his head. Even the magic words, "G—d d—n," had no other effect than certain words had upon the tail of the Abbess of Andouillet's mule; he only shook his head. At last a Portuguese officer set us right, and we got what we wanted. The old fellow knew well enough, but was in hopes that we might go farther, but here he was disappointed. From this officer we got the names of a number of things and some Portuguese phrases, which I wrote down and committed to memory. In a short time I did very well, as I had little difficulty afterwards to make myself understood, and was improving every day.

In the course of the afternoon, the other officers of our party joined; we amused ourselves by relating the adventures of the day. One of them, a young ensign, had no other animal than a small donkey to carry everything. Going through a piece of bad road, poor donkey stuck fast, and could neither get one way nor the other; he had to unload him, and drag him out with ropes, by which means he was completely covered from head to foot with mud.

We of course passed through the famous lines so long occupied by our troops, and which caused so much grumbling among the *quid-nuncs* at home, because the army was lying there quietly without fighting; John Bull never being pleased unless they were moving, and thinking nothing of a battle without a long list of killed and wounded. But the long rest given to the army was, perhaps, one of the best things their great commander ever did, as they wanted for nothing, while the enemy wanted everything. After passing the lines, the country had the appearance of being what our soldiers called a good deal *rompé'd*.

Having rather a long day's march before us to Santarem, we determined over night to be off as early as possible in the morning, and agreed that whoever woke first was to alarm the others. I happened to be the watchful one, and observing it to be very light, roused the others. We were soon up, had the baggage loaded, and when just ready to start, the town clock struck *two;* however, we determined to proceed, as there was a fine moonlight; but had not gone above three or four miles, when we lost our moon, and found ourselves upon a large moor, at the crossing of four roads, and no sign-post. What was to be done? We were preparing to bivouack, when we espied a light at a distance; two of us set off immediately towards it, but in an instant again it was dark. In a little time, as we were quiet, it appeared again, and we succeeded in getting up to it, and discovered that it proceeded from a house, or rather hovel. On turning the corner, I found one end of a pitch-fork presented to my face; at the other end was an old man; my comrade was saluted in a similar manner by an old woman, with some other implement.

We came to a parley, but could get no other answer than "*Nao comprendo.*" I made a movement upon the old gentleman's flank, which I contrived to turn, and got between him and the door, but by doing so I left myself exposed to the attack of his right wing, or wife, who made a vigorous charge upon the posteriors of my horse, which he returned *instanter*, and laid the old lady sprawling, luckily without doing her any injury. My comrade having then nothing to do, came to my assistance, as the old gentleman had made a spirited attack upon me, having nearly dismounted me, by charging with the pitchfork against my side, and succeeded in fixing it in my coat; however, just as the old lady had recovered her legs, and was commencing another attack, our infantry, in the shape of a couple of servants, came up, and attacking the old man in the rear, which my manœuvre upon the centre had left exposed, they were obliged to surrender; we then had no difficulty in making him comprehend that he must show us the road to Santarem. With some trouble we prevailed upon him to accompany us, and show us the road; had we been going to hang him, he could not have made much more fuss. The old lady went with him. After he had put us on the road, we gave them a glass of rum each, and left them to return thanks to St. Antonio and the other saints they had been invoking for the last hour. They never quitted the pitchfork and hoe they had at first armed themselves with; though they were regularly made prisoners of war, the victors had the generosity to allow them to retain their arms.

It was late when we arrived at Santarem, considering the early hour we started, as the old couple, out of revenge for their defeat, had put us on the longest track; the road, besides, was very tedious, as it wound round a number of points, at each of which we expected to get a view of the town, but found that we had still another bay to go into. What made it, perhaps, appear longer than it otherwise might, was our early rising, and having had no breakfast, besides a very hot sun. Though this place had been Massena's head-quarters, it was, nevertheless, a good deal *rompé'd*. It was a hospital and commissariat station, where we drew rations. We went on to Abrantes, where we again drew rations, and halted a day to refresh our cattle, as they had got but bad feeding on the road, and not being very long from England, were not accustomed to the forage of the country. Here, as was generally the case in large towns, we had some difficulty in getting a billet, and that but a bad one; besides, being a hospital and commissariat station, there was a garrison of Portuguese troops.

We each got separate billets, but soon all got into one, the best—but bad was the best; neither table, chair, nor window-glass. These inconveniences we did not much mind, as a more serious one appeared in view—no fuel to cook our rations: a neighbouring stable supplied this want—we made an attack upon the manger, and soon set our pot boiling. By the time our soup and *bouilli* were ready, it was quite dark; an embassy was dispatched to the old woman for a light, which she absolutely refused, though she did not hesitate to boil her pot by our fire. I attempted to take the lamp from where it hung; she very deliberately commenced boxing my ears—I gave the lamp a kick and upset her oil. Shortly after, her husband came in, and began to swear and mutter something, not highly flattering to us or creditable to himself, but finding us a rather large party, servants and all, he soon got quiet. The next morning the old woman wanted to be paid for her oil and lamp, but that was quite out of the question, as we had only a few shillings amongst us, which we had other use for than to give it to uncivil people, though, literally speaking, they were not obliged to provide anything for us, not even a chair; yet, it was generally customary for them to give a light, and the use of their cooking utensils; when civil, they were seldom losers, as they generally got something—meat, spirits, bread, &c., though money was rather a scarce commodity.

The next town we came to was Gaviao, a place considerably *rompé'd;* but here we had an addition to our mess that was a treat, for all the time since we left Lisbon we had nothing but tough beef, and that not always of the best quality, and to us, who, like our horses, were not accustomed to the country fare, the addition of a fowl was a luxury. Where it came from I never knew; whether it had been killed by *accidentally* throwing stones at it, or whether it tumbled, without being aware, into our camp-kettle, was no business of mine to inquire. The doctor's servant acted as mess-man for our party, and drew our rations. Some of our party began to grow sickly, the light country wine not agreeing with them; we were afraid we should have been obliged to have left one officer behind, but he contrived to get through.

After leaving Abrantes, we lost all the fine country of Portugal, and got into bleak moors covered with gum cistus, a rank shrub, with a most unpleasant smell; it was almost suffocating to go a day's journey through it, especially in hot weather.

At Nisa, a nice little town, having much the appearance of an English one, and about the cleanest in Portugal, we again drew rations. There was a large colony of storks in the steeple of the church. The commandant asked us to dine with him: he had been wounded and left in charge of this station; he gave us an excellent dinner, which in those times was a good thing—indeed, when is it not?—but when a man is campaigning, it is pleasant were it only for the sake of variety.

Near Nisa is the celebrated pass of Villa Velha; no person that has ever gone through this is likely to forget it. The road winds down an immense hill, with rocks above and below it, which seem every moment ready to fall upon and crush the passenger; all at once you come upon the pass, taking a sharp turn to the right; then you are fairly in; it is almost impossible to get back—a horse may turn, but no kind of carriage can; the road is so rough and steep, that horses are in danger of falling at every step. About two hundred yards down is a sharp turn to the left, or rather to the left about, as it runs nearly parallel for some distance; then a sudden and steep turn to the right, so steep that it is difficult to keep upon it; at the foot of this it leads to a deep ford and to a narrow bridge; the ascent again is not so difficult. On the top of the hill is the miserable village from which the pass takes its name. Once when I was quartered there, I asked the Juiz de Fora whether the place he shewed me was for me or my horse; he replied, "*Por ambos dois*"—for both.

A few days' march from this is Sabugal, a place more *rompé'd* than any we had yet seen; it is on the Coa, a very rapid and deep river. A very severe action was fought here; in such case the town is sure to suffer. We were told here to billet ourselves where we could; the first house we knocked at was opened by a squalid-looking woman—we soon saw that she and her family were ill of a fever. In the next house we went to, there was a dead man; the third had neither door nor window, and but part of a roof; at last, we went back to one which, from its miserable appearance, we had passed; as we found neither dead nor sick, so we determined upon taking our quarters there. We got some dinner cooked and eat it outside, as we did not much admire the interior, and would not have gone in it at all but that we thought the night rather cold for a bivouac, though a few nights after we were obliged to do it in worse weather. At bedtime we went in.

In one end slept our landlord and family, some six or seven children; next to them came our party of officers; the servants next to them again, not forgetting a cat and a pig that shared beds with all at times: immediately under were our horses and mules. We did not sleep much, as may be supposed; so after breakfasting upon goat's milk and boiled chesnuts, which our landlord gave us, we departed, leaving him in return some beef, a bone of ham, and the remains of our soup, for which he was very thankful.

Sabugal is situated near the frontiers of Spain and Portugal, which are divided here by a small stream. The first town of consequence in Spain is Ciudad Rodrigo; here we began to find symptoms of the neighbourhood of the army, having met but one officer and his servant on the way to Lisbon; he had been some days on the way, and could give us but little intelligence, farther than that we were losing a great many men before Burgos.

At Ciudad Rodrigo there was a great deal of bustle; a great many sick and wounded soldiers, their bandages and clothes still bloody—everything seemed in motion. A Spanish regiment was mounting guard, officers and orderly dragoons arriving and departing in all directions; everybody seemed to have something to do and was in a hurry. At last we met Lieutenant Robe of the horse artillery, who told us that the siege of Burgos was raised, and that the army was retreat ing as fast as it could; also, that his father, Colonel Robe, was badly wounded, and on his way to Lisbon for England.

We waited on the colonel, who had been hit near the knee by a grape shot, of which he never recovered, but lingered, suffering great pain for some years. His son was killed at Waterloo, after behaving most gallantly. He was a most promising officer.

We stopped that night at Ciudad Rodrigo, and went on next morning, but everything was in confusion. We could get no quarters, or anything to eat; the roads were strewed with sick and wounded. Not being attached, we were, in a measure, our own masters; so halted to rest, as we found it of no use to go any further, and saw the army pass us. Such a set of scarecrows were never seen. It was difficult to say what they were, as the men's coats were patched with grey; some had blankets over them, and most of them were barefoot; every step they took was up to the knees in mud; women and sick men were actually sticking in it; if a horse, mule, or donkey stumbled, there the poor starved (I was going to say *half* starved) creature fell, stuck fast, and the baggage had to be abandoned.

A brigade of artillery that had just come out from England was, with cavalry and light troops, covering the rear. This brigade had left Lisbon but a short time before, and was in high order. The clothing of the men scarce soiled, and the horses sleek and fat, made a strange contrast with the others, especially the company of artillery that had served in the batteries before Burgos. We at first took the latter for prisoners, as they were mostly in French clothing, many of them riding on the carriages, sick and wounded, drawn some by oxen and some by mules and horses. I never saw British soldiers in such a state.

One afternoon after the march, a very brisk firing was heard towards the right; everybody thought it was an attack, and stood to their arms. An attack it certainly was, not by the enemy, but by our men upon some hogs which were feeding in a wood. Upon them our hungry soldiers made a most vigorous attack; and many a porker had to rue the shooting of that day. Some general officers coming to see the cause of the firing, made a great fuss, and put a stop to the sport, though they laughed in their sleeves at the time, as I have been credibly informed that some of the staff *actually had a fresh pork griskin for supper, and voted it excellent.* The French were also much surprised at the firing, as they could not imagine what it was at, and were kept on the alert all night, but had no pork for supper.

Our Lisbon party here broke up. I having got through my provisions, and being without quarters, not being yet attached, thought it best to go where I could get something to eat, so returned to Ciudad Rodrigo. To do this I had to pass over most shocking roads. They were in a much worse state than when I had passed over them a few days before, and the number of dead men and animals that now lay by the road-side was shocking. I heard my name called from the ditch, and looking round I saw an officer lying on the road-side, who had been a cadet with me a few years before at Marlow. Some ammunition carriages going by at the time, I got him placed upon one of them. He died that evening, and I buried him soon after, digging the grave myself, with the assistance of one man only. The ceremony was not long, nor the mourners many. I cannot now recollect his name.

It had been raining all this time, and I had nothing to eat except the nuts I gathered by the road-side, which I shared with my horse, as he was nearly as badly off as myself, the grass and everything that he could have eaten having been destroyed by the numbers who had gone before. We came to a place which, a few days before, had been a small commissariat station, where I fully expected something, but the commissaries were off, and had burnt some biscuit. Some soldiers scrambling for what they could get, I joined them, and succeeded in getting out half a biscuit only a little burnt, which was the only regular food I had tasted for two days. That afternoon my servant found me out. We had separated in the bustle. He told me he had got a ration of beef and bread for us both, which we ate with great gusto, though we hardly waited to warm it.

I soon arrived at Ciudad Rodrigo, where I drew proper rations, though given very stingily, and went on towards Almeida. On my way, I passed a division of the sick from Salamanca hospital. Many of them were in carts drawn by oxen, jolting over rough roads, the poor fellows in them screaming at every jolt. Such as were able were obliged to walk, some with their heads bandaged up, others with their arms in slings, many fainting by the way, exhausted and lying down to die.

I remember two Portuguese soldiers sitting leaning against the same tree. One of them looked so miserably at me that I got off my horse to give him some rum out of my canteen. He muttered something and pointed to the other man, who, I supposed, was his brother from what I could understand. He was already dead in a sitting posture. I returned to the first, but before I could offer my canteen he fell down by the tree dead.

Soon after, I mounted and rode on, when I saw before me a British soldier kicking with all his might at a Portuguese carter, who was thrashing at him with his long ox goad. I moved up to see the cause of this combat, which I found originated in the cruelty of the driver, who would not replace a sick soldier properly in his cart. The poor fellow had slipped out behind, and his legs were dragging on the road. The driver, afraid of being late, would not stop to put him in properly; the soldier could not, having been wounded in both arms. I made the Portuguese place the man properly in the cart, and then belaboured him soundly with a good stout oak sapling till I was tired, and more comfortably warmed than I had been for days before.

This achievement performed, I rode on to Gallegos. I got a good billet, and thought to be pretty comfortable, especially as I saw a couple of good beds in the room. I was just settling which I should appropriate to myself, or whether, to make up for lost naps, I should not take both, not having had my clothes off for four nights; but here I was disappointed, as a soldier came in and said that he could not get quarters anywhere for his master and another wounded officer, whom I had passed on the road in a cart. I told him to bring them in, and I would provide for them. I found that I was acquainted with them both, being likewise old cadets. It was curious that in less than three days I had assisted as many old cadets, they being sick and wounded. I determined on giving up my *beds,* as I thought I might be in the same situation myself, which was the case afterwards, when one of these officers gave me some assistance, though my case was not a very bad one. After regaling on some fried ham and eggs, I again mounted my horse for Almeida, desiring my servant to follow, taking a blanket under my saddle in order to secure a bed. When I arrived I found some officers just sitting down to dinner, which I joined and did ample justice to in spite of the ham and eggs; but as I had been several days without that essential meal, I thought it no harm to take two in one. At bedtime I called for my blanket, but it was gone. I never saw it more. A servant lent me his great-coat, I put on my own, and slept upon a tarpaulin.

It was above a week before I got a blanket; some came for the men; there were two over, which I got. I also got some straw, and with a pair of sheets had a most luxurious bed. It was the first night for a fortnight that I had taken off my clothes; generally, instead, pulling on my great-coat, not always dry. Talk to me of down beds! I never knew luxury before.

SEVEN WEEKS' CAPTIVITY IN ST. SEBASTIAN, IN 1813.*

THE following narrative of scenes which passed in the interior of St. Sebastian,† after the failure of the first assault, in July, 1813, and until the surrender of the castle in the following September,

* By Lieutenant-Colonel Harvey Jones, R.E.

† The town of St. Sebastian, containing nearly ten thousand inhabitants, is built on a low peninsula, running north and south; the defences of the western side being washed by the sea, and those on the eastern side by the river Urumea, which at high water covers four feet of the masonry of the scarp. The works of the land front, across the Isthmus, consist of a single front of fortification, exceeding 350 yards in length, with a flat bastion in the centre, covered by a hornwork, having the usual counterscarp, covered-way, and glacis; but the defences running lengthways of the Peninsula, consist merely of a simple rampart, indifferently flanked, without either ditch, counterscarp, glacis, or other obstacle in its front; and further, this naked scarp wall, on the eastern side, is seen from its summit to its base, from the Chofre range of sand hills on the right of the Urumea, at distances from five hundred to a thousand yards."—JONES'S JOURNAL OF THE SIEGES.

is drawn up from notes inserted in my journal immediately after the capture of the place. In describing scenes which I witnessed, or relating the substance of conversations or anecdotes, I shall nothing "extenuate nor aught set down in malice." The regular order of events as they occurred, has not been adhered to, it being considered unimportant, so long as the facts were faithfully reported. The narrative commences at the place to which the gallant and eloquent historian of the Peninsula war conducted his readers,—that is, to the breach, where he left me disabled by wounds, on the morning of the 25th July, 1813.

After witnessing the unsuccessful efforts of Lieutenant Campbell, 9th regiment, and his gallant little band, to force their way on to the ramparts, and their retreat from the breach, my attention, a short time afterwards, was aroused by an exclamation, from the soldier lying next to me,—" Oh, they are murdering us all!" Upon looking up, I perceived a number of French grenadiers, under a heavy fire of grape, sword in hand, stepping over the dead, and stabbing the wounded; my companion was treated in the same manner: the sword withdrawn from his body, and reeking with his blood, was raised to give me the *coup de grace*, when fortunately the uplifted arm was arrested by a smart little man, a serjeant, who cried out, " Oh, mon Colonel, êtes-vous blessé!"* and immediately

* The serjeant must have mistaken my rank, from seeing a large gold bullion epaulette on my right shoulder, and the blue uniform rendering it more conspicuous.

ordered some of his men to remove me into the town. They raised me in their arms, and carried me, without the slightest difficulty, up the breach on to the ramparts of the right flanking tower: here we were stopped by a captain of the grenadiers, who asked some questions, then kissed me, and desired the party to proceed to the hospital. On passing the embrasures of the high curtain, we were exposed to a very sharp musketry fire from the trenches; and here it was that we met the governor and his staff in full-dress uniforms, hurrying to the breach. He asked if I was badly wounded, and directed that proper care should be taken of me.

After descending from the curtain into the town, and proceeding along the street leading to the hospital, we were accosted by an officer, who had evidently taken his *goutte :* he demanded my sword, which was still hanging by my side. I told him he had the power to take it, but that he had no right to do so, as I had not been made a prisoner by him; and, moreover he had not been at the breach. This appeared to enrage him, and with great violence of manner and gesture, he unbuckled the belt and carried away my sword.* Upon reaching the

* During the battle of Vittoria, having accompanied one of the battalions which carried the village of Gamarra Major by storm, we soon found ourselves in the midst of the French, when, by not sabring a soldier that crossed my path, but merely striking him with the flat of my sword, I had a narrow escape of my life, as he ran and dashed across the river, then turned round and deliberately fired at me; I escaped

hospital, the chirurgien-major was very kind in his manner; after enlarging my wounds according to the French system, and then dressing them, I was carried across the street, and put into a bed in one of the wards of the great hospital, which a soldier was ordered to vacate for my use; this man returned in the course of the morning for his pipe and tobacco, which he had left under the pillow. Soon after I was placed in bed, two officers of the Royals, Lieutenants Alston and Eyre, were brought in, both severely wounded. In the course of the morning we were visited by the governor, who made inquiries as to our wounds, and whether we had been plundered of anything. I then learned that a great number of English soldiers, not wounded, had been taken, and were lodged in the town prison. The two officers above named, and myself, were committed to the charge of Monsieur Joliffe, a civilian, attendant upon the hospitals, and his wife; from both individuals we received every attention that the situation we were placed in permitted them to show us. They were both killed during the second siege, at least I must conclude

with merely a graze on the elbow. I then determined, (not taking delight in cutting men down,) not to draw my sword except for self-defence) when going into action again; and it was acting upon this determination that my sword remained in the scabbard. On passing through the trenches, advancing to the assault of the breach, I armed myself with a fascine picket, and it was fortunate I did so; before I was knocked down, a splinter of a shell struck the steel scabbard, and cracked it, but the blade of the sword saved my leg.

so, as I could not learn anything about them after our removal into the castle.

On the morning of the 27th, Lieutenant M'Gill, 38th regiment, was brought into the ward severely wounded, having been taken prisoner in the trenches, during the sortie of the night. The soldiers and officers who were captured, and not wounded, were lodged in the town-jail along with the prisoners taken at the assault of the 25th. The only persons permitted to visit us were some staff officers, occasionally some of the engineers, a few Spanish ladies, and a Spanish barber; from the former I was made acquainted generally with everything passing in the British lines, at least as far as conjecture on the part of the French enabled them to communicate; there is every reason for supposing they did so in the expectation of ascertaining what might be the actual state of affairs in the British lines. Notwithstanding boats arrived nightly from Bayonne, bringing shells, medicine, charpie, (a substitute for lint,) artillerymen, and engineers, and returning with some of the wounded, the garrison remained in great ignorance of the movements of the two armies, Soult invariably sending word that he would soon raise the siege. Thus, by promises of immediate relief, keeping up the spirits of the garrison, and rewarding the gallantry displayed by particular individuals during the assault, and in the sorties, by promotion, or by sending them the decoration of the Legion of Honour.

In the French army, there appeared to have

been a system of reward for good and gallant conduct by removal into the grenadiers, or voltigeurs, which had an excellent effect. A French soldier was extremely proud of his green, yellow, or red epaulettes: they were badges of distinguished conduct, and none but those who had shewn great gallantry in action were admitted into their ranks. The non-commissioned officers were generally selected from these companies, and then came the highest honour a Frenchman knew or coveted, which was, the Cross of the Legion of Honour, and it was liberally bestowed. What with the success attendant upon the sorties, and the numerous decorations which had been distributed amongst the officers and private soldiers, such a spirit of daring and enthusiasm was created, that I believe before the batteries opened the second time, the garrison, individually or collectively, would not have hesitated attempting any enterprise, however difficult or dangerous. The idea of a surrender never was entertained by them at any period previously to the capture of the town.

After the stones had been extracted, which had been blown into my legs and thighs, by the bursting of shells and grenades, I was enabled to move about, and get into the gallery running round the court-yard of the hospital, which was in a house of considerable size, built in the usual Spanish style, having a court-yard in the centre, with a large entrance-door from the street, galleries from each story running round it, and into which all the doors and windows of the rooms respectively opened, excepting on the side of the street. The gallery of the floor on which our ward was situated, was the only place where we were allowed to breathe the fresh air; and had it not been for the great height of the castle above the town, which enabled us to see the donjon and some of the batteries, our view would have been bounded by the sky, and the four interior walls of the hospital. One day, whilst sitting in the gallery, I observed a table placed in the one below me, and on the opposite side of the court-yard; immediately afterwards, an unfortunate French gunner was laid upon it, and both his arms amputated, his hands having been blown off by an accident in one of the batteries. In the course of the morning, whilst conversing with the surgeon who had performed the operation, he told me that he had acted contrary to his instructions, which were, never to amputate, but to cure if possible. And upon asking the reason for such an inhuman order having been issued, his reply was, the Emperor did not wish that numbers of mutilated men should be sent back to France, as it would make a bad impression upon the people. I replied, "You must be a bold man to act in opposition to this order." He said, "Affairs are beginning to change, and, moreover, circumstances make it necessary that *the soldiers* should know they will be taken proper care of in the event of being wounded, and not left to die like dogs; we send as many as we can at night to Bayonne by the boats—thus we clear out the hospital, and are relieved from a great deal of labour."

In conversations with many of the officers, they detailed acts committed by their soldiers in Spain, so revolting to human nature, that I dare not commit them to paper; the reader would be disgusted with the recital, and my veracity impeached; and equally incredulous should I have been, had not the narrators declared they had witnessed the scenes which they had described.

A chef de battalion once asked me how we managed with our soldiers when we wanted them to advance and attack an enemy. My reply was, "Forward!" "Ah! that way will not do with us; we are obliged to excite our men with spirits, or to work upon their feelings by some animating address: and very often, when I fancied I had wrought them up to the fighting pitch, some old hand would make a remark which in an instant upset all I had effected, and, consequently, I was compelled to recommence."

In discoursing about the expeditions that detachments of their troops frequently made from the great stations, for a period of eighteen or twenty days, I inquired how they managed to provision them for so long a time. The answer was, " Our biscuits are made with a hole in the centre, and each biscuit is the ration for a day; sometimes twenty are delivered to each individual, who is given to understand that he has no claims upon the commissariat for the number of days corresponding with the number of biscuits he receives." I observed it was not possible for the soldier to carry them. "We know that very well; but then he has no claim upon the government for that period, and we do not inquire how he lives in the interim!"

It appeared that there was a very great difference in the accuracy of firing by the troops in the trenches. The chief of the staff, Monsieur Songeon, inquired what description of troops we had that fired so well. "He said, "Some days I can look over the parapets without the slightest molestation; on other days it is not possible to shew my nose, without the certainty of being shot."

Donna M—— and her mother were very kind, and used frequently to pay us visits. The daughter was a remarkably fine and handsome young woman. Unfortunately, one day, when they were sitting with us, the governor arrived. He laughed and joked with Donna M——; but when he left the hospital he gave an order to the corporal of the guard not to admit any more Spaniards. It was understood that a few days afterwards the governor sent to say that he wished to see Donna M——, but she declined the invitation. Upon my release I made anxious inquiries for my fair friend, and ascertained that she was living with an English officer. It appeared that during the sack of the town, in order to save herself from the violence of the soldiers, who had forced their way into her house, she had thrown herself for protection into the arms of a British officer, who was passing at the moment, and heard her cries. She continued to live with him until the end of the war. Her protector was a captain in one of the regiments forming part of the division to which I was attached, and, consequently, Donna M—— was often fated to see me pass her on the line of march. Her downcast looks spoke plainly of painful recollections, and she never would recognise me.

From my first entrance into the hospital I had been attended by a Spanish barber, in whose house a French officer was billeted. As I could speak Spanish fluently, we had a great deal of conversation. He used to communicate to me all he heard and saw of what was passing both inside and outside the fortress. When he learnt that I was an engineer, he offered to bring me a plan of all the under-ground drains, and aqueduct for bringing water into the town. Monsieur Joliffe, our attendant, although a good-natured man, kept a sharp eye on the barber, and in consequence it was difficult for him to give me anything without being detected. At last, one morning, when preparing for the operation of shaving me, he succeeded in shoving a plan under the bed-clothes. I anxiously seized the earliest opportunity of examining it; and, from the knowledge I had previously acquired of the place, soon became acquainted with the directions of the drains, &c. From that moment my whole attention was fixed on the means of making my escape. I knew that the hospital was situated in the principal street, the ends of which terminated upon the fortifications bounding the harbour or sea; if once I could gain the street, I had only to turn to the right or left to gain the ramparts, and to make my escape from the town in the best manner I could.

One evening, just at dusk, when the medical men took leave of us for the night, one of them left his cocked-hat on my bed. As soon as I made the discovery I put it on my head, hurried down stairs, and made direct for the great door. I found it so completely blocked up by the guard, that, unless by pushing them aside, it was not possible to pass without being discovered; I therefore retreated up stairs in despair, and threw the hat down on the bed. Scarcely had I done so when in rushed the doctor, inquiring for his *chapeau*.

We were more than once visited by the crews of the boats which arrived nightly from France; the sight of us appeared to afford them great gratification, but there was nothing in their manner or demeanour which could in any way offend us. Of course the object in bringing them to see the prisoners was that they might mention the circumstance when they returned to Bayonne. Very unexpectedly, one evening, about nine o'clock, the governor's aid-de-camp appeared at the prison, and told the officers to prepare immediately to go to France. A Portuguese captain, one of the party, was dreadfully in fear of being sent there, and, with great warmth of manner, told the aid-de-camp that Lord Wellington would soon be in possession of the place, and that if the prisoners were not forthcoming he would make the governor answerable in his own person. It is supposed that the aid-de-camp went and reported this conversation to the governor, as he did not return for some time, and then told them that it was too late to embark that night, as the boats had sailed. They were never afterwards threatened to be sent away. Being very anxious to know how these boats escaped the vigilance of our cruisers, I was told that at dusk they started from Bayonne, sailed all night direct into the Bay of Biscay, at day-break hauled up, and ran parallel to the Spanish coast, and at nightfall stood in for St. Sebastian, thus avoiding our vessels, which stood off and on the coast between the town and Passages. These nightly communications were of essential service to the defence, keeping alive the spirits of the garrison, and bringing supplies. A colonel of engineers arrived a few days previously to the first assault, to replace one who had been wounded and sent to France. A considerable quantity of shells and stores were brought by them; and also medicines and articles required in the hospitals, particularly bandages and charpie.

About the middle of August, the garrison began to flatter themselves that the siege was turned into a regular blockade, and that they would be relieved by the successes of Marshal Soult: their spirits were high, and their hopes elated. The 15th of August, the birth-day of Napoleon, was observed as a day of rejoicing among the garrison, and at nightfall the letter N, of a very large size, was brilliantly lighted up on the face of the donjon. When the operations of the second siege commenced, a captain, who was an almost daily visitor, kept me *au fait* of all that was going on. I learned from him the nature of the intrenchments made in the rear of the breach, and likewise that a great quantity of *combustible materials* had been placed in the houses around and adjoining it. To this cause I have ever attributed the destruction of the town by fire, and not to wanton mischief on the part of the assailants. It would obviously be the interest of the garrison to destroy the cover the houses would afford an enemy in making his approaches against the castle. The impression upon my mind was, and always has been, that the town was burned by the combustion of the materials previously arranged for that purpose. When the successive accounts of the progress of the fire in the town was communicated to the inmates of the hospital, a savage and exulting laugh would be heard from the officers who happened at the moment to be present, visiting their wounded comrades. Nothing could exceed their apparent delight when a Spanish captain, an *Afrancesado*, who had retired into the castle with the garrison, came into the hospital, in the evening of the assault, wringing his hands, tearing his hair, and declaring he had heard the shrieks of his wife and daughters, and saw his house in flames. Both were subjects for great merriment to the French; and the poor Spaniard must have bitterly regretted the day when he sided with them. The French officers did not fail to taunt him with having done so, and ridiculed his frantic actions. One morning early we were disturbed by a party of men, bringing in an officer of the Brunswickers dreadfully wounded by a grape-shot. He had been taken in a sortie made during the night, with several soldiers, who were swept into the town from the trenches. In the course of the day I was asked whether I would like to speak to a corporal of sappers, who had been made prisoner during the sortie. I was delighted at the prospect of seeing one of my old friends, but was greatly astonished, in the afternoon, by seeing a fine tall young man, a stranger, walking into the ward, dressed in a red jacket. He was the first sapper I had seen in the new uniform, as blue was the colour worn when I was taken prisoner. Upon inquiring when he had joined the army from England, he replied, " Yesterday morning; I was put on duty in the trenches last night, and was shortly after brought into the town by the enemy!"

From the daily accounts we received of the extent and position of the different works carrying on in the trenches, it was evident that the same nature of attack would be observed as at the first siege. Knowing well the length and difficulty of the approach to the breach, and how strongly it had been intrenched within, I was fearful for the result, and the hopes of being released vanished. One morning, a captain of artillery, whom I had never before seen, came into the ward, and commenced conversing about the siege, addressing himself particularly to me; he observed that the whole second parallel was one entire battery; and if there were as many guns as there were embrasures, he said, we shall be "joliment f——." My reply was, "Most assuredly you will; depend upon it there are as many guns as embrasures; it is not our fashion to make batteries, and stick logs of wood into the embrasures, in the hopes of frightening an enemy." He made a grimace, and, with a shrug of his shoulders, walked out of the ward. The following morning the surgeon came, as usual, to dress our wounds; this was about half-past seven; all was still, and he joyously exclaimed, as he entered, "So we have another day's reprieve!" In about half an hour afterwards, and whilst I was under his hands, the first salvo from the breaching batteries was fired; several shot rattled through the hospital, and disturbed the tranquillity of the inmates; the instrument dropped from the surgeon's hands, and he exclaimed, "Le jeu sera bientôt fini!" and then very composedly went on with his work.

The opening of the batteries made a great stir amongst all hands. We soon got an intimation to prepare to be removed into the castle: a private hint was given to me to be "sage" on the way up, as the captain of the escort was "très méchant," and that we must be quiet and orderly. This I suppose was intended to deter any of us from making attempts to escape. The wounded prisoners, as well as those not so, were moved in one body up the face of the hill to the entrance of the castle. Under the Mirador Battery they were exposed to a sharp musketry fire; some of the party were wounded, and amongst them the Portuguese captain severely in the thigh. Before passing through the gateway, I turned round to take a view of the batteries and trenches, but was soon faced to the right about by the captain of the escort, and conducted into the building on the sea-side, which had been constructed for a powder-magazine, but was now converted into an hospital: the interior was fitted up with wooden bedsteads similar to those in English guard-rooms ; here the wounded were lodged ; and in the area surrounding the building were placed those prisoners, 150 in number, who were not. As the number of wounded increased, the hospital filled rapidly, and in the hopes of preventing the fire from the batteries being directed against it, some of the prisoners were desired to hoist a black flag on the roof of the building. While they were doing so, I told the French officer it was labour in vain, as it would not have the effect desired, but in all probability the contrary, as we had always considered, and been given to understand, that the building was their great depôt for powder, and consequently hoisting a flag would be regarded as a ruse to preserve their ammunition, and not to protect the wounded. And little benefit did we receive from the ensign flying over our ill-fated heads. After the capture of the island Santa Clara, it was almost impossible for any person to move about that part of the castle opposite to it without the risk of being killed or wounded : the discharges of grape and shrapnells from it swept the whole of the interior, and it was only at night, and then with great risk, that fresh water could be obtained from the tank, which was situated on that side.

The garrison always entertained the idea that the assault would take place during the night; therefore each succeeding morning, when light dawned upon them without having been aroused from their slumbers by the shouts of the assaulting columns, they felt as if they had obtained a reprieve for another twenty-four hours. On the 31st of August, when the first rattle of musketry was heard in the castle, an inquiring look pervaded each countenance; but all were silent. As the firing continued, and the rattle of it increased, little doubt remained as to the cause; every soldier seized his musket and hurried with alacrity to his post. I was then debarred from speaking or holding converse with the unwounded prisoners outside. One day, after the breaching batteries had opened their fire, I was asked by a French officer whether I thought that the prisoners would remain quiet when an assault of the breach should take place; and he added, if they were to make any attempts, they would all be shot. I replied, " You may depend upon it that, if an opportunity offers, they will not be backward in taking advantage of it: do not fancy you have a flock of sheep penned within these walls; and happen what may, shoot us or not, you will be required to give a satisfactory account of us when the castle is taken." On the 31st of August, during the assault of the breach, the appearance of boats with troops pulling for the sea front of the castle, created considerable alarm, and had the attempt to land been made, I have little doubt but it would have succeeded: the effect would have been great; the capture of the castle, in all probability, the result; and the troops in the town, upon learning that their retreat was cut off, would have surrendered at discretion.

From the commencement of the assault, until the rush into the castle upon the capture of the town, not the slightest information could we obtain as to the state of affairs at the breach. The period that intervened was one of the most anxious and painful suspense: at last the tale was told, and who can describe the spectacle the interior of the hospital presented? In an instant the ward was crowded with the wounded and maimed; the amputation-table again brought into play; and until nearly daylight the following morning, the surgeons were unceasingly at work. To have such a scene passing at the foot of my bed, was sufficiently painful; added to this, the agonizing shrieks and groans, and the appearance of the grenadiers and sappers, who had been blown up by the explosion on the breach—their uniforms nearly burnt off, and their skins blackened and scorched by gunpowder—was truly appalling, the recollection of which can never be effaced from the memories of those whose ill fate compelled them to witness it. The appearance of these men resembled anything but human beings: death soon put an end to their sufferings, and relieved us from these most distressing sights. Of all wounds, whether of fractured limbs or otherwise, those occasioned by burns from gunpowder appeared to be accompanied with the most excruciating pain and constant suffering.

In the rear of the donjon there was a small building, in which was deposited a considerable quantity of gunpowder. Shells were falling fast and thick around it; and there being every appearance that it must soon be destroyed, a detachment of soldiers was sent to withdraw the ammunition. This dangerous service they were performing in a most gallant manner, and had nearly completed their work, when some shells fell into the building, exploded the few barrels that remained, and blew the building with some of the soldiers into the air, not leaving a vestige to show that such an edifice had ever been erected.

There were three French ladies in the garrison— the widow and two daughters of a French commissary-general who had died in Spain: they were on their way to France when the investment took place. These ladies were permitted to enter the hospital, and were allowed a small space at one end of the wooden bedstead; here they remained for several days and nights; the only water they could obtain to wash since the island of Santa Clara had been in the possession of the besiegers, was the same that we had, sea-water, which the attendants contrived to procure by descending the rocks at the back of the castle. The small quantity of fresh water obtained from the tank during the night was reserved for cookery or drinking, which was greatly needed by the troops during the fatigue and heat to which they were exposed at this very hot season of the year (August). As the number of the wounded increased, so the accommodation in the hospital became more restricted. Some of the officers who were lying upon the floor were loud in their complaints that Madame and her daughters were occupying the space which properly belonged to them : they succeeded in getting the ladies turned out, to find shelter from shot and shell where best they could! The day the castle capitulated, I went in search of my fair companions, and found them nearly smoke-dried under a small projecting rock. One of the young ladies was extremely pretty, and shortly after the siege was married to the English commissary appointed to attend upon the garrison until embarked for England. The change from the hospital to the naked rock relieved them from witnessing many a painful scene, as the amputating-table was placed at the foot of the bedstead in that part of the room allotted to us.

After the capture of the town, a heavy bombardment of the castle took place, by salvos of shells from upwards of sixty pieces of artillery : the short interval of time which elapsed between the report of the discharge of the guns and mortars, and the noise of the descent of the shells, was that of a few seconds only. The effect of these salvos by day, terrific and destructive as they proved, was little heeded in comparison with the nightly discharges.

Those of the wounded and mutilated who were fortunate enough to have found temporary relief from their sufferings by sleep, were awakened to all the horrors and misery of their situation by the crash of ten or a dozen shells falling upon and around the building, and whose fuzes threw a lurid light into the interior of the ward: the silence within, unbroken save by the hissing of the burning composition; the agonizing feelings of the wounded during these few moments of suspense are not to be described. No one could feel assured of escaping the destruction which was a certain attendant upon the explosion, to be immediately succeeded by the cries and groans of those who were again wounded.

Many an unfortunate soldier was brought to the amputation-table to undergo a second operation; and in the discharge of this painful duty the medical men were engaged nearly the entire night. As to rest, none could be obtained or expected with such scenes passing around a person's bed. The legs and arms, as soon as amputated, were carried out, and thrown away on the rocks. It was a novel and by no means an agreeable sight, but one which I was daily compelled to witness.

It is but justice to the French medical officers to state, that their conduct during the whole period of their harassing and laborious duties was marked by the greatest feeling and kindness of manner, as well as attention to the relief of the unfortunate sufferers who came under their hands. Scarcely had the ward been restored to tranquillity, when another salvo would be heard, and the repetition of the same scenes would take place.

The unfortunate prisoners who were not wounded had been placed in the area around the hospital, and consequently were exposed to the fury of each successive discharge, without the slightest cover or protection from its destructive effects. Knowing their exposed situation, I exerted myself in every possible way to obtain a few pickaxes and shovels to enable them to throw up some sort of traverse or splinter-proof. All my applications were unheeded; and, in consequence, fifty were killed or wounded out of a hundred and fifty who were confined within the enclosure walls.

With the single exception of an act of brutality on the part of a French officer to myself, the wounded prisoners had no cause for complaint, though their confinement might have been less rigorous. From the surgeon who attended us, and the hospital attendants, we experienced great kindness. Our diet was regulated in the same manner, and of the same quality and proportions, as that of the French wounded soldiers in the adjoining ward. The greatest luxury allowed was occasionally three stewed prunes.

The only officer of French engineers who escaped being killed or wounded was Lieutenant Goblet,* who commanded the company of sappers at the great breach, the post of honour which they claim. The greater number of this company were

* Minister of war in Belgium, after the separation of that country from Holland, in 1830.

destroyed by the explosion during the assault. This officer was the only individual of the garrison Lord Wellington permitted to return to France. He carried despatches from General Rey, the governor, to Marshal Soult, to make known to him the surrender of the castle.

The effects of the vertical fire in the interior of the castle immediately after the capture of the town were so destructive and annoying, that, had it been continued six hours longer, the garrison, I have no doubt, would have surrendered at discretion. The officers were loud in their complaints at the obstinacy of the governor, as they said, in uselessly sacrificing the lives of the soldiers. They had lost all hope, or nearly so, that Soult could make any successful attempt for their relief. During this period everybody sought shelter where best he could among the rocks; still no nook or corner appeared to be a protection from the shrapnel shells. A serjeant of the royals, standing at the foot of my bedstead, was killed by a ball from a shrapnel shell, and fell dead upon me. An Italian soldier, who had been appointed to attend upon the wounded prisoners, whilst endeavouring, close to the hospital door, to prepare some *bouillon* for our dinner, was, with his *marmite*, blown into the air: and so ended, for the day, all our hopes of obtaining a little nourishment. Life and bustle had disappeared: scarcely an individual was to be seen moving about.

This state of affairs continued until the batteries in the trenches slackened their fire. Nothing was done: everybody sought shelter from the tremendous fire of shells which was poured into the castle, and to escape from the terrific effects and havoc caused by their explosion. The whole interior was ploughed up; and, had this stream of fire been continued a few hours longer, the garrison would have obliged the governor to surrender.

The shriek of the bullets from the shrapnel shell is very different from the whistle of a musket-ball; and oft repeated were the exclamations, "Ah! ces sacrés bullets creux!"

It may not be unworthy of remark, that the bullets discharged from a shrapnel shell assume the form of a polygonal prism. A French officer showed me one that had just been extracted from a wounded man: he anxiously inquired whether they were of that form when put into the shell. I afterwards observed the same in many others, which, at my request, were handed to me by the operating surgeons.

The excellence of the British artillery is well known. Nothing could surpass the precision with which the shells were thrown, and the accuracy with which the fuzes were cut. It is only those who have had the opportunity of witnessing their fire, and comparing it with that of the French, that can speak of its superiority. During the siege, we little heeded the lazy French shells thrown into the batteries or trenches. From the length of the fuzes, sufficient time was almost always allowed, before bursting, to put ourselves under cover; and, when they did burst, the splinters flew lazily around. On the contrary, when the sound of an English shell was heard in the castle, or when the man stationed in the donjon cried, " Garde la bombe," everybody was on the alert. The velocity of its flight far exceeded that of the French. Touching the ground and bursting were almost simultaneous; and then the havoc and destruction caused by the splinters were tremendous.

None but those who have been exposed to the effects of shrapnel shells can fully appreciate the advantages of possessing such a terrific and destructive missile. It appeared to be of little avail where a man placed himself for protection. No place was secure from them; and many a soldier was wounded without having been aware that any shell had exploded in his neighbourhood.

A French officer of Engineers, who was very badly wounded, and lying on the opposite side of the ward, was well supplied with the best professional books. He kindly allowed me the use of them. Many were works which I had never been able to procure; and much pleasure and instruction did I derive from the perusal of them. Upon inquiry, I was given to understand, that the French engineers were always supplied with them by the *government, and their* generals with the best maps of the country where they were employed.

One day, before the great battery in the hornwork opened its fire against the castle, I was called to the door of the ward by a French officer, who exclaimed, " Voilà les fiacres qui viennent nous chercher." I was puzzled to know what he meant; when, upon looking out in the direction he pointed with his hand, I beheld a most cheering and beautiful sight, in the appearance of a large convoy of transports under full sail. The officer was a true prophet, for those vessels conveyed the garrison from Passages to England.

When it was communicated to me that we were no longer prisoners, I looked around for the best sword in the ward, to replace the one taken from me. Having discovered a handsome sabre belonging to a wounded staff-officer, I sent and desired that it might be taken down from the place where it was hanging, as I wanted such a weapon. I have it still by me. It was the only sword I wore until the end of the war; and often, when at the outposts with a flag of truce, have I seen the French officers regard the eagles on the belt with anything but a gratifying look.

In July, 1813, who could foresee that, in two years from that time, such a change would take place in my position as afterwards was the case. In 1815, I was quartered in Paris, and was engineer in charge of the fortification on Mont Martre. During that period I frequently saw several of the officers who had formed part of the garrison in St. Sebastian; and from my old friend, the chirurgien-major, I received frequent visits. We both agreed, that, notwithstanding the tables were turned, our present position was more agreeable than when our acquaintance commenced in St. Sebastian.

ARROYO DE MOLINO.*

WHETHER we consider the foresight, skill, and perseverance displayed in the affair at Arroyo de Molino, or reflect upon the important results which ensued on its accomplishment, it must at once be esteemed one of the most brilliant and decisive services which took place during that eventful war. It was a service carried into effect without any great loss on either side—attended with the surprise and defeat of one of the most experienced generals in the French army, and with the capture of nearly two thousand of their finest soldiers.†

The small town, or rather village, of Arroyo de Molino, where the main body of the French, as

* By Major Patterson, late of the 50th, or Queen's Own regiment.

† " A brigade of Girard had marched two hours before, but Dombranski's infantry and Briche's dragoons were only falling on the Medellin road, when the alarm was communicated by a videt. Girard was at first incredulous; but above the howling of the storm, the rush of infantry was heard, and, in a few minutes, the 71st and 92nd regiments burst into the

they imagined, lay secure, is situated at the base of a range of hills, which extend to the north and east in the form of a crescent, and so precipitous as to be nearly inaccessible. In the neighbourhood of this chain of heights are two roads by which the enemy might escape, and an extensive plain, somewhat thinly planted, which afforded, also, cover for their retreat and from our pursuing fire. General Hill's object was, therefore, to place his troops in such a manner as to cut off the line of their retreat by all these routes.

The troops intended for the enterprise advanced in one column, when, on arriving within half a mile of the enemy's position, they closed up, under cover of a bridge, and were separated into bodies for the particular objects of attack. General Howard's brigade marched directly on the town, the remaining columns breaking off, so as to turn the enemy's right should he appear upon the plain; while the cavalry, by a rapid movement along the Merida road that skirts the wood, might act in front, or on the flanks, as circumstances demanded.

street, while the wild music of their bag-pipes was heard amid the cheering of the Highlanders, playing the apposite tune, " Hey, Johnny Cope, are ye waukin yet?" Girard and part of the dragoons had not quitted the village, but they now galloped off, making a bold and irregular resistance, while the infantry formed a square. The English guns had now got up, and opened a crashing fire on the French infantry; the cavalry were dispersed by a charge of the allied dragoons, and the 13th rode bravely forward, and captured the artillery."—MAXWELL'S LIFE OF WELLINGTON.

Although, on arriving before the village, it was approaching that period of the morning when daylight should appear, yet it was nearly dark at the time we halted, after our long and weary march. Heavy black clouds were rolling along the sides of the sierra, which, enveloped in a gloomy and almost impenetrable mist, seemed, as it were, to frown upon the forest underneath. Every now and then the wind, with a fierce and angry howl, swept across the plain—its hollow and melancholy gusts, in like manner, echoing even beyond the far-off mountains; but, after the tempestuous night we passed since leaving the village and cheerless bivouac (for we had orders to light no fires) of Alcuesca, we were by this time pretty well inured to drenching weather, and prepared to encounter the very worst the elements might have in store.

We stood at our position cold and shivering, wondering what was to come on next, and looking almost as black as the dismal squall that menaced us, when the matter we had on hand soon beginning to wear a business-like appearance, the whole current of our ideas assumed another aspect: we forgot the pelting of the storm, with all its dire accompaniments, and, with one exciting *impulse*, (an impulse which, before the enemy, ever has that effect with British soldiers,) were filled with life and animation, when, without much unnecessary delay, we were in full pursuit of Girard's flying columns.

During the advance, the light troops, consisting of the light companies of the 50th, 71st, and 92nd regiments, under the command of the Hon. Colonel Cadogan, of the 71st, made onwards to the village, and halted on some high ground near a chapel. About which time, Lieutenant and Adjutant Law, of the same regiment, was ordered in advance to reconnoitre, when, on arriving nigh the place, he perceived a dismounted picket of the enemy's cavalry, with their horses near them, seated round a fire, composed of the chapel-doors and window-frames piled up in heaps. As the daylight gradually appeared, those pickets mounted and retired, which was the signal for the general formation of the columns of attack.

Law, being anxious to get into the village, pushed on, in order to find out what was going forward there. The warfare of the elements still continued, while the clouds, gathered into one dark mass, rendered it almost impossible to distinguish objects clearly. Assisted, however, by the lurid glare of fires, which the rain had but partially extinguished, he obtained a full view of a scene amongst the enemy, the interest of which it would be no easy matter to describe. Officers and soldiers, both of cavalry and infantry, whose voices and footsteps were distinctly heard, and whose movements were illumined by the aforesaid glare, were running wildly in all directions. They had no time to "forge their weapons for the fight;" confusion reigned, where all a little before was wrapped in gloom and stillness. Some were calling for their horses, others seeking for their knapsacks, while consternation and dismay were pictured on every countenance. In trying to make their escape, and scarcely aroused from their dreams and reveries, instead of keeping to the main street, they levanted, some by the back premises, and many more by different loop-holes which the straggling nature of the place afforded.

The lieutenant, a man of great coolness and determination, not quite satisfied with the extent of his discoveries, was resolved to penetrate still further, when, perceiving one of the Frenchmen enter a gateway, which stood most invitingly open at the time, he incautiously rode in after him; on which the soldier, finding no outlet for escape, perched, or rather esconced himself up within a corner of the court-yard, and screwing up his courage desperately, he also upraised his piece in order to prevent the officer closing on him; there was no space or time, however, to present his musket. Instead of cutting on one side, firing, or parrying off the blows which probably, had there been room, would have taken place between them, they both stood gazing, as if doubtful in what manner to proceed, grinning and growling awfully at each other, like Jeffrey and the cat; until at length, seeing there was nothing to be done in such close quarters, and the Frenchman, who was a fellow of gigantic strength, having no inclination to surrender, though modestly invited thereunto by the British officer, and no assistance or support at hand, the lieutenant turned his horse, (a grey steed—his companion on many a hard day's march,) sharply round upon his heel, when, applying the spurs lustily to his flanks, he galloped through the gateway, saluted on his passage by a salvo from the astounded soldier, which caused the mortar and splinters of the mason-work to come tumbling about his ears.

Proceeding hurriedly through the village amidst the retiring enemy, many of whom were trying to make resistance, while sharp and sudden reports of musketry came now and then upon the ear, he was joined by Major Clement Hill of the blues, brother and aide-de-camp to the general of division; when, both passing through a narrow road enclosed by walls and olive-trees, some of the French grenadiers who were retreating parallel with the road popped their muskets over the wall, and fired a volley on the officers, at the same time desperately wounding the major's horse.

Law, seeing the dangerous plight of his companion, who had fallen beneath the animal, made a sabre cut upon one of the nearest Frenchman, when some of our skirmishers arriving opportunely to his aid, the enemy soon drew back among the trees, and bolted hastily in all directions.

Major Hill, who, by this time, assisted by his friend, was remounted on a French dragoon horse, which seemed to be in quest of a new master, continued to lead on the troops, in front of which, however, being somewhat in advance, and the daylight not being clear enough to distinguish friend from foe, he was mistaken by a soldier of the 71st for a French officer, and called on to surrender or his life would be the forfeit. It was not without considerable difficulty and explanation that he could convince the man he was a British officer, and aide-de-camp to the general, when the surprise and consternation of the soldier may be much more easily imagined than described.

When the prisoners were marching by next day, on their route to Lisbon, it was remarkable with what indifference and gaiety they went along. The dispirited countenance, or clouded brow, which might naturally appear under the circumstances of their late defeat and consequent surrender formed no part of their expression on the journey. On the contrary, the loud laugh of independence, mirth, and glee was more evident and rife among them. Though mostly young men full of health and vigour, their features bore the stamp of service in many climes. They formed, withal, a motley assemblage. The specimens of sundry nations were here collected—the brown Italian, the fair-complexioned German, the hardy Swiss, the muscular Swede, the light gay-hearted Frenchman, all abandoned, as it were, even by the very hope of returning to their homes or country; and, as before observed, pursued their way under the motto of " sans souci," as though they were themselves the favourites of fortune, and not the vanquished party.

Prince d'Aremberg, commanding the 27th regiment of chasseurs à cheval, (a corps that was raised in Brussels,) was endeavouring to make his escape during the *melée* which took place before the enemy left the village, when Corporal Dogherty, of the 71st, perceiving his manœuvre, charged his bayonet, and stopped the prince in his career. Muffled up in a large green cloak, which almost extinguished him, (for he was a very little personage,) he was but indifferently prepared for an encounter with the stalwart Irishman, who, suddenly reining back the Frenchman's horse, the force of the bit, which was very powerful, threw the animal upon his haunches, the rider at the same time falling on the pavement.

Dogherty, at once perceiving the advantage of his own position, resolved to profit by it, when, presenting his weapon, he called out to the prince for his surrender. The latter, prostrate on the ground, and therefore in no condition for a contest, sung out, "Peccavi!" when, throwing the ample folds of his cloak aside, he exposed the honours and decorations by which his breast was covered, which he thought would protect him (and he judged rightly) from being transfixed by the corporal's bayonet. Making signs to him to rise, Dogherty marched him in a prisoner to Captain Clements, of the 71st, into whose charge he was delivered. The corporal was a fellow remarkable for his bravery in many battles, where, being often wounded, he was discharged with a liberal pension.

It was observed during the attack upon the village that the chief of the "Etat Major" was, in a most affecting way, leading about his son, a remarkably fine boy, by the hand, asking protection for him from all the British officers to whom he could get access.*

---

* Lieutenant-Colonel Cadell, in the account of his campaigns, relates an extraordinary instance of cool bravery on the part of Captain Irwin of the 28th grenadiers:—

"At this period, our gallant comrade, Lieutenant Irwin, (now lieutenant-colonel,) fell senseless, from fatigue and exhaustion, and it was with great difficulty he was restored. Seven or eight Frenchmen, while endeavouring to make their escape down the mountain, were taken in an extraordinary manner by Lieutenant Irwin, of the grenadier company, the first in the pursuit. He took up what they call in Ireland 'a couple of two-year-old stones,' about half the size of a man's head, which he aimed so well with his left hand, that he brought down two of the Frenchmen, one after the other. The others, seeing their comrades so roughly handled, quietly surrendered, and he brought them all in prisoners."

THE TWENTY-NINTH AT ALBUERA.

On the afternoon of the 15th of May, 1811, after a long march, the English army took up their ground on the heights in rear of Albuera; but as the Spanish army had not arrived, General Houghton's brigade, consisting of the 29th, 57th, and 1st battalion of the 48th regiment, were moved to the right and formed *en potence*. The Spaniards having come up during the night, our brigade, after standing some hours under arms, was ordered about six or seven o'clock on the morning of the 16th, to resume its place in the line. We had scarcely time to get a little tea and a morsel of biscuit, when the alarm was given—" Stand to your arms! The French are advancing!"

We accordingly instantly got under arms, leaving tents and baggage to be disposed of as the quarter-master and batmen best could. We moved forward in line to crown the heights in front, which were intended for our position, and which may be shortly described as follows. The rivulet of Albuera ran nearly parallel to the front of the heights, at about six hundred yards distance, which sloped down to it, these being perfectly open for all arms; but beyond our right, they swelled into steeper and more detached ones. The village of Albuera was nearly opposite the centre of our line, and on the same side of the water, at which point was the only bridge. The banks of the rivulet were at some places steep and abrupt. On the opposite or French side, they were rather low, and the ground flat and open for some little distance, then gradually rose to a gentle height, covered with wood, particularly at some distance from the bridge up the river, where the French army lay concealed from our view, they having only some detached parties of cavalry in the open ground.

In occupying the position, the army was formed as follows:—The Portuguese (in blue) on the left: the English (in red) in the centre—viz., General Houghton's brigade, the 29th, 57th, and 1st battalion of the 48th regiment; General Lumley's, 28th, 39th, and 34th regiments; Colonel Colburn's, the 3rd, the 2nd battalion of the 48th, 66th, and 31st regiments; and the Spaniards (in yellow or other bright colours) formed the right. The whole drawn up as for a grand parade, in full view of the enemy, so that Soult could see almost every man, and was also enabled to choose his point of attack, which would not have been the case if we had been kept under cover, a few yards farther back, behind the crest of the heights, or had been made to lie down, as we were used to do on former occasions, when under the Duke of Wellington. That part of the 4th division under Sir Lowry Cole, which had just arrived from Badajoz, were posted in second line in our rear.

Before we had time to halt in our position, we observed two large columns of the enemy, supported by cavalry and artillery, moving towards the bridge and village of Albuera, which was occupied by the light corps of the German Legion, under Colonel Hacket. The first attack here commenced, under cover of a heavy cannonade, upon the village and our line in its rear. The Germans made a gallant defence, and maintained their post. But as the enemy *apparently* seemed to make a push at this point, Colburn's brigade was ordered to move down in support of the troops in the village.

Soult must have been much delighted on observing this movement: it no doubt was precisely what he most wished, because the columns which *appeared* to threaten the village and our line, was only a *ruse* to distract our attention and neutralize the English force, which he most dreaded. Our skilful adversary was in the meanwhile throwing his masses directly across our right flank or Spanish army, which extended to a great distance from us; and it was with no small surprise that we most unexpectedly heard a sharp fire commence in that quarter.

The error our chief had been led into now became evident. We were suddenly thrown into open column, and moved rapidly along the heights to our right flank, for nearly a mile, under a tremendous cannonade, for the French had already established themselves on some commanding heights, which raked us as we advanced, Captain Humphrey and several men being killed. They were, at the same time, attacking the Spaniards with great vigour, having thrown them into some confusion when in the act of throwing back their right to meet this flank attack. Colburn's brigade, also, which had moved to cover the village (as above stated) had been recalled, and brought up in a hasty manner, in column, obliquing to their right towards the heights now occupied by the enemy, and formed line at a right angle, and perpendicular to the first position. It has been understood, that Colonel Colburn wished to move to the attack with the two flank regiments, in quarter-distance columns, and the two centre ones in line; but Sir William Stewart, anxious to shew a large front, was deploying the whole. The 3rd, 48th, and 66th regiments, were in line, and the 31st regiment still in column, when a body of French lancers, taking advantage of the thick weather and heavy showers of rain, got round the right of this brigade, made a dash from the rear through those regiments which were in line, breaking them, and swept off the greater part as prisoners into the French lines. The 31st regiment stood firm, and fortunately escaped the disaster; and the Spaniards contended with some difficulty to hold their ground. Just as this misfortune had occurred, our brigade came up (the 29th leading regiment): we closed up into quarter-distance columns, under cover of the heights, and deployed; but before the 57th and 48th regiments had completed the formation, a body of Spaniards in advance of our left flank gave way, and in making off ran in our front, and then came rushing back upon us. We called out to them, urging them to rally and maintain their ground, and that we would shortly relieve them.

On these assurances, with the exertions of some of their officers and of our adjutant, who rode amongst them, they did rally and moved up the hill again, but, very shortly afterwards, down they came again in the utmost confusion,—mixed, pell-mell, with a body of the enemy's lancers, who were thrusting and cutting without mercy. Many of the Spaniards threw themselves on the ground, others attempted to get through our line, but this could not be permitted, because, we being in line on the slope of a bare green hill, and such a rush of friends and foes coming down upon us, any opening made to let the former pass would have admitted the enemy also. We had no alternative left but to stand firm, and, in self-defence, to fire on both; this shortly decided the business; the lancers brought up and made the best of their way back to their own lines, and the Spaniards were permitted to pass to the rear.

The formation of our brigade being now completed, and Lumley's brigade having taken post on the left, and all being now ready for the attack, Sir William Stewart rode up to our brigade, and after a few energetic words, said, " Now is the time—let us give three cheers!" This was instantly done with heart and soul, every cap waving in the air. We immediately advanced up the hill, under a sharp fire from the enemy's light troops, which we did not condescend to return, and they retreated as we moved on. On arriving at the crest of the height, we discovered the enemy a little in rear of it, apparently formed in masses or columns of grand divisions, with light troops and artillery in the intervals between them: from the waving and rising of the ground on which some of these stood, the three or four front-ranks, in some cases, could fire over the heads of one another, and some guns posted on a bank fired over one of the columns. Notwithstanding this formidable array, our line went close up to the enemy, without even a piece of artillery to support us (at least near us there were none): we understood that the nine-pounder brigade had been withdrawn in consequence of the disaster above related; while Soult has since stated that he had forty pieces of cannon vomiting death at this point. The 29th regiment being on the right of this line, its flank was *en l'air* and completely exposed, without any strong point to rest upon, while the Fusileer and Portuguese brigades of the fourth division, which had also been brought up to the new front, were a considerable way to our right in the plain below.

This was the moment at which the murderous and desperate battle really began. A most overwhelming fire of artillery and small arms was opened upon us, which was vigorously returned; there we unflinchingly stood, and there we fell; our ranks were at some places swept away by sections. This dreadful contest had continued for some time, when an officer of artillery (I believe German) came up and said he had brought two or three guns, but that he could find no one to give him orders (our superior officers being all wounded or killed). It was suggested that he could not do wrong in opening directly on the enemy, which was accordingly done. Our line at length became so reduced that it resembled a chain of skirmishers in extended order, while, from the necessity of closing in towards the colours, and our numbers fast diminishing, our right flank became still further exposed. The enemy, however, did not avail himself of the advantage which this circumstance might have afforded him.

We continued to maintain this unprecedented conflict with unabated energy. The enemy, notwithstanding his superiority of numbers, had not obtained one inch of ground, but, on the contrary, we were gaining on him, when the gallant Fusileer brigade was moved up from the plain, bringing their right shoulders forward; they thus took the enemy obliquely in flank, who, although already much shattered, still continued to make a brave resistance, but nothing could withstand the invincible and undaunted bravery of the British soldiers. The enemy's masses, after a desperate struggle for victory, gave way at all points, and were driven in disorder beyond the rivulet, leaving us triumphant masters of the field.

To the credit of the troops engaged, it ought to be recollected that, in all other battles fought either before or afterwards in the Peninsular, our gallant army, under a skilful commander, had only either to march up to the enemy or to await his attack, and that after a conflict of more or less duration, the victory was won; but in this terrible contest, error, confusion, and misfortune, attended our first disposition. Victory had to be retrieved from a brave and experienced foe under many untoward and disheartening circumstances, and it seems universally agreed that the annals of war scarcely afford an instance of so bloody a battle, in proportion to the numbers engaged, having ever been fought.

Mustering the living, and recording the dead, became afterwards our melancholy duty. On reckoning our numbers, the 29th regiment had only ninety-six men, two captains, and a few subalterns remaining out of the whole regiment; the 57th regiment had but a few more, and were commanded out of action by the adjutant; the first battalion of the 48th regiment suffered in like manner; not a man of the brigade was prisoner; not a colour was lost, although an eloquent historian, most unwarrantably, stated that the 57th had lost theirs— the 57th lose their colours!—never! Major-General Houghton, commanding the brigade, and Lieutenant-Colonel Duckworth of the 48th regiment, were killed; Lieutenant-Colonel White of the 29th regiment mortally wounded; Colonel Inglis of the 57th, and Major Way of the 29th regiments, very severely. In fact, every field-officer of the whole brigade was either killed or wounded, so that at the close of the action the brigade remained in command of a captain of the 48th regiment, and, singular enough, that captain was a Frenchman (Cemetiere).

The field afterwards presented a sad spectacle—our men lying generally in rows, and the French in large heaps, from their having fought principally in masses, they not having dared to deploy, (as they afterwards told us,) from a dread of our cavalry, having supposed that we would not have ventured to act in such an open country without a great superiority in that description of force.

The French were driven in such confusion from the field, that their brigades and regiments lost all order, and were completely mixed, so that numbers of our men, and several of the officers who had been taken prisoners, made their escape out of the enemy's bivouack during the night, and many deserters came over. But notwithstanding their great disorder, which must have been known to our chief, we remained all the next day looking at one another, while the enemy was actively employed in reorganizing their shattered forces. It struck many people that, if only a demonstration of advancing had been made, even on the following morning, their total rout would have been complete, because General Hamilton's division of

Portuguese were almost still entire, nor had Hacket's fine corps, or even Lumley's brigade, or our cavalry, been rendered unserviceable, and the remaining part of the 4th division, which had been detained at Badajos, were momentarily expected to arrive. On the third day, even after the enemy had recovered their order, they, as soon as they observed that we were about to advance, immediately commenced their retreat without offering the smallest resistance.

Some affecting incidents, which occurred on this memorable occasion, may not prove uninteresting.

When in our first position, Major-General Houghton was on horseback in front of the line, in a green frock-coat, which he had put on in the hurry of turning out: some time afterwards his servant rode up to him with his red uniform-coat. He immediately, without dismounting, stripped off the green and put on the red one; and it may be said that this public display of our national colour and of British coolness actually was done under a salute of French artillery, as they were cannonading us at the time.

There had been a general court-martial held some time previously to the action. The prisoner, Lieutenant Ansaldo, was found guilty and sentenced to be *suspended* for six months; he, however, instead of quitting his corps during that period, remained with the army, and gallantly went into action by the side of his prosecutor—

they both fell! And what is still more extraordinary, the President, (General Houghton, (the Judge-Advocate, (Captain Binning, 66th regiment,) and many of the members and witnesses were also killed, and were almost all of them entombed near the same spot.

A few days after the battle, *five* regiments, who suffered most, were embodied into *one!* forming a provisional battalion—viz., the 3rd regiment, one company; the 66th, one company; the 29th, two companies; the 57th, three; and the 31st, three companies, placed under the command of Lieutenant-Colonel L'Estrange of the 31st regiment.

The Duke of Wellington, on hearing of Soult's advance, used the utmost possible exertions to come up, and to have commanded in person: he only arrived the second day after the action—unfortunately *too late*. Some days afterwards, I have been told, his Grace, while inspecting the hospitals at Elvas, said to some of our men, "Oh, old 29th, I am sorry to see so many of you here!" They instantly replied, "Oh, my lord, if you had only been with us, there would not have been so many of us here!" so implicit was the confidence of even the humblest individuals in this great man.

OUT-POST ANECDOTES,

ETC.

In talking over old scenes and by-gone times with other officers who had served in the Peninsular, the conversation has frequently turned upon the pleasant way in which the out-post duty was carried on towards *the close of the war;* and, as I was serving in a light infantry company at the time that the army was in the south of France, and was therefore very constantly upon out-post, I had many opportunities of personally remarking the courteous manner in which the duty was performed between the French and British armies; and, perhaps, a few anecdotes that came under my own immediate observation may not be deemed wholly uninteresting to the general reader.

I never knew an advanced sentry of either army to be *wantonly* shot at the out-posts; and I have often myself, when strolling too far in advance of my own picket, been waved back by the French, but in no one instance was I fired upon.

The outposts of the division to which I belonged were furnished by mixed pickets from the light companies of the different regiments, and two battalions of German riflemen, known in that part of the army as "Halket's Green Germans." They were excellent soldiers, and their officers were a remarkably gentlemanlike, well-informed set of men.

At the time that the allied army were in front of St. Jean de Luz, and shortly before the battle of the Nivelle, it was very difficult—nay, almost impossible—to procure any good wine; and, being one day on out-post duty at a post which we used to call the Chapel Hill picket, it occurred to a German officer and myself that, being on good terms with the French, and in the habit of often chatting with their officers at the out-posts, we might be able to get a case of claret by their means. On going to the front we were immediately joined by a French officer, who expressed every wish to oblige us; but he said that he really could not afford to purchase the wine himself, with the chance of losing his money, in case any movement should take place in either army; but that, if we chose to take the risk upon ourselves, and would intrust him with the price of it, his regiment would be again at the out-post in three days' time, and that we should then have our wine. He was true to his word. On the third day there was a case of most excellent claret waiting for us, which he had been kind enough to bring upon a mule from St. Jean de Luz; and we parted, after exchanging names, and mutually expressing a wish that we might renew our acquaintance at some future period under happier auspices. When at Paris in 1830, and living on terms of intimacy with many French officers who had served in the Peninsular war, I made particular inquiries about my Chapel Hill acquaintance, but could never learn any tidings of him. If, however, by any strange accident, this work should find its way into his hands, he will not be displeased to see that his kindness and good-nature are duly appreciated after the lapse of so many years.

At the Chapel Hill post there was a small open chesnut grove between the French and English pickets, which was not occupied by either party during the day, but at night our sentries were pushed forward close to each other amongst the trees. One fine moonlight night our advanced sentry called the attention of Colonel Alexander to the French sentry in his front, who was distinctly seen in the moonlight leaning against a tree, and fast asleep with his musket by his side. Alexander went quietly up to him, and took possession of the musket, and then awoke him. The man at first was much frightened upon finding himself disarmed, and in the hands of an English officer. Alexander gave him back his firelock, merely remarking that it was fortunate for him that he had found him *asleep on his post instead* of one of his officers. The poor fellow expressed the greatest gratitude; and, by way of excuse for such an unsoldierlike act, said, that his regiment having been moved from the extreme left of the French army, he had been marching for many hours through bad cross roads, and having been immediately put upon out-post duty, he was overcome by fatigue.

It was at the same post that one day seeing a French officer coming towards us, another officer and myself went out to meet him. He said he was aware that Prince R—— belonged to that part of our army, and inquired whether the prince happened to be then on out-post. We answered that he was so, and was, moreover, field-officer of the day, and that we would punctually deliver any message which he might have for him. He replied, "Well, then, I have most important news for him. There has been a great battle fought in the north of Europe, in which his elder brother has been killed, and the prince serving in your army is now the head of his family." A few days after this occurrence, I was informed that Prince R—— had obtained leave to return to Germany for the purpose of looking after his affairs.

I remember once, after a trifling skirmish, when the firing had ceased on both sides, that we observed a Portuguese advanced sentry, belonging to a regiment of Caçadores, who had been pushed forward as a vidette, amusing himself by fighting a sort of duel with the French sentry in his front. After they had exchanged three or four shots, down dropped the Portuguese to all appearance dead; and the Frenchman, without waiting to reload his musket, ran up in the hope of securing the dead man's knapsack before any one could reach the spot from our side. But the Portuguese proved too cunning a fellow for "Johnny Crapaud!" He allowed him to come within a few yards of him, when, jumping up, he shot him dead, and then quietly resumed his duty as a sentry.

Shortly after the battle of the Nive, Colonel Alexander, in returning from the front, on a very dark, stormy night, missed his way, and his horse falling over a bank, both horse and rider came clattering down heels over head into a lane, and close to a French sentry, who instantly challenged. Alexander hearing the *qui vive*, and the click of his musket, thought that he was going to fire, and called out, " C'est l'officier du poste Anglais—ne tirez pas!" " Non, non, mon Colonel," replied he, "j'espere que vous n'êtes pas blessé!" The same corps was in our front at this time that had been opposed to us at Chapel Hill, where Alexander had awoke the sentry who was sleeping on his post; and if that story was known amongst the man's comrades, it may possibly have been the reason of the Frenchman's forbearance in the present instance.

These anecdotes, but trifling in themselves, still tend to shew that feelings of respect and courtesy may exist between two gallant and chivalrous nations, although opposed to each other in a stern and bloody warfare.

MARSHAL BERESFORD.

In that brilliant scene of the great Peninsular drama enacted on the hills of the Arrepiles, now nineteen years ago, I performed the humble part of assistant-surgeon in the —— regiment of foot. Like all military men, I was anxious for promotion, and had been long trying, through every interest I could move, to obtain a staff-surgeoncy in the Portuguese army—an appointment then open to officers of my rank. My exertions, however, had proved fruitless, and I had almost given up the pursuit.

It was near sunset; the opposing armies were in fierce collision, and as detached masses from either side rushed forward to occupy the various vantage-grounds of the position, the two lines seemed to mingle, yet, for a moment, to repel each other, like meeting torrents. A long and twisted stream of grey curling smoke marked the indentations of the combat, whilst the sharp continuous tearing of the musketry, and the deep interrupted roar of the cannon, formed an awful concert.

The surgeon of my regiment and myself had held a little council of war in the rear of our division, then moving into the fight, and it was settled by mutual consent, that he should remain where he then was, with the main body and reserve of our Æsculapian stores, to receive the more serious cases from the front, whilst I was to keep close in with the regiment, to afford the "*premiers secours*" to our wounded comrades before they passed to the rear. I happened to be tolerably well mounted. *En croupe*, I carried a pair of capacious "*Alforges*," or Spanish saddle-bags, containing, on one side, a plentiful supply of the minor apparatus of surgery, and on the other, such "*provent*" as Captain Dougald Dalgetty would have laid in for a like occasion. Suspended to my saddle-bow was a "*borachio*," or leathern bag, of country wine. Thus accoutred, I rode on with my regiment.

We had just turned a rising ground, and had come into near view of the lesser Arrepiles, which was still crowned by a strong body of French infantry. A Portuguese brigade was in the act of storming the hill as we came up, and were gallantly mounting its side; but that most commanding point of the adverse position was quite as gallantly defended by the enemy, who as yet maintained their ground on its crest. A division of the Portuese army, led on by Sir William Carr Beresford in person, was closely engaged at its base, nobly rivalling the feats in arms of their British allies.

As we pressed on towards this interesting scene, a mounted officer, in Portuguese staff uniform, galloped towards us from the front, shouting at the top of his voice, "A surgeon, a surgeon—a British surgeon!" In an instant I was at his side, and recognised him to be Colonel Warre, one of the marshal's aides-de-camp. "Follow me," were the only words pronounced by him, as he wheeled round his charger, and again spurred him towards the line of fire.

After a few minutes' gallop we drew up at a covered wagon, to which the colonel pointed with eagerness as he dismounted. I had already drawn the curtains of the vehicle aside, and perceived that it contained two persons: one in the uniform of a serjeant, the other I immediately recognised as the marshal himself. He was lying on his back, dressed in a blue frock-coat and white waistcoat. Just below the left breast was a star of blood, bright and defined as a star of knighthood. It was about the size of that chivalrous decoration, and occupied the exact spot where it is usually fixed. There was a small rent in its centre, black and round. The eyes were half-closed; the countenance in perfect repose, perhaps a little paler than when I had last seen it.

The situation of the wound, just over the very fountain of life; the stillness of the wounded general; the appearance of his companion, whose lower limbs were literally mashed; the commander-in-chief and the non-commissioned officer laid side by side, silent, motionless, and bloody;—all struck me at the moment as a prelude to the equality of the grave. I asked no questions, for I had come to the conclusion that there might be no tongue to move in answer. In an instant the marshal's dress was torn open, and my fore-finger, that best of probes, was deep in his side. Not a muscle moved, not a sound was uttered; I felt the rib smooth and resisting below, whilst the track of the bullet led downwards and backwards, round the convexity of his ample chest. I now spoke for the first time since I had entered the wagon, and said, "General, your wound is not mortal." This observation of mine, which I made quite sure could not fail to be particularly interesting to my patient, seemed to have been heard with perfect indifference; for without taking the slightest notice of the very agreeable intelligence I had just communicated, he looked up, and asked, "How does the day go?" "Well," said I, "the enemy has begun to give way." "Hah!" rejoined the marshal, "it has been a bloody day."

During this brief conversation, I had traced the course of the ball by a reddish wheal, which marked its *trajet*, and I felt the missile itself deeply lodged in the flesh of the left loin. The preliminaries for cutting out were arranged in a moment, and the marshal had turned on his right side, when the wounded serjeant, having by this time, as I suppose, discovered my trade, began most lustily to call upon "*Nossa Senhora*" and the doctor in the same breath. I requested of him, in his own language, to be silent; telling him, at the same time, that his general was lying wounded by his side. Upon this the marshal turned round his head, and, with a reproving look, said to me, "Sir, if that poor fellow's wounds require dressing more than mine, dress him first." Both the words and the manner in which they were spoken, then made a strong impression on me, and impressions stamped on the field of battle are not easily erased. I assured his excellency that nothing but amputation could be of any service to the serjeant, and that I had not the necessary instruments by me for such an operation.

All parties were again silent, and I proceeded to cut out the bullet. My knife was already buried in the flesh, its point grating against the lead, when the marshal, feeling that I had ceased to cut, and calculating, perhaps, that my steadiness as an operator might be influenced by the rank of my patient, again turned round, and with as much *sangfroid* as if he had been merely a spectator, said, in an encouraging tone, " Cut boldly, doctor; I never fainted in my life;" almost at the same instant I placed the bullet in his hand.

When the wounds had been bound up, the patient demanded what steps he should next adopt. To this I replied that it would be prudent to have himself bled after some hours. " But who is to bleed me ?" quickly rejoined the marshal. I was in some measure prepared for this question, and had already determined on the course I should follow.

From the moment I had recognised the commander-in-chief of the Portuguese army lying wounded in a wagon, close in with the enemy, and had ascertained that his wound was not necessarily mortal, I saw that my being on the spot, at such a moment, might lead to my promotion. A fair, unimpeachable opportunity of tendering fresh services to him on whom the accomplishment of my ambition seemed to depend, was now afforded me. But such is the influence of an unflinching, unaffected firmness of character in a chief over those below him, and such the impression left on my mind by what I had just witnessed, that I felt convinced I should establish a higher place in the marshal's good opinion by remaining in the fight, than by volunteering to leave it, even for the purpose of attending to his own wound. I therefore respectfully submitted to his excellency, that my regiment was then probably in action; that I should be sorry to be out of the way when my friends and comrades might need my assistance, and that I hoped he would be kind enough to permit me to join them. " Most certainly," was the reply.

I saw no more of the marshal for many weeks, and when I had the honour of being again presented, I found him very ill, suffering much from inflammation in his side, and a profuse discharge from his wounds, kept up, as was afterwards discovered, by some portions of woollen cloth, which the bullet had carried forward from the breast of his coat, through the loose folds of which the missile had passed before it entered the flesh.

In quitting the marshal on the field, under the circumstances and with the impressions I have just described, I followed the course most consonant to my feelings, my sense of duty, and even my views of my own interest at the time. Whether I judged rightly upon the latter point or not, certain it is that, when I appeared in the next great battle-scene at Vittoria, the following year, I had already, for some months, filled the station of staff-surgeon in the Portuguese army.

THE PYRENEES, IN 1813.

After our successful defence of the key of the British position, on the 28th July, 1813, in the Pyrenees, against an enemy's force so very superior to our own in point of numbers, we enjoyed one day's rest, which was greatly to be desired, having been engaged with the enemy on the 26th, at Linzoain, (on which occasion the 40th lost six officers and nearly 100 men, and on the 28th, five officers and 123 men;) in bivouack the two previous nights, exposed to torrents of rain, and our baggage in the rear—both officers and men, owing to the mountainous country over which we had been marching for several days back, nearly without shoes—a day of rest was invaluable to us, for the purpose of repairing our damages and drying our saturated clothes. On the morning of the 30th we were again ready for any service that might be required of us. We were not long without occupation: about ten, A.M., an order arrived for the troops to cross the ravine at the foot of our position, and attack the enemy on the summit of a range of high and steep mountains in our front. The day was broiling hot, and it required great exertion to ascend these rocky heights: it was, however, effected; and, after much gallantry on both sides, the enemy were driven at all points to defend as ineffectually every subsequent position which they took up to their rear. At this moment, the 40th regiment was ordered, by Lieutenant-General Sir Lowry Cole, commanding our division, to proceed down the mountain to our left, and arrest the progress of a column of the enemy who were retiring in the valley. The road, if so it can be called, by which it was necessary to descend, which in winter was evidently a watercourse, was obstructed by masses of rock and deep gulleys. Under a smart fire from the retiring force, we at length reached the bottom of the mountain, and a rush being made with the bayonet, we succeeded in taking prisoners the whole of the 32nd French light battalion, consisting of twenty-four officers and nearly 700 men—more than double the numerical strength of the 40th regiment at that time. The commanding officer, *chef-de-bataillon*, a very gentlemanly man, who had been wounded in the arm that morning, presented me his sword, which is still in my possession. How often has it recalled to my memory the glorious days of that period, when we had abundance of occupation for the mind as well as the body!—not like this inactive period of time, in which so many Peninsular men of my standing, as well as myself, are—vegetating, I will not say, for we are, I fear, too old for that, but—withering, upon an insufficient half-pay. Shortly after this piece of good fortune, and the prisoners were collected together, the Duke of Wellington arrived in the valley, and, in person, I reported to his Grace the fruits of our exertions, requesting to be informed how I was to dispose of them; when his Grace, smiling, said, "What! the 40th again?" and desired that they should be sent to the rear, under an escort of the regiment, on their way to Vittoria.

It was a curious circumstance that, upon inspecting the prisoners' knapsacks, a quantity of drinking cups were found, which the quartermaster of the 7th fusileers, in our division, had sent for to England for the officers, and which it is supposed had been landed at Passages, but on their way through the mountains to the fourth division, had been taken by the enemy: as I heard no more of them, I presume they at length reached their original destination, the quartermaster of the 7th having been informed of the circumstance. Amongst the officers taken prisoners by us was one of almost gigantic size. A short time previous, he had been the tambour-major of his battalion, and had been recently promoted to the grade of sous-lieutenant. I found him extremely troublesome, making several attempts to escape; and it was not until severely rebuked for it by his commanding officer that he desisted from his attempts. On the return of the escort from conducting the prisoners to the rear, I learned that our troublesome friend had, during the morning of the action, been the bearer of an eagle, which, upon our approach, he had thrown into a rapid stream, along the left bank of which the corps to which he belonged was retiring. It is needless for me to say how greatly annoyed I was, that all hope of discovering so valuable a trophy was thus irretrievably lost. This piece of information explained to me Sir Lowry Cole's motive for inquiring of me, during our pursuit of the enemy that day, whether the 40th regiment had not taken an eagle with the prisoners.

How many circumstances occur during the heat of battle which are worth recording for their singularity! Amongst this number are the following:—Whilst I was giving some directions to a serjeant of the regiment, during the time we were under a smart fire from the enemy's guns on the 28th, he was suddenly wheeled about by the effect of a round-shot, which struck the end of his knapsack, and, tearing it from his back, scattered the contents of it in the air without doing him the smallest injury. At the same moment, I received a musket-ball, which struck the front of my cravat, which it tore, and, passing under the collar of my coat, grazing the skin of my shoulder, escaped through an aperture of its own making. Not so fortunate was Lieutenant Galway, who, during our first charge, received two musket-balls in his body, from the effect of which I found him, on returning to our ground, lying upon a heap of stones, and bleeding rapidly to death. Whilst we were rendering him every assistance, (no medical man being with us,) we were called away from our exertions by the return of the enemy, and when they were again driven back, and we regained our former ground, Lieutenant Galway was discovered lying upon his back where we had left him: his pulse had ceased to beat, and life to all appearance had passed away. " Is he beyond all hope, and can nothing be done for him?" inquired one of the party. The reply was, " Nothing—he is dead!" At that moment, to our astonishment, he rose upon his seat, and, staring wildly about him, with apparent surprise, said, " Dead!" It was the last effort of nature: he had no sooner uttered this, than, falling upon his back, he died without a struggle.

THE 40TH REGIMENT IN THE PYRENEES.

When the 4th division, under Sir Lowry Cole, occupied, on the evening of the 27th July, 1813, the heights in front of Pampeluna, with a very superior force, under Marshal Soult, in position in its front, the 40th regiment, at this time under my command, which, from previous losses, was reduced to one captain, nine subalterns, and less than four hundred men, was directed by the Duke of Wellington in person to occupy the summit of a rocky hill, which was considered to be the key of the British position. Two Spanish regiments and the 40th composed the entire force placed there, with which I was directed to keep the hill to the last. We passed the night under the continued fire of four small guns, without sustaining any material loss. On the morning of the 28th, about ten o'clock, the enemy made their attack with a powerful force, as I was subsequently informed, consisting of several thousand men. Our line was formed across the hill, with a space of about eighty yards in our front, the two Spanish regiments being posted upon our flanks. No sooner did the enemy's fire reach us, than the Spaniards retired in the utmost confusion, and scattering themselves over the face of the mountain in our rear, (on the summit of which the duke and his staff were stationed,) were seen no more, leaving the 40th totally unsupported. As soon as the head of the attacking French column had reached the brow of the hill and formed, a volley was fired by the 40th, and a charge of bayonets made, which drove them down again in the utmost confusion. Four times the enemy renewed the attack, and each time they were driven back at the point of the bayonet, leaving the 40th in final possession of the hill which they had so resolutely defended; not, however, without their having sustained considerable loss. His Serene Highness the Prince of Orange, who conveyed to the regiment after the second charge the thanks of the Duke of Wellington, narrowly escaped, and the brigade-majors of Sir Lowry Cole and Sir William Anson, Roverea and Avemen, who came down shortly afterwards, were both killed near me in the struggle which took place. The day following a French officer of rank came to me with a request that he might have his wounded carried off, and after speaking in the highest terms of the gallantry displayed on the 28th in defence of the hill, he assured me that several hundred of his men were placed *hors de combat* on that occasion. Severe as this loss appears, I cannot, when I consider the position of the enemy, crowded as they were on the brow of the hill, without the power of immediately retiring, when the several charges were made, for a moment suppose that this statement, from such an authority, was an exaggerated one, more particularly as I was a witness of the severe loss sustained by the enemy on that occasion from the bayonet alone, to which we considered ourselves solely indebted, placed as they were in the hands of brave men, for the successful defence of the position entrusted to us.*

MILITARY RETRIBUTION.

About five o'clock on the morning of the 9th of December, 1813, the inhabitants of the little town of St. Jean de Luz were roused from their sleep by the drums beating to arms, and the merry bugles of the light infantry sounding "the assembly" in the streets. All now was bustle and military preparation, which, to an inexperienced eye, might seem to partake of considerable confusion, as the soldiers of the different corps were seen hurrying to their respective parades.

In about three-quarters of an hour our rolls

* S. Stretton, Colonel, H.P.

were called, three days' rations served out, and the first division on its march towards the outposts. As soon as the different corps had taken up their ground, the attack was commenced by the whole of the light troops; but it is not my intention to give an account of the operations of the army during the first day of the passage of the Nive, but to confine myself to the events that occurred to the light infantry company to which I belonged. After a sharp but successful skirmish over about four miles of country, we were stopped by a large force of French posted behind an embankment. Just at this moment a young staff-officer rode down on a fine well-fed horse, with a white flowing plume in his hat, and ordered me instantly to cease firing. I listened to him with infinite surprise, looking at the same time with the greatest admiration at the neatness of his dress and general appearance, my unfortunate regimentals being considerably the worse for wear, and my nether garments nearly in rags and much patched; but not feeling the same respect for his military talents that I did for his spruce turn-out, I positively refused to obey his orders. Nevertheless, he rode down my line of skirmishers and stopped their fire. One blast, however, from my bugles set the company at work again; and then, much to my delight, I saw him ride on to the next light company, commanded by Captain Burnet, where I well knew he would meet his match, for a better soldier or a funnier fellow you will not meet with "on a summer's day." What passed between them I know not; but the result was, that Burnet continued his fire.

Our staff friend, finding that he could make nothing of us, rode up to Colonel Alexander, and the following conversation took place between them:—

"Pray, sir, do you command the light companies in the road?"

"Certainly," replied Alexander.

"Well, then, sir, I have ordered the two officers there to cease firing, and they will not obey one word that I say to them."

"Of course they did not," said Alexander; "and they were quite right."

"Right!" replied the staff man; "why, sir, they are firing upon our fifth division!"

This Colonel Alexander knew to be nonsense, and he replied—

"I do not care who we are firing at: they have been firing at us for the last three hours, and I do not care a d—n who they are!"

The staff-officer rode off. Very shortly after he was gone, I heard the bugles in the rear sounding the advance, and I repeated it upon mine, but still the company did not move. The fact was, that it was very difficult to do so, for in our front was a strong quickset hedge, which was no trifling obstacle to tired soldiers, with knapsacks on their backs, and three days' rations in their havresacks; and the fire from the enemy at this moment was very severe. Colonel Alexander galloped down to know why his orders were not obeyed; but his quick military eye instantly saw the difficulty as well as the remedy, and he ordered me to get through a hedge on my left with the left sub-division, and carry a house from which we had been considerably galled. With some difficulty I forced myself through, cheerfully followed by the men, who gave a good British cheer, and the house was soon in our possession, with very trifling loss on our part. The fifth division was now seen steadily advancing over the crest of the hill. This settled the business, and the French fled down the Bayonne road.

It may readily be conceived that, after a long skirmish over an inclosed country, a light company is not quite in such good order as when it started, and our pursuit now very much resembled a pack of fox-hounds running into a fox after a long run. One fine young soldier, of the name of Holmes, outstripped the rest of the company with the speed of a greyhound, and dashed by himself into the rear of the retreating French. A scuffle and two or three shots had taken place before we reached him, when we found him panting for breath with one French soldier in his grasp, whom he had knocked down with the butt of his musket, and two others lying dead at his feet: one of these he had bayoneted, and the head of the other was blown to atoms. Poor Holmes was himself badly wounded in the knee three days afterwards. I was standing by him when he received his wound, and upon my saying that I hoped he was not badly hurt, he replied, " Yes, sir, I am, very ; but

I do not care : I have just shot three officers." I have no doubt in my own mind that this was perfectly true : he was one of the best shots in the company ; and the French were so near that their officers were easily distinguished. I believe that Holmes is still living on his pension with his family in Staffordshire.

But to return to the Bayonne road. A few minutes after Holmes had been sent to the rear with his prisoner, much against his will, we passed some wounded French lying by the road-side ; one of whom raised himself on his elbow, and said, in English, " Is there no d—d Light Bob here who will give me a drink of water ?" A man of the name of Jones, who had been many years in the company, looked him hard in the face, and then, without a moment's hesitation, drove his bayonet through him, saying, " Give *you* a drink of water ; you shall have my bayonet, Mr. Evans !" This, of course, appeared to Colonel Alexander, who was out of hearing, to be a savage act of wanton cruelty towards a poor helpless French soldier. He rode up, burning with indignation, and said, " You scoundrel, what do you mean by bayoneting a wounded man ?" It was well for Jones that his answer was prompt and Alexander's sword in the scabbard, or he might have felt the edge of it. " This man," replied he, " is Evans, sir, who deserted from this company the night before the battle of Corunna !" This proved to be the case. Evans lived for two days in our hospital, and was fully identified. It is but justice to say that I verily believe, had the like appeal been made to Jones by a French soldier, he would have given him the last drop of water in his canteen; and it may be as well to mention, for the benefit of those who are not military, and who may, therefore, feel a little squeamish at such summary justice as that which Jones administered with his bayonet, that Evans would equally have died without his assistance. His thigh was dreadfully shattered by a musket-shot, and too high up to admit of amputation. The enemy retired into the intrenched camp in front of Bayonne, and thus ended our skirmish.

In the evening, reports were spread that the 1st division and Lord Aylmer's brigade were to return to their former quarters; the 1st division to St. Jean de Luz and its neighbourhood, and Lord Aylmer's brigade to its cantonments higher up the river. But this report seemed so improbable, because it was evident that Soult would make every effort the next day to oblige the Duke to recross the Nive with the right of his army, that Alexander actually betted ten guineas that we should not move to the rear.

About dusk we were delighted by the sight of Jem Hughes (Alexander's batman) coming down the road with the picket canteen on his shoulders. Jem was employed unpacking it in a cow-shed, which we had promoted to be our dining-room, when I observed him stop short in his proceedings, and saw plainly by his countenance that something was wrong. I trembled for our supper;

but one comfort was, that there lay the beef and the four snipes which we had killed a few days before on the banks of the Bidassoa. "Confound the fellow, (thought I,) he has forgotten the cigars and the grog-bottle!" But my anxiety was soon relieved. "If you please, sir," said Jem, "I have left the candles behind; but I can easily make one while the beef is boiling." Now both Alexander and myself entertained the highest respect for Jem's ingenuity, but we thought that this effort of genius was beyond even his powers of contrivance. He, however, proved as good as his word. By the time that the beef was boiled, and the snipes grilled, Jem produced his candle, and not a bad one either. He had twisted some dry rushes together, and saturated them with grease, which afforded us plenty of light to eat our supper by. As soon as we had discussed the good things before us, and had smoked our cigars, and finished a comfortable tumbler of grog, we repaired to the company fire. It was a fine starlight night, and we had just curled ourselves up in our cloaks, with the prospect of a good snooze after all our fatigues, when the rascally bugles were heard sounding the assembly, and in a short time we were retracing our steps towards St. Jean de Luz, leaving the 5th division to take charge of the outposts. Our night-march, and the subsequent operations of the army, are to be found in the pages of "The Subaltern."

I know no sight more affecting than that of a military hospital after a general action. There lies a gallant soldier, who, a few hours before, had stood by your side in the full enjoyment of health and youthful vigour, now a poor mutilated wretch on his death-bed, with the cold drops of perspiration standing on his brow, and occasionally may be heard a suppressed groan, wrung from him by intense suffering. He has, however, the proud consciousness of having done his duty by his country as a brave and faithful soldier, and dies respected and regretted by his comrades.

Far different are the feelings of that miserable renegade to his country, Evans. Writhing in mortal agony, with his French voltigeur uniform by his bed-side, he has no one to pity him! He knows that he is regarded with abhorrence and contempt by all his fellow-sufferers in that melancholy room. Even the hospital orderly, in giving him the necessary medicines, turns from him with disgust. You will often see a rough but kind-hearted soldier, seated for hours by the bed-side of a wounded comrade, administering to his wants, smoothing his pillow, and tending him with all the gentleness and affection of a woman.

A soldier's life is a merry and a happy one; but such scenes as these will force deep reflection, and graver thoughts, even upon the most light-hearted.

ANECDOTE OF BAROSSA.

After the battle of Barossa, the wounded of both nations were, from want of means of transport, necessarily left upon the field of action the whole night and part of the following day. General Rousseau, a French general of division, was of the number: his dog, a white one, of the poodle kind, which had been left in quarters upon the advance of the French force, finding that the general returned not with those who escaped from the battle, set out in search of him; found him at night in his dreary resting-place, and expressed his affliction by moans, and by licking the hands and feet of his dying master. When the fatal crisis took place, some hours after, he seemed fully aware of the dreadful change, attached himself closely to the body, and for three days refused the sustenance which was offered him.

Arrangements having been made for the interment of the dead, the body of the general was, like the rest, committed to its honourable grave; the dog lay down upon the earth which covered the beloved remains, and evinced by silence and deep dejection his sorrow for the loss he had sustained. The English commander, General Graham,* whose fine feelings had prompted him to superintend the last duties due to the gallant slain, observed the friendless mourner, drew him, now no longer resisting, from the spot, and gave him his protection, which he continued to him until his death, many years after, at the general's residence in Perthshire.

* The late Lord Lynedoch.

ANECDOTE OF SIR WILLIAM INGLIS.

I am tempted to record instances of coolness and intrepidity in Sir William Inglis, during the sanguinary struggle of Albuera. The regiment formed line on its destined position from open columns of companies. Sir William, close to and immediately in front of the colours, was dressing the line on the centre: he had finished with the right wing, and having turned to the left, was coolly scanning the men as they formed, when a shot brought his charger to the ground, leaving his master erect on his feet. At that critical moment I observed his unchanged countenance, and that while he extricated his feet from the stirrups, he never once turned his eyes from the line he was continuing to perfect, and not until that was completed did he cast a glance on the remains of his noble steed. When subsequently struck down by a grape-shot, which had perforated his left breast and lodged in his back, he lay on the ground close to the regiment, refusing all offers to be carried to the rear, and determined to share the fate of his " die-hards," whom he continued to cheer to steadiness and exertion; and who, encouraged by the voice of their brave commander, continued to close in on their tattered and staff-broken colours, as their comrades fell in the line in which he had formed them. So destructive was the fire of the enemy, that in a short time the few survivors must have slept in peace with their fallen brothers, had not the Fusileer brigade come up to their support by a forced march from the trenches before Badajoz, and by a brilliant charge turned and decided the day. The wreck of the 57th, cheered on by their prostrate and almost exhausted chief, was on the point of joining in the charge, when Marshal Beresford exclaimed, "Stop! stop the 57th; it would be a sin to let them go on!" and when the remnant of the "die-hards" retired, they carried with them the colours shot to ribbons, but unpolluted by a moment's grasp of a foeman.

SANTAREM.

The vineyards around Santarem were now teeming with delicious grapes ready for the wine-press. The "black cluster" and "sweet amber," rich as the honeycomb, hung in tempting bunches by the road side. It is hardly necessary to say, that our soldiers helped themselves, without control or reserve, to as many as they chose to take away with them. This was also the season when the orange comes to perfection, and Santarem could boast some of the finest orange groves of any near Lisbon. These, too, were thinned of their golden fruit, lest it should quench the thirst of the invaders.

The troops were in high spirits, and the Portuguese portion of them, who knew no more of the lines of Torres Vedras than the French or the English, amused themselves with stories on the probabilities of their future destiny. Some said they were going a fishing with the English for *Bacalháo* (salt-fish) ; some that they were about to embark for Mauritania, in quest of Don Sebastiano; but they all agreed in one thing, and that was, that they would fight the French when and where *O-grande-Lord** would lead them on.

By far the greater portion of the people of Santarem had gone by water to Lisbon before we arrived, and the few who remained were flocking rapidly out of it as our troops defiled through the streets on the morning of the seventh. I had just descended from the upper town, and had reached a *quinta,* or gentleman's pavilion, on the Villa Franca road, when three young ladies, of the class of Portuguese gentry, came from the quinta and surrounded my horse. Whether they judged that I was a commissary, or thought they could discover more of the charities of our nature in my countenance than those of other men, is what I do not pretend to determine ; certain it is, that the elder of the ladies gently took my horse by the bridle, while the two younger ones caught hold of the skirts of my coat with one hand, and of my stirrups with the other, and all three implored me, *é por amor de Deos,* (for the love of God,) not to be deaf to their entreaties. I at first endeavoured to put on the Stoic, and to be as repulsive and uncompromising as the Cynic of Sinope, particularly as we were in public, and there was a good deal of

* Literally, " the great Lord," meaning Wellington.

tittering around me; but if there be a something irresistible in the tears of one pretty woman, what must there have been in the tears of three? While I was deliberating with myself whether I would listen to their supplication or not, I had somehow resigned my horse to their guidance, and they had conducted us both to the quinta door; so that without coming to any resolution as to what I would do, I dismounted, and was led by the three young ladies into the front saloon. There, after craving my forgiveness for having made me their captive, they told me that they were three sisters, that their parents had been dead for some time, and that their maternal grandmother, who had been bed-ridden for many years, and had returned, with age, to second childishness, was then in an adjoining apartment, quite unconscious of the miserable death that awaited her, should they be obliged to leave her behind, and abandon her to the merciless invaders. They had been endeavouring, they said, for several days past, to prevail on some of their friends to afford her some kind of conveyance to Lisbon, and had even applied to the Juiz-de-Fora for his assistance; but that everybody had been so occupied about their own affairs, and there had been so many cases of a similar nature to provide for, that they had not succeeded in any quarter, and were at length driven to the distressing alternative of leaving her behind to perish alone, or of remaining with her, now that the army was nearly passed, to be insulted and maltreated by the French. They had already, they continued, as a last resource, endeavoured to interest several officers, English and Portuguese, in their situation. Some had treated their supplications with indifference, others with ridicule, all had passed onward, and left them and their aged parent to their fate, till they had seen me, in whom they had placed their last hope.

"Well," thought I, for I saw that apologies would be useless, " here's a pretty scrape I have got into." Wheel transports I had none at command, and the commissariat brigades of mules were gone forward in front of the column, and to get one of them back against such a stream of men was no trifling affair. I foresaw, indeed, that it would be one and the same thing in the end to leave the old lady to perish in the quinta, or to send her forty or fifty miles on the back of a mule towards Lisbon, exposed by the way, as she necessarily would be, to the effects of change of air, to the fatigue of sitting up, and to the want of a comfortable bed at night; yet there was so much of self-sacrifice in the conduct of the young ladies, so strong a sense of filial duty and affection, that I could do no less than everything in my power to preserve her life, so I sent for one of the largest *machos* (he mules) of a brigade, and had it provided with an *albarda*, or broad-seated pack-saddle. The servant of the house, a sturdy fellow, then brought the old lady forth, mounted the *macho*, and placed her before him so as to support her in his arms. She more resembled a being torn from the mansions of the dead than an inhabitant of this world. She was worn by long suffering almost to a skeleton; her long silvery locks had got loose from the bandage which had confined them, and were flowing in wild disorder over her neck and shoulders. As the troops passed her by in rapid march, she gazed on them fervently, dropping the while the beads of her rosary in unison with the motion of her lips, as she supplicated *Nossa Senhora dos Viandantes* (our Lady of Travellers) to protect her on the long and perilous journey that lay before her. Alas! the Virgin was deaf to her supplications. Our soldiers, as they passed, cracked their jokes at the appearance of our group; but this was a matter of little consequence. To alleviate the weight of a mite of the intolerable load of Portuguese suffering, more than compensated for the passing ridicule of the thoughtless. The young ladies, seeing their aged parent placed beyond the reach of the enemy's cruelty, took each of them a little bundle of necessaries, and after thanking me a thousand times for what I had done, and promising to send the *macho*, on their arrival at Lisbon, to the address which I had given them, followed the old lady and servant on foot, and soon disappeared amidst the retiring fugitives.

Here terminated the adventure of the quinta for the present. I shall have occasion to revert to it, and to conclude it hereafter; but as the order of time interposes other matter, we will leave the young ladies, their grandmamma, the servant, and the macho, to make the best of their way towards Lisbon, while we continue our retreat towards Villa Franca.

At Villa Franca, Azambuja, and Cartaxo, the vintage was more advanced than in the towns further in the interior of the country. The wine was already fermenting in the vats when the retreating troops made their appearance in those towns. I had then, for the first time, an opportunity to learn that Virgil, in his Georgics, pointed to a fact, and not to a fiction, when, in apostrophising Bacchus, he sung, as Dryden has it,—

> "To thee his joys the jolly Autumn owes,
> When the fermenting juice the vat o'erflows.
> Come, strip with me, my god; come, drench all o'er
> Thy limbs in must of wine, and drink at every pore!"

I observed men employed in the vats to tread out the juice of the grapes, whose bodies and limbs were dyed of a fine rich mahogany tint by frequent immersion in the must of red wine. There exists a something more or less of this practice throughout Portugal. The process may not be entirely to the taste of our fastidious wine-bibbers; but they may allay the qualms of offended imagination in the consoling reflection, that fermentation and filtration are powerful purifiers of wine.

Unfortunately for the people of those towns, they lay without the defensive line which the army was about to occupy, and consequently within the range of the enemy's depredations. Fatigue parties were therefore sent out to draw the taps, and beat in the heads of all the wine tuns they could find. Our men, in the performance of this duty, waded, in some instances, breast high in the sunken *adegas* (wine stores), to destroy the wine, and the streets were literally deluged with it. Upwards of forty thousand almudes* were destroyed in this manner. At Villa Franca our soldiers could not resist the temptation to drink their fill of the luscious juice as it flowed in torrents down the streets. They came in crowds to fill their canteens, and many, very many of them, threw themselves prostrate before the bubbling fountain of Bacchus, and worshipped the drunken god till they were unable to stand, in which state they were, in some instances, lashed, like wineskins, upon the backs of mules, and carried forward, lest they should fall into the hands of the enemy.

The wines destroyed in this way composed but a trifling portion of the produce of those districts. The major part of the vintage was kept in the adegas at such distances from the high roads that no time could be allowed to destroy it; and it remained, among a thousand other goodly gifts of Providence, to fall into the hands of the spoliators of Lusitania.

The weather, which had been delightful throughout the retreat, broke up on the evening of the 7th of October, one day only before our corps of the army reached its position in the line of defence. The retiring multitude of fugitives had, in general,

* A Portuguese wine-measure, containing in Lisbon thirty-six English wine pints.

by this time, housed themselves in some way or other within the protecting line, in which they were so far fortunate. Had the rains, which were extremely violent, set in ten days sooner, vast numbers of them must have perished of cold, and by the obstacles of the way.

On the 8th of October we had a good view of the then, to us, for the first time discovered, but now celebrated lines of Lisbon, stretching from Alhandra on the Tagus, by Calhandriz, Bucellas, and Sobral, to the north-west. The portion of these lines that fell to the defence of Hill's corps extended from Alhandra on the right to Bucellas on the left, being flanked on the Tagus by British gun-boats, and on the left by the fortified heights of Sobral. In the rear of this line was an easy and direct communication from the Tagus to Bucellas, through the village of Alverca, and between the first and second line of defence. Fort Sobral, on the height to the left of Bucellas, was a formidable work, topping like a mural crown the strong ground beneath it, and commanding the Lisbon road everywhere within reach of its artillery.

The sight of these stupendous field-works,* connecting the line of defence from the Tagus to

---

* Sixty-nine works of different descriptions fortified this line. In these were mounted 319 pieces of artillery, requiring upwards of 18,000 men to garrison them. From plank to plank the lines of Lisbon extended five and twenty miles. The timber for palisades, platforms, &c., consumed upwards of 50,000 trees.—ED.

the sea, astounded some of the would-be wise ones in the British army, who had ventured to predict, or at least to persuade themselves and their friends, that they should witness in this retreat a repetition of the closing and disastrous scenes of that of Coruña. The nature of the warfare carried on between the belligerents kept Massena also in the dark as to the existence of those formidable bulwarks of Portuguese independence, so that Lord Wellington seems to have thrown a magic veil over them till the day on which his army took possession of the formidable barrier that intervened between Massena and the object which he, the day before, vainly imagined to be within his clutch.

"The defensive power of these lines was never tried," say some: granted; but Massena's respect for them has established their celebrity, for he knew by the lesson taught him at Busaco what he had to expect from such works defended with the united courage of the British and Portuguese nations, and by the skill of their commander.

VENTURINHO DO POÇO.

On the morning of the 10th of October, as I was wending my way between Calhandriz and Alverca, (the village which I have already mentioned as being behind Alhandra,) I heard at some short distance from the road a plaintive moan, as that of a child in distress. I stopped to listen, the noise seeming to come from a little chapel, or *Ermida*, standing a few paces from the road side. On looking into the chapel all therein was silent, and I could discover no traces of anything living. Proceeding a little beyond the chapel, the sound became louder, and seemed to come from the earth. I went on till I came to a well, and on looking over its brink saw a child at the bottom of it sitting upon a mass of soft mud. The well was one of that kind which is generally used in Spain and Portugal for the purpose of irrigating gardens. It was ten or twelve feet in diameter, and about fifteen feet deep. The child was quite naked, and evidently too young to have climbed over the parapet of the well, from which it was clear that it could not have fallen in by accident, and that some evil-disposed person had cast it in for the purpose of destroying it. Fortunately, the well was entirely free from water, having nothing in the bottom of it but a bed of soft mud to a considerable depth, to which the child owed its preservation. On seeing me and my servant looking over the brim of the well, it raised its little hands towards us, and cried aloud, "Mài! mài! mài! ay, minha mài!" tantamount to "Mother! mother! mother! oh, my mother!" I made my servant disengage as much as possible of the bell-rope of the chapel, with which, and the chain-halters of our horses, I lowered him down into the well, and drew up the child. It was a boy; and its skin was incrusted over, as one may readily imagine, with the contents of the well. It appeared to have bled profusely at the nose, but had no bones broken, nor contusion about its person that I could discover, save a slight bruise on the forehead. It had arrived at an age to be able to toddle about, but could say nothing articulate more than the words already explained, so that it could afford me no clue whatever to the names of its parents, or how it had come into the well. My servant, having chafed its limbs, enfolded the child in his cloak, and placed it on the pommel of his saddle, in which guise we carried it to Alverca, where I handed it over to the civil jurisdiction of Dame Halbard, the wife of a serjeant attached to my establishment, who literally stitched the urchin up in a blanket, till she could make him a dress, and provide him with necessaries.

I published the circumstance far and wide, and caused placards to be put up in Lisbon and other large towns, describing the child, and the manner in which I had found it; but I never could succeed in obtaining any tidings of its parents, or any information by which I might be led to form a conjecture upon the mystery of its being in the well. It is hard to believe that a parent, and a mother too, (for the child had evidently been used to the cares of a mother,) could have been prevailed upon, under the pressure of any degree of misery and misfortune, to act towards it so cruel and unnatural a part; and yet if it had not been the act of a parent, one would have thought that somebody would have come forward and claimed the child. Be this as it may, the boy throve amazingly, and with the pliability of infantine affection, soon became familiar with his new quarters. In a few weeks he could say many words in English; could ask for bread and butter, and bread and wine; but if I mentioned the well in his presence, or talked of putting him again into it, he turned pale, and seemed ready to faint with terror. In fine, he was a pretty little creature, with dark-brown curly hair, a clear olive complexion, and a pair of large sparkling eyes, black as the feathers in a raven's wing. Every day weakened my hopes of finding any clue to his parents, and strengthened the interest which I, and all those about me, took in his well-being; and as he could give no account of his name, the Portuguese about my establishment christened, or rather named him, "Venturinho do Poço," and the English, "Little Fortunatus of the Well."

The extraordinary circumstances attending the discovery of little Fortunatus, soon became generally known in that part of the army to which I belonged, and came to attract the attention of Major ——, of the —— regiment. One day, as the major and I were confabulating upon different, subjects, he purposely drew the conversation to that of the little foundling, and inquired, with some earnestness, how I meant to dispose of him in case his parents or relations should not be eventually discovered. "The question," said I, " is a poser; I have as yet come to no resolution upon that point; but if I can do nothing better, I may take him home to England with me, to commemorate my Peninsular campaigns, and give him the run of my house in common with some half-dozen urchins of my own." Hereupon the major volunteered his services to relieve me from my charge of foster-father, undertaking to provide for the child, and perhaps to adopt him, if he might be allowed to dispose of him as he should think proper. Now the major was a gentleman of affluent fortune, who, if married, had no children, and the offer seemed to promise so many goodly results in favour of little Ventura, that I did not hesitate a moment to comply with his request. Before we parted, I transferred to him the person of the little stranger, with all my paternal rights and privileges. The major, as I understand, sent the boy to Ireland to be brought up and educated, whence I heard nothing more of him during the lapse of six or seven years. In the mean time, the boy had been kept at school, and had developed talents which appear to have fixed the major's attachment for ever, and to have induced him to apply to me for every particular which had attended his discovery in the well, which I readily afforded him, in the manner in which I have herein detailed them. I have not since heard of the major or of Ventura, who must by this time have arrived at manhood; but I hold it as more than probable, that he is now looking forward to a station in society far more elevated than that in which his progenitors moved, and which he never could have expected to enjoy, but for the disasters which had befallen his country, through which the guiding hand of an Omnipotent Providence brought to him, without any merits of his own, supreme good out of overwhelming evil. The publishing of this anecdote will be the touchstone of his disposition; if he be of a character open, manly, and generous, he will come forward and acknowledge his obligations to, and cultivate the good opinion of him, to whom, under Heaven, he owes the first and most important step towards his present lot and future expectations; but if he be of a turn of mind proud and vainglorious, he will be ashamed of the mystery that hangs over his birth and parentage, and we shall hear nothing more of little Fortunatus of the Well.

ESCAPE AT ALBA DE TORMES.

At Alba de Tormes, a town where, during the time that we remained, all the horrors of starvation stared us in the face, Lieutenants Law and Cox, of the 71st regiment, had a most extraordinary, and, it might be added, miraculous escape. It was at that period when Soult cannonaded the place, in October, 1813, before the retreat of Salamanca.

While the officers referred to were seated, as quietly as the state of things admitted, in the act of discussing their scanty fare, in one of the attic rooms where they were billeted, a shell from the French lines came tumbling in, with the precipitation usual with such visitors, through the shingled roof of the apartment, when, falling upon Law's boat-cloak, which happened fortunately to be on the floor, the violence of its progress was somewhat checked; but, coiling itself quite snug within the ample foldings of the cloak, it continued whirling round in a most amusing manner, though a dangerous customer to joke with, until, at length, allowing sufficient time for the astounded lodgers to escape, it burst with such an awful crash, that the officers, in their consternation looking about, perceived the upper story of their tenement in fragments, and all their goods and chattels (cloak included) scattered to the four winds of heaven.

THE HEAVY CAVALRY AT SALAMANCA.

Among the many instances of their brilliant attacks, enough stress certainly has never been laid on the conduct of the brigade of heavy cavalry at the battle of Salamanca, on which memorable day they with equal steadiness and impetuosity burst upon the infantry of the French left, and literally swept them from the ground, overthrowing column after column, and sending to the rear above three times their own number as prisoners. The battle of Salamanca formed the closing scene of such a series of able and well-combined manœuvres, and the turning of the French left, by the rapid and admirably concerted march and attack of the third division, was so prominent a feature, that it is only upon these considerations we can reasonably account for the slight mention made in the Duke of Wellington's despatch of the consecutive attacks of the heavy brigade of cavalry, which are merely noticed as " a successful charge under the orders of Sir S. Cotton (Lord Combermere)." It may be well to give a short and explicit statement of what actually took place as regards the attacks in question, leaving the impartial reader to judge for himself how far the heavy brigade may lay claim to having contributed materially to the successful execution of the bold and splendid manœuvre by which the left of Marshal Marmont's position was turned, the whole plan of his operations completely checked and reversed, and his army subjected to one of the most signal discomfitures sustained by the French in the Peninsula. In proceeding to give this narrative, however, it must first be clearly announced and explained, that not the slightest detraction is attempted from the well-earned laurels of the third division, whose behaviour at Salamanca will be recorded as long as the memory of that celebrated conflict, is either intended or thought of for an instant. The intention of this statement is merely to claim for the brigade of heavy cavalry the tribute to which it is conceived they are justly entitled, for their effective and prominent co-operation with the infantry at that part of the position in the defeat of the left wing of the French. It would be idle to assume that the cavalry could have performed this alone, but they ought to have the full credit of having made the very best advantage of the confusion which arose among the French when they found their flank was turned, by so resolutely following up what the third division had begun; because it is well known, that after the first onset at five o'clock, until about seven, when the cavalry halted, that division advanced with little opposition, securing the prisoners whom the dragoons were sending to the rear by whole battalions.

To proceed to the statement of facts, it will be recollected that, in the middle of July, 1812, Marshal Marmont, who was on the right bank of the Douro, after making various demonstrations to deceive Lord Wellington as to the point where he desired to effect his passage across that river, at length executed it on the night of the 17th. As soon as this was known at the British head-quarters, orders were issued for the whole army to march towards their right, in order to counteract the intentions of the French general, whose object had been all along to force back his opponents by threatening their flanks and communications. On the morning of the 18th, the movement of the French towards their left, in order to prosecute that object, was gallantly kept in check by Major Bull's and Ross's troops of horse artillery, with the light dragoons and part of the light division, while a larger force was brought forward near the village of Torrecilla della Orden. There being, however, no position at that place, Lord Wellington caused everything to fall back upon the heights between Carrigal and Fuente della Peña, which was not executed without some partial fighting, in which three or four hundred men on both sides were either killed or wounded.

On the 19th of July nothing of any moment occurred till towards evening, when it being discovered that the French were again in motion towards their left, some corresponding movements were made by Lord Wellington, the result of which was, that the two armies appeared opposite to each other in order of battle at daybreak on the morning of the 20th. No engagement, however, ensued; but Marmont continuing his flank march to his left, the British army moved accordingly in the same direction. On the 21st, both armies, still prosecuting their parallel movements, crossed the river Tormes, and next day took up their respective positions on two opposite heights, near the village of Arapiles, about five miles from Salamanca, thus bringing to issue a brilliant and most skilful series of manœuvres, which had now lasted for several days, without the French having been able to gain their object.

Under cover of a heavy cannonade, (he outnumbered us in artillery,) Marmont followed his former plan of extending towards his left, until about three o'clock in the afternoon, when Lord Wellington, attended by a single aide-de-camp, having from the right of his own position reconnoitred the march of the French columns, determined on turning their left, and instantly caused the third division to be brought forward for that purpose.

They accordingly came into action on the flank of the French soon after five o'clock. They were received by a brigade of infantry, who, with numerous skirmishers, attempted to check their attack, and give time for bringing up a heavier force to meet it. This resistance was, however, soon overcome, and they drove the French over the crest of the heights at the point of the bayonet.

It was at this critical juncture that the heavy cavalry brigade, 3rd and 4th dragoons, and 5th dragoon guards, received from Sir Stapleton Cotton their orders to advance; and moving rapidly forward between the flank attack of the 3rd and the more direct one of the 5th division, which was the right of our infantry line, came first into contact with the 66th (French) regiment, consisting of three battalions, and formed in a sort of column of half-battalions, thus presenting six successive lines, one behind the other. Strange to say, though drawn up in that formidable manner, their fire was so ill-directed, that it is believed scarcely a single dragoon fell from its effects; and no check taking place, the cavalry bore vigorously forward at a gallop, penetrating their columns, nearly the whole of which were killed, wounded, or taken, leaving the broken infantry to be made prisoners by the 3rd division as they cleared the ground before them, to assist in which one squadron of the 4th dragoons was for the moment detached. They presently came upon another column, however, of about 600 men, who brought down some men and horses by their fire, but attempted no stand of any consequence, and falling into confusion, were left as before to be captured by the advancing infantry.

The nature of the ground, which was an open wood of evergreen oaks, and which grew more obstructed as they advanced, had caused the men of the three regiments of cavalry to become a good deal mixed in each other's ranks; and the front being at the same time constantly changing as the right was brought forward, the whole had now crowded into a solid line, without any intervals. In this order, but without any confusion, they pressed rapidly forward upon another French brigade, which, taking advantage of the trees, had formed a *colonne serrée*, and stood awaiting their charge. These men reserved their fire with much coolness, till the cavalry came within twenty yards, when they poured it upon the concentrated mass of men and horses with a deadly and tremendous effect. The gallant General Le Marchant, with Captain White, of his staff, were killed; Colonel Elley was wounded; and it is thought that nearly one-third of the dragoons came to the ground; but as the remainder retained sufficient command of their horses to dash forward, they succeeded in breaking the French ranks, and dispersing them in utter confusion over the field. At this moment Colonel Lord Edward Somerset, discovering five guns upon the left, separated from the brigade with one squadron, charged, and took them all.

Here terminated the series of attacks we have

endeavoured to describe; for by this time, (about forty minutes after the first charge, which took place soon after five o'clock,) it was with difficulty that three squadrons could be collected and formed out of the whole brigade, and any further advance would have been unnecessary as well as imprudent. The spot where Lord Edward captured the guns was about three miles from where the first shot was fired by the third division.

Meantime the British attack along the whole front was in progress; the infantry went gallantly on to the attack of the heights with general success; and by seven o'clock the French were entirely driven from their position, nor could anything but the approach of night have enabled Marshal Marmont in any degree to rally his dispersed and discouraged troops.

The circumstances we have detailed speak for themselves; and it is hardly necessary to disclaim again any idea of detracting from the glory so gallantly gained by the British infantry in general, and especially by the 3rd division, at Salamanca. But what unprejudiced man can talk of our cavalry being deficient in impetuosity or resolution after what we have recalled to the recollection of the military reader? It may certainly be argued that the French did not prepare for receiving the attacks of our heavy cavalry brigade, by forming squares; and possibly, if they had, a better stand might have been made by them: but whatever suppositions we may make, or whatever conditional results we may imagine, one thing is perfectly obvious, namely, that if nothing but their actual annihilation could have stopped the career of the heavy brigade of cavalry on this occasion, the serious loss they suffered at the time General Le Marchant fell would, in all common probability, have done so.

CAPTURE OF THE ENEMY'S PICKET AT BLANCHEZ SANCHEZ.*

Having read an account of the capture of the enemy's picket at Blanchez Sanchez, on the 25th July, 1812,—" whilst they were carousing in a wine-house," by a corporal's patrol, I then promised that I would avail myself of the first opportunity, when I should leave the service, of giving an accurate and faithful account of that occurrence, not only for the honour of the patrol, which I then commanded, but also for the honour of the regiment in which I have served these last four and thirty years, having accompanied it with the expedition to Portugal, in 1808, and being present with it during the Peninsular campaigns, from the passage of the Douro at Barca de Avintas, 12th of May, 1809, until the battle of Toulouse, 1814; and subsequently accompanied the expedition to North America, and

* By William Hanley, late serjeant-major 14th light dragoons.

was present in the general engagement before New Orleans, 8th of January, 1815.

"It was about one o'clock, P.M., 25th of July, 1812, that the brigade, consisting of the 1st German hussars and 14th light dragoons, arrived at Arevola, where it halted and bivouacked. Patrols were sent out on the several roads; the one that I was ordered to command, consisted of four men of the 1st German hussars, and four men of the 14th dragoons, with orders to proceed on Blanchez Sanchez, and ascertain whether the enemy occupied that town or its neighbourhood. As we journeyed, we passed through a small village about two leagues on the road. Here I halted, and inquired of the alcalde for any information he might have obtained respecting the enemy. He replied, that he knew for a truth they were in Blanchez Sanchez, from which we were then distant about two leagues. Finding our horses rather fatigued, and the distance greater than had been expected, I felt anxious to feed before we proceeded further; and as the alcalde expressed himself with much warmth in favour of the British, I requested, if it were possible, he would be so good as procure us a small feed of corn for our horses, which would greatly refresh them: he replied, we should have it immediately. It was accordingly brought into the praça, where we then sat. Having placed a sentry on the church-top as a look-out, we unbridled and fed; after which, we mounted and moved off, sending forward three men in advance, one, fifty yards in front; a second, fifty yards to the right;

and the third, fifty yards to the left front, with orders to halt as soon as they should come in sight of the enemy, town, or any strange object.

"The advance moved on in this order until they reached the summit of a hill, from which could be seen the town of Blanchez Sanchez, and halted; I beckoned them to fall back and join the patrol, when all dismounted. I now walked up to the brow of the hill, and observed to the east of the town a column of infantry on parade. We remained dismounted about fifteen minutes, during which time the troops were undergoing an inspection, after which the column took ground to its right, broke into the Madrid road, and totally disappeared behind the hill on which it had assembled. I mounted the patrol, and galloping over their camp-ground, the fires of which were then cheerfully burning, having piled on broken furniture which they had carried from the village; we made for that side of the town whence they had marched, hoping to secure any stragglers or followers of the column. I should here observe, that Blanchez Sanchez is a small village of only one street, and stands on the open plain, without either hedges, walls, or enclosures. We rode cautiously down the street, when turning to the right, three dragoons were observed running from a barley-field, in which they had been cutting forage, and making for a house that stood isolated on the plain : we gave our horses the reins, galloped after and secured them. The house had a high wall, extending from its gable-ends, forming a yard or fodder-shed for feeding cattle in its rear, and into which there was but one means of ingress or egress, and this by the door of the house, through a narrow passage. We found this door closed, but by firing into it, it was soon blown open. It so happened, that at this time the dragoons were feeding their horses, and attending to their stable duties for the night.

"I ordered the men to keep up a brisk fire down the passage, as I considered by so doing it would create a conviction that our strength was greater than it really was, while it also prevented the enemy from getting more than an occasional shot at us up the passage.

"As I sat in front of the house, giving orders, my right shoulder parallel with the bed-room window, which was on the ground floor, the officer who commanded suddenly sprang up and fired his pistol through the window in my face, dropping down again, having been hitherto concealed beneath the window-sill. I instantly thrust my arm through the broken frame, pistol cocked, and pointed it directly down upon him, when he exclaimed, "Prisoner! Anglaise." I desired him to arise, and bring me his sword and pistol, which he did. I must not omit to observe, that his bed-room door opened into the passage, so that had he made an attempt to escape, he must have been that instant shot. I ordered one of the German hussars, who spoke French fluently, to dismount and accompany the officer into the yard, and summon the picket to surrender, assuring them that the cavalry brigade was close at hand, and that I insisted upon an immediate surrender before its arrival: in case of refusal, I should immediately fire the premises, (which were thatched,) and that no man should escape. In the course of a few minutes the hussar and officer returned, acquainting me that the men would surrender—provided I allowed them to retain their valises—to which I consented. There existed an old understanding between both armies, that had been established by long practice, that once a prisoner, all effects were relinquished; of course this surrender was an exception to the rule, and was strictly observed.

"The prisoners were now ordered to leave their swords in the yard, each man to lead his horse up the passage, which could admit but one at the same time; and on arriving at the door, to deliver his arms over to a dismounted dragoon, who broke the butts, throwing them some distance from him; each followed in succession, until the whole, in number twenty-eight horses, went out. As they passed the door, they were formed in rank of fours, stirrups up across their saddle-seat. My patrol I divided on each flank, with one man and myself in the rear. The lieutenant I allowed to ride by my side, part of his horse's reins being placed on my bridle-hand.

"We had just moved off, when a French colonel, mounted on a plain saddle, rode up on my right, and giving me a slap on the shoulder, accompanied it with, 'Bon jour, Anglaise.' I turned quickly round, and, seizing his sword, drew it from the scabbard, telling him he was my prisoner. He appealed, with a look of astonishment, to the officer in charge, with a ' Mon Dieu !' and, as I had neither time nor inclination to parley, I ordered him to proceed. His servant coming up at the same time, with two mules and baggage, numbered with the rest, and all marched on. It was about seven, P.M., when we left Blanchez Sanchez. The colonel told me afterwards that he had mistaken us for prisoners,—that he had preceded a column then on the march for Blanchez Sanchez; the dust arising from its march we could plainly distinguish.

"The officers and men expecting to meet the cavalry brigade, as I had said, expressed their astonishment at the disappointment. I told them that no doubt the brigade had fallen back for the night to a village not far distant; and I persuaded the men to increase their pace, so that they might get in before dark. My chief object was, however, to weary them as much as possible, and hurry them onwards to the village, on arriving within a short distance of which I sent a dragoon forward to acquaint the alcalde that I was marching in several prisoners, and to request he would open the chapel for their reception for a short time, and also to have lights placed within.

"It so occurred, that high mass had been celebrated that morning. The candles at the altar &c. were all lighted, and in marched men and horses, producing a most singular contrast with its congregation, in less than twelve hours. The prisoners complained that they were hungry, not having had any supply of rations since Salamanca. I once more called upon the goodness of the kind alcalde, who immediately ordered the villagers to collect bread, and wine was brought from his own house. The alcalde, priest, and myself, distributed to each his share—the wine rather sparingly. The old men, young women, and children, vied who should assist the most.

"It was at this village I fed our horses on grass, and having rested and refreshed the men, I told the officers that we must now move on until we reached the brigade, which I was certain was near at hand. We accordingly turned out, formed in the same order as before, and moved off with the repeated *vivas* of the villagers; and—what cheered us most—conducted by a beautifully bright moonlight.

"At length we arrived within sight of the advanced videttes of the 14th light dragoons, who challenged. The reply, 'The patrol,' being satisfactory, we proceeded; but, on our closer approach, the videttes, discovering by the moon's light such a numerous group of long-tailed horses, supposed the enemy were playing off some stratagem, and fired, and retired towards their picket, which came up with swords drawn, at a brisk trot, led by Lieutenant Ward, to whom I explained how matters stood. He congratulated one and all on our good fortune, and accompanied the patrol to Major-General Baron Alten, who commanded the brigade, with whom the officers remained. The dragoons and horses were lodged in a chapel close to our bivouack, where we were all received by the cheers of officers and men. The prisoners were marched, dismounted, to head-quarters.

"His Grace the Duke of Wellington was pleased to order that the cavalry regiments then in front should take a proportion of these horses fit for duty on their strength, paying the general regulation price—viz., 25*l*. for each, which was divided among the men of the patrol. The duke was also further graciously pleased to express his approbation by a donation to each man of twelve dollars, and twenty-four to myself when at Madrid, and also condescended to mention this capture in his despatches to England.

"Thus, I have endeavoured faithfully to relate the capture of the enemy's picket at Blanchez Sanchez, consisting of one officer and twenty-seven dragoons, with their arms, accoutrements, &c., complete, and also a lieutenant-colonel (mounted), his private servant, with two mules and baggage, by the patrol under my command; and as an honourable testimony of which I was presented with a medal at the head of the regiment.

"In conclusion, I must be allowed to observe, that had this picket been 'carousing in a winehouse,' there would have been no possibility of securing and marching them such a distance. The truth was, they were surprised; and they had not so soon forgotten the panic and confusion into which they had been thrown a few days before at the battle of Salamanca.

"For the authenticity of the above, I can with confidence refer to Lieutenant-Colonel Townsend, now commanding the 14th light dragoons, or to Colonel Brotherton, Commandant, Cavalry Depôt, Maidstone."

THE END.

T. C. Savill, Printer, 107, St. Martin's Lane.

INDEX

(Compiled by S. Monick)

Introductory notes:
(1) The terms which comprise the Indices to Volumes I and II are selected on a keyword basis;

ie the key terms on each page are entered. As is commonly the case, these terms are ordered in an alphabetical sequence. However, it is readily apparent that the sequence incorporates main terms, beneath which subordinate entries are contained.

In Volume I the main terms are:

Badajoz; **Battles, Campaigns, Wars**; **Casualties**; **Cuidad Rodrigo**; **Lisbon**; **Spain/Spaniards**; **Tactics**; **Uniforms and accoutrements**; UNITS AND FORMATIONS; **Weapons and Ammunition**

In Volume II the main entries are:

Battles, Campaigns, Wars; **Casualties**; **Shipping/Ships**; **Spain/Spaniards**; **Tactics**; **Uniforms and accoutrements**; UNITS AND FORMATIONS; **Weapons and Ammunition**

It is equally apparent that the entries under these main headings are further sub-divided. This aspect is an especially notable feature of the heading UNITS AND FORMATIONS; due to the need for specificity in complex military organisations.

(2) The obvious relationships between terms (as in the case of geographical locations which are also the site of battles, Salamanca and Badajoz being obvious examples) necessitates the extensive use of cross references.

(3) The use of annotation has, in theory, no place within an index. However, careless editing has resulted in confusion with regard to several terms, obvious examples being:
– The references to the two Paget brothers in Volume I, no distinction being made between Generals Edward Paget and Lord Henry Paget (cf INTRODUCTORY ESSAY - **Maxwell as editor**].
– The reference to the 7th Hussars as the 1st Hussars [cf INTRODUCTORY ESSAY - **Maxwell as editor**].
– The variation in the spelling of place names (often within the context of the same chapter) [cf INTRODUCTORY ESSAY - **Maxwell as editor**].
– The misspelling of names of prominent personalities (Pack and Crauford in Volume I being obvious examples).

In the interests of historical accuracy, and with a view to providing the reader with clarity on these points, notes have thus been added in such circumstances where it has been deemed necessary.

(4) The use of square brackets indicates that the indexer has completed the name of an individual, where the Christian name, etc has been excluded in the text.

(5) Where the authorship of a particular chapter has been identified, both the author and title of the chapter are separately indexed. However, where a chapter is anonymous, it has not been indexed.

(6) Occasionally, a term has been more closely identified by the indexer. For example, where the author has referred to a division or regiment as 'our division' or 'our regiment' and it is possible to more accurately define the formation in question, the term has been more specifically identified. This practice has also been adopted with regard to place names (eg rivers, towns, etc).

INDEX TO VOLUME II

A

Abercrombie, [Col Alexander], 238
Abisbale, Count d' [see: D'Abisbale, Count]
Abrantes, 188, 198,,203,204,244,277
Abrantes, Duke of [see: Junot, General Jean-Androche]
Acqs, 165
Adour (River), 134,148,164,165,169, 171,181
   Bridge, 181
   Pontoon bridge, 168-169,180
Africa
   Coast, 250
Agueda (River), 27,28,30
Alba de Tormes (River), 3,17,18,19, 31,372
   Bridges, 17
Albuera (River), 231,233,236,237,240
   Bridge, 231,236,321,323
   Fords, 237

Ferdia, 233
[see also under: **Battles, Campaigns, Wars**]
Alby, 121,122
   Mayor, 122
Alcale (University), 11,12,14
Alcuesca, 314
Aldea de Figueras, 33
Alexander, Col, 164,172,173,175,176, 177,334,336,350,353,354,355
Alhandra, 366,367
Ali, 50
Almarez, [1]
Almeida, 251,283,284
Alpedriz, 249
Alps, 9
Alston, Lt, 289
Alten, Maj Gen (later Field Marshal), Sir Charles (Karl) von, 28,87,386
Alverca, 366,369
America [see: North America, South America]
Animals,3,6,7,19,56,70,74,259,282
[see also specific types; eg: Bullocks, Donkeys, Horses, Mules, Pigs]
Anseldo, Lt, 330
Anson, Gen Sir William, 348

INDEX 391

Aragon, 61,62,115
Aranaz, 93
Aranjuez, 12,15
Arapiles (Mountains), 19,40,48,50
[see also under: **Battles,
Campaigns, Wars** - Salamanca]
Arbuthnot, Col, 238
Aretesque, 78,79
Arevala/Arevalo/Arevola, 3,15,381
Arga (River), 60,61,79
Arganda, 12,13,14,15
Arinez, 42
Ariyez, 48
Arronchos, 209
Arroyo de Molino (village), 312,314, 315
[see also under: **Battles,
Campaigns, Wars**]
Arroyo de Molino (Maj Patterson), 312-320
Asses, 7,53,232
Asturia (Province), 74
Asturias (Mountains), 38
Aveman, Gen, 348
Awards
Legion of Honour (France), 290,291
Aylmer, Lord, 364
Azambuja, 364

B

Badajoz, 209,213,221,231,235,330
[see also under: **Battles,
Campaigns, Wars**; Ramparts]
Bridge, 221,227,228
Baggage, 3,6,15,19,22,35,39,40,44,47, 52,56,61,88,94,110,169,170,271, 273,280, 321,343,384,387
Bagneras, 164
Banos, 30
Barba del Puerco, 251
Barka de Avintas, 380
Barnes, Maj Gen (later Gen) Sir Edward, 136,138,139,141,142,143
Basque, 73
Peasantry, 66
Bastan (valley), 60,65
Basterreche (chateaux), 181,182,183

Battles, Campaigns, Wars
[see also: **Casualties**]
Aboukir Bay [see: Nile]
Albuera (1811), 126,233,236-240, 321,358
Arroyo de Molinos (1811), 312-320
Badajoz (siege) (1812), 210,232,322
[see also in general section]
Breaches,210
Barossa (1811), 356
Bayonne (1813-1814), 133-149,171,183
Citadel [see: Fortress]
Dockyard, 178
Fortress, 134,181,181,182,185
Garrison, 166,171,178,179,180
Burgos (siege) (1812), 12,279,281
[see also in general section]
Burgos (retreat) (1812), [1],12-27,30,260
Busaco (1810), 114,367
Campo Major (1811), 125
Corunna (retreat) (1808-1809), 125,367
Fort St Christoval (siege) (1811), 221,222,223,226,227,228,230, 231,232
Fortifications, 229
Garrison, 222,224
Ramparts, 222,227,229
Trenches, 223,226,227,229
Fuentes d'Onoro (1811), 114,126
Garris (1814), 151-160
Gibraltar (siege) (French Revolutionary Wars, 1792-1802), 243
Linzoain (1813), 343
New Orleans (1815), 381
Orthes (1813), 120
[see also in general section]
Pampelona (1813), 347
Peninsular War (1808-1814), 96, 97,107,113,126,163,187,193, 194,239,260,287,312,371,380
[see also: individual battles, campaigns]
Pyrenees (1813), 78,133,135
[see also in general section]
Russia (1812)
Moscow, 256

Sabugal (1811)
Sahagun (1808) [see also under: **Casualties**]
Salamanca (1812), 114,126,373,374-380,386,387
  Arapiles (heights), 337,338,376,378
San Sebastian [see: St Sebastian]
St Sebastian (siege) (1813), 76,80, 291,294,297,298,299,303,305, 308,309,311
  Breaches, 78,287,288,299,302, 303,307
  Castle, 286,290,292,298,300,301, 302,303,304,305,308,309, 310
  Fortifications, 286,295
  Fortress [see: Castle]
  Garrison, 290,291,297,302,305, 308,309,311
  Governor, 288,289,294,296,297, 308,309
  [see also: Rey, General Louis-Emmanuel]
  Ramparts, 287,288,296
  Trenches, 288,289,290,294,298, 299,301,308,309
Talavera (1809), 105,114,125
  [see also in general section]
Torres Vedras (Peninsular War), 272,273,359,366,367
Toulouse (1814), 120,121,125,380
  [see also in general section]
Vimiero (1808), 113
Vittoria (1813), 28,42-54,56,59, 61, 62,103112,113,114,115,135,180, 288,343
  [see also in general section]
Waterloo (1815), 148,179,269,280
Batty, R
  Campaign of the left wing of the Allied Army in the Western Pyrenees, 180
Bayas (River), 41
Bay of Biscay, 76, 297
Bayonne, 70,76,106,133,134,136,138, 148,150,163,180,184,290,292,296, 297,352,353
  Camp, 354
  Consul, 185
  [see also under: **Battles, Campaigns, Wars**]

Beaucourt, 171,178
Beef, 276,279,282,355
Beira, 188,260
Belem,29
Belgium
  Minister of War, 307
Berens, 119
Beresford, Marshal [Sir William Carr], 108,209,231,236,337,338,339,340, 341,342,359
Beunos Ayres, 243
Bidassoa (River), 62,65,66,67,68,69, 70,71,76,78,80,82,87,91
  Bridges, 65
    Lazaca, 68,81,82,83
    Sunbilla, 68,91
    Yanzi, 68,93,94
  Fords, 72
Bidouse (River), 165
Bigorre, 164
Bilboa, 61,104
Binnie, Capt, 331
Birmingham, Maj, 227,228
Biscarret, 72
Biscuit, 25,29,38,58,73,95,195,282, 293,321
  Bags, 81
Blake, General [Joachim], 237
Blakeney, -, 235
Blancho Sanchez, 381,382,385
  [see also under: Pickets]
  Alcalde [see: Mayor]
  Mayor, 381
Blankets,17,29,55,208,284,285
Bloye, Mr, 167
Boars, 5,16
Bock, Baron, 105 [spelt 'Boch']
Bonaparte, Joseph [see: Joseph Bonaparte]
Bonaparte, Napoleon [see: Napoleon Bonaparte]
Boncoux (chateaux), 181,182,183
Boots, 90
  Hessian, 16
Boardeaux, 171,180,181
Bradley, Dr James Byron, 188
  A night in the Peninsular War, 187-204
Braganza (royal house of Portugal), 108
'Branco' (dog), 203

INDEX 393

Bread, 218,230
Briche, General, 312
Bridges, 14,35,58,69,123,313
  [see also under: name of specific place/ river; eg Adour]
  Pontoon, 169
  [see also under: name of specific river; eg Tagus - Pontoon bridge]
Britain/British [see: Great Britain]
British Isles [see: Great Britain]
Brotherton, Col, 388
Bruce, Lt Col (later Maj Gen), Sir Charles, 158,160
Buchan, Brig Gen, 137,144,146
Buenzo, 89
Bugle horns, 13
Bugles, 212,213,227,233,350,351,355
Bull, Maj, 375
Bull fights, 5,255
Bullocks,29,188,217,226
Bulls, 6,29
Burgos, 16,37,99,270,279
  [see also under: **Battles, Campaigns, Wars**]
  Bridges, 12
  Castle, 12,37
Burcellas, 366
Burnet, Capt, 350,351
Burrard [Lt Gen] Sir Harry, 113
Burroughs, Capt William, 185
Busaco (Mountains), 250
Byng, Maj Gen (later Gen) Sir John, 78,79, 89,137,139,146,147

C

Cadell, Lt Col, 320
Cadogan, Col the Hon, 315
Cadiz, 14
Caldas [see: Las Caldas]
Calhandriz, 365,367
Cambo, 139
Cameron, Col [John], 142
Campaign of the left wing of the Allied Army in the Western Pyrenees (R Batty), 180
Campan, 164
Campbell, Gen, 78
Campbell, Lt C, 287

Campbell, Capt (later Maj) Duncan, 159
Campo Major [also referred to as Campo Mayor], 209,214
Cantonments, 27,354
Capistras/Capitras [see: Muleteers]
Captaras [see: Muleteers]
Capture of the enemy's picket at Blancho Sanchesz (Sgt Maj William Hanley), 380-388
Cartaxo, 364
Carriage, 53,99,110,244,275,281
Carrigal, 375
Carts, 3,188,226,244,283,384
Carvajales, 33
Castanos, [General Franciso Xavier], 237
  [Spelt 'Castonos' in text]
Castello Branco, 188,189,201,202
Castille, 251
Casualties
  Albuera, 233
  British
    King's German Legion, 237
    57th Regiment, 235
    Portuguese, 235
    Spaniards, 235
  Fort St Christoval
    British, 228
  Linzoain
    British
      40th Regiment, 343
  Vittoria
    French, 113
Cat, 279
Catalonia, 61
Catholics [see: Roman Catholics]
Cattle, 383
  [see also: Bullocks, etc]
Celerico, 251
Cemetiere, Capt, 329
Cheyne, Lt, 168
Chofre (sand hills), 286
Christians, 215,216
Cholera, 243
Churches, 4,10,206,209
Churchill, Maj, 138
Churchyard, Tpr, 123,124
Clausel, Marshal Bertrand, 43,62,104
Clements, Capt, 319

Coa (River), 251,278
  Bridge, 251
Coimbra, 244,249
  University, 249
Colborne, Col (later Field Marshal Sir) John, 322,324
  [misspelt as 'Colburn']
Cole, Gen [Sir Galbraith Lowry], 78, 79,205,235,238,323,344,346,347, 348
Collier, Lt Col G, 185
Colours,153,327,328,358,359
  King's Colour
Column [see under: Tactics]
Combermere, Lord [see: Cotton, Maj Gen (later Gen) Sir Stapleton]
Conductors [see: Muleteers]
Constantinople, 254
Continent [see: Europe]
Convents*, 3,7,10,37,39,171,172,175, 176,206,246,257,258,267
  [*Note: Term used interchangeably with monasteries]
  [see also: Monasteries]
  Aolcobaca, 245,247,248,249
  Abbot, 247
  San Antonio, 201
  St Bernard, 181,182
  St Martin's, 247
  St Vincent, 270,271
Convicts, 223
Cor, Marescal del Campo Le, 135,145
Coria, 27,28
Corn, 32,56,65,70,74,116,130,218, 261,381
Costa, Brig Gen Da [see: Da Costa, Brig Gen]
Cotton, Maj Gen [later Field Marshal Sir Stapleton], 79,105,374,377
Cotton, Lt Col (later Lt Gen) Sir Willoughby, 167
Cox, Lt, 372
Crofton, Capt the Hon W G, 185
Cuidad Rodrigo, 20,26,27,30,279, 280,281,282
  [see also under: **Battles, Campaigns, Wars**]
Cumberland, 268
Currie, Lt Col, 144
Curry, Capt Hunter, 107,108

Cymbals, 55

D

Da Costa, Brig Gen, 137,143,145
Dalgetty, - , 247
Dalgetty, Capt Douglas, 338
Dalmatia, Duke of [see: Soult, Marshal Nicholas]
Dalrymple, Gen Sir Hew [Whiteford]
  Memoir...Proceedings as connected with the affairs in Spain, 113
D'Aremberg, Prince, 318,319
De Comissari (Mountains), 69
D'Erlon, [Marshal Jean-Baptiste Drouet], 78,79,87,89
D'Espada (Mountain), 164
De Gagan, Count [see: Gagan, Count de]
Devonshire, 262,263
Dogherty, Cpl, 319
Dogs, 178,194,196,203,261,264,357
Dombrowski, [Gen Jan Henryk], 312
Donkeys, 56,199,272,280
Donna Maria (Mountains), 90,91
Don Pedro [see: Peter I]
Douro (River), 12,14,15,32,33,34,97, 130,268,375,380
Douze (River), 164
Drums, 55,91,167,232,258,349
  Drum calls
    'Assembly', 340,355
Dryden, John, 364
Duckworth, Lt Col, 235,328
Duennas, 97,99
Duke of Wellington [see: Wellington, Duke of]

E

Eagles (birds), 180
Eagles (French standards), 345,346
Earl of Hopetoun [see: Hopetoun, Earl of]
Ebro (River), 38,61,62,103
Echelar (heights), 68,71,81*
  [sometimes spelt 'Etchelar']
  [*Spelt 'Echalar' on this page]

INDEX 395

Echelar (Mountain), 95
  Pass, 94
Elgoriage, 91
Eliot, Capt, 167
Elley, Col, 378
El Teatro del Principe, 11
Elvas, 210,211,214,226,231,331
  Drawbridge, 210
  Forts
    La Lippe, 210
    Ramparts, 211
Emerson, J
  Recollections of the late war in Spain and Portugal, 205-242
England/English, 2,28,56,61,105,108, 114,128,130,145,387
  [*see also:* individual place names]
Entrenchments, 4
Escurial, 4,16
  Palace,5
Esla (River),33,34,125
Estramadura, 27,28,214,259
Estrella (Mountains), 261
Etchelar [*see:* Echelar]
Europe, 131,200,247,251
Evans, Lt, 155,156
Evans, Pte, 353,354,356
Exeter, 262
Eyre, Lt, 289

F

40th Regiment in the Pyrenees, The (Col S Strelton), 347-349
Fancourt, Bde Maj, 154
Fearon, Col, 156
Ferdinand II (King of Aragon, 1479-1516), 37
Ferdinand VII (King of Spain, 1814-1833), 257
Fishlock, Tpr, 119
Font-Arabia, 71,165
Forage (town), 76
Forage, 7,52,74,99,116,275 [*see also:* Corn, Hay, Straw]
Fordice, Maj
Fortifications [*see also under:* **Battles, Campaigns, Wars** - St Sebastian - Ramparts, Trenches; Paris - Mon

Martre; *see also:* Forts - St Christoval - Ramparts; Torres Vedras in general section]
Forts/Fortresses, 61
  [*see also under:* Jurumanha]
  Conception, 251
  Sobral, 366
  St Christoval, 221,222
    Ramparts, 222
Foy, [General Maximilien-Sebastien], 104
France, 49,62,65,69,76,96,104,187, 252,292,296,297,332
  [*see also:* French]
Frontier, 61
Frazer, Col Sir Augustus, 165
  [spelt 'Fraser' in text]
French★, 4,9,12,13,14,16,17,18,19, 20,21,24,25,31,33,34,37,38,39,40, 41,43,44,45,47,49,50,51,52,54,55, 56,59,60,61,70,71,72,82,83,87,91, 92,93,96,97,99,100,102,104,106, 107,108,109,111,112,113,115,118, 119,120,123,125,126,133,136,138, 139,140,141,142,143,144,145,146, 148,151,152,153,154,155,156,157, 159,165,167,171,172,176,177,178, 182,205,206,207,208,209,211,212, 213,214,219,226,227,228,231,233, 236,237,238,239,273,281,288,289, 290,298,299,312,313,317,320,321, 323,324,325,327,328,329,330,332, 333,339,341,344,345,346,347,348, 349,350,351,351,352,353,359,360, 363,364,365,372,374,375,376,377, 378,379,381,383,386
  [*see also:* France; UNITS AND FORMATIONS - France - Army]
  [★ Note: The term 'enemy' is entered under 'French']
Frias, 40
Fuentes d'Onoro, 202 [*see also under:* **Battles, Campaigns, Wars**]
Fuentes de Guinaldo, 27
Fullen, Sgt, 229

G

Gagan, Count de, 99

Gale, Capt, 152
Gallegos, 27,28,284
Galway, Lt, 346
Garda, 250
Garris, 151,153
[see also under: **Battles, Campaigns, Wars**]
Gave de Mauleon, 165
Gave de Pau (River), 118,119,164,165
  Ford, 119
Gave d'Oleron (River), 118,165
Gaviao, 276
Georgics (Virgil), 364
Germany, 335
Gil Blas (Le Sage, Alain Rene), 68
Girard, [General Jean-Baptiste], 312,314
Goatherders, 202
Goats, 53,54,73
  Goats' flesh, 220
Goblet, Lt, 307,308
Gold, 55
Gomecha, 49
Graham, Gen Sir Thomas, 32,44,50, 60,61,80,85,90,103,106
Granada, 164
Grant, Lt Col Colquhoun, 99,109
Great Britain [see also: England], 76,367
  Government, 186
Guadiana (River), [1],211,213,214,232
  Ford, 226
Guadarama (Mountains), 4,5
Guarena (River),6,15
Guinaldo
  Plains, 254

H

Halbard, Mrs, 369
Halbard, Sjt, 369
Halkett, Col [later Gen Sir Hugh[, 323,330 [misspelt 'Hacket' in text]
Hamilton, Capt, 143
Hamilton, Gen, 329
Hamilton, Lt, 143
Hanares (River), 12,14
Hancox, Capt, 120
Handspikes, 67
Hanley, Sgt Maj William
  Capture of the enemy's picket at

  Blancho Sanchez, 380-388
Harispa, General, 159
Harvey, Capt J V, 185,186
Hasparen, 115,117,138
Hawkeshaw, - , 235
Hay, 7,116
Hay, Maj Gen [Andrew], 182
Helebra (River), 23,24
Hill, Maj Gen [later Gen Sir Rowland], 12,33,34,50,62,78,79,80,87,88,106, 133,135,136,137,138,143,144,145, 151,158,159,313,317, 318,366
Hill, Maj Clement, 317
History of the war in the Peninsula and the South of France (Lt Gen Sir William Napier), 91,168
Holkar [Indian ruler opposed to Wellington], 113
Holland, 307
Holmes, Pte, 352,353
Hope, [Lt Gen] Sir John, 66,243,259
Hopetoun, Earl of [see: Hope, [Lt Gen Sir John]
Horse flesh, 113
Horses, 2,4,13,17,20,21,31,33,36,43, 53,56,57,68,74,75,82,85,93,98,99, 100,105,107,110,115,116,117,124, 129,130,143,148,155,164,176,189, 190,192,193,194,197,201,202,203, 209,213,227,240,255,284,315,316, 317,319,336,338,350,358,361,377, 378,381,382,383,384,386,387
Hospitals, 188,201,275,283,288,290, 291,292,294,295,297,298,300,301, 303,305,306,307,308,331,355
  Attendants, 307,356
Houghton, Gen, 235,238,321,322, 328,330,331
Howard, Gen, 313
Hughes, Pte Jem, 354,355
Humphrey, Capt, 323

I

Iberian Peninsula, 60,286,328,332,374
  [see also: **Battles, Campaigns, Wars** - Peninsular War; Portugal, Spain]
Incas, 55

Ines [see: Sor Juana Ines de la Cruz]
Inglis, Col (later Lt Gen Sir) William, 235, 329,358
Ireland, 215,216,264,320,371
Irish, 233,319
Irthing (River), 268
Irun, 69,70,80
Irwin, Capt, 320
Isabella (Queen of Aragon, 1407-1504), 37
Ituren, 91

J

Jaca
  Pass, 62
Jarama (River), 12,14
Joliffe, Monsieur, 289,295
Joliffe, Mrs, 289
Jones, Col
  Account of the war in Spain and Portugal, 113
Jones, Pte, 353,354
Jones, Lt Harvey
  Seven weeks captivity in St Sebastian, in 1813, 286-311
Jones, [Maj Gen Sir John Thomas]
  Journals of the sieges undertaken by the Allies in Spain, 113, 286
Joseph Bonaparte (King of Naples (1806-1808) and Spain (1808-1813), 7,12,26,34,44,46,60,62,72, 104
Journals of the sieges undertaken by the Allies in Spain (Col Jones), 113,126
Junot, General [Jean-Andoche], 114
Jurumanha, 211,214,232
  Fortress, 211

K

Kearney, Mr, 188,201
Kempt, Gen [Sir James], 46
Kent, Capt, 11
Kettle, 29
Kettle, - (servant), 169,170
Kildare,107

L

Lamego, 32,268
Lanz (River), 79
Lanz (town), 80,87
La Rhune (Rock), 69,70,76
Las Caldas, 244,245
Law, Lt, 315,316,317,372,373
Lazaca [see under: Bidasoa (River) - Bridges]
Le Brun, Capt, 118,120
Le Cor, Marescal del Campo [see: Cor, Marescal del Campo Le]
Lecumberri, 90
Leira, 249
Le Marchant, Capt, 145
Le Marchant, Maj Gen [John Gaspard], 378, 380
Leon, 33,251
Lerin (valley), 92
L'Ers (River), 121
Le Sage, Alain Rene [see: Sage, Alain Rene La]
Life of the Duke of Wellington, The (W H Maxwell), 12,42,72,134,169,233,235
Line [see under: **Tactics**]
Lisbon, 114,194,202,203,243,244,259,270, 271,276,279,280,281,318,359,360,3 61,362,363,365,369
  Magistrate, 271
Logrono, 62
Lonsdale, Mr, 199
Lord Combermere [see: Combermere, Lord]
Lord Lynedoch [see: Lynedoch, Lord]
Los Alduides (mountain pass), 79
Los Passages [see: Passages]
Luaza de Alva, 49
Lumley, Gen [Sir William], 322,325, 320
Lusitania, 365
Lynedoch, Lord [see: Graham, Gen Sir Thomas]

M

Maclean, Mr, 188

Madrid, 4,7,8,12,14,15,16,26,30,
34,254,259,382,387
　Beuno Retiro, 9,15
　Plaza Major, 8
　Prado, 15
　Royal Palace, 9
　Streets, 9
Manzanares (River), 7
Marchant, Capt [*see:* Le Marchant, Capt]
Marchant, Maj Gen [John Gaspard] [*see:* Le Marchant, Maj Gen John Gaspard]
Marches/marching, [1],13,16,21,22,
26,29,32,34,35,37,41,55,62,63,64,
72,74,79,80,82,83,87,88,92,96,232,
238,244,254,259,265,267,273,278,
295,314,316,328,335,343,350,355,
359,363,373,375,376
Marganta, 48
Marlow (military college), 74,282
Marmont [Marshal Auguste-Frederic-Louis], 114,374,375,376,379
Marsan, 164
Massena, [Marshal Andre], 245,249,367
Matadores, 5
Mauritania, 360
Maxwell, William Hamilton
　The life of the Duke of Wellington, 12,42, 72,134,169,233,235
Maya (mountain pass),
71,78,80,91,158★
　[★Spelt 'Maia' on this page]
Medellin, 312
Mergua, 43
Merlin, General [Philippe-Antoine], 104
Miranda de Duoro, 32
Monasteries, 3,7,201,247
　[*see also:* Convents]
Mondego (Bay), 248,250
Mondego (River)
Monks, 203,245,246,248,249
　Benedictine, 247
Monreale, 246
Montgaillard, 164
Montijo, 214,220,221
Monuments
　Officers killed at Bayonne

　Coldstream Guards, 184,185
　1st Foot Guards, 185
　2nd Foot Guards [*see:* Coldstream Guards]
　3rd Foot Guards, 185
　60th Regiment, 185
Monzarbes, 19,20
Moors, 55,195
Morales, 34
Mules, 2,7,13,14,29,53,56,74,110,116,
129,170,188,195,206,217,226,232,
271,272,279,280,281,333,362,365,
385,387
Muleteers, 11,13,14,29,129,194,
195,196,204,226

N

Nanclara [see under: Zadora (River) - Bridges]
Napier, Col [later Lt Gen] Sir [William Francis Patrick], 287
　History of the war in the Peninsula and the South of France, 91, 268
Napoleon Bonaparte, 9,72,98,113,
118,182,183,187,258,292,297
Navarre, 59
Night in the Peninsular War, A (Dr James Byron Bradley), 187-204
Nisa, 202,203,204,275
Nive (River), 115,134,135,138,143,
165,350,354
　Bridge, 134,135,138
　Fords, 135
　　Cambo, 133
　　Villa Franche, 134
Nivelle (River), 69
North America, 244
Nuns, 37, 257,258

O

O'Callaghan, Col (later Lt Gen) Robert W, 154,155,159
Olabarre, 42
Olaque, 73,79★,89★
　[★Spelt 'Olacque' on these pages]
Olaz, 79

INDEX   399

'Old Tom' (horse), 100,101
Oliveira, 261,262,265,267,268
Olivenza, 213,214,232,235
　　Garrison, 214
Olla, 244
Oporto, 130,265,268
Orange, Prince of, 348
O'Reilly, Capt, 167
Orthes, 118,119,130
　　[see also under: **Battles,**
　　Campaigns, Wars]
Ortiz, 80
Osma, 40
Oxen, 52,281,283
Oyarzum, 69

P

Pack, [Maj] Gen [Sir Denis], 83
★Paget, Gen Sir Edward, 22
★Paget, Lord Henry, 125
　　[★**Note**: cf note under these entries
　　in Index to Volume I]
Palencia, 37
Pamplona, 52,53,60,62,64,65,71,
　　72,78,79,80,81,82,85,87,90,113
　　[see also under: **Battles,**
　　Campaigns, Wars]
　　Citadel [see: Fortress]
　　Fortress, 60
　　　Ramparts, 60
　　Garrison, 72,113
Pantaloons, 16
Panurge (character in Rabelais's
　　Pantagruel), 250
Paris, 183,256,311,333
　　Mon Martre
　　　Fortifications, 311
Paris, General, 133,136,138,147,159
Passages, 69,297,311,345
　　Garrison, 61
Patrolling/patrols, 97,121,131,213,254,
　　380,381,384,387
Patterson, Maj
　　Aroyo de Molino, 312-320
Pau, 179
Pedro I (Emperor of Brazil and King
　　of Portugal, 1822-1831], 245,249
Pedro de Peralta Barnuevo Rocha y

Benavides
　　Tomb, 247
Peninsula [see: Iberian Peninsula]
Percival, Capt, 93
Perthshire, 357
Picadores, 5
Pica du Midi (Mountain), 164
Pickets, 70,81,82,94,98,100,117,118,
　　119,120,125,129,130,175,176,181,
　　182,212, 222,315,333,386
　　Blancho Sanches, 380,383,387
　　[see also in general section]
　　Chapel Hill, 333,334,336
Picton, [Lt] Gen [Sir Thomas],
　　47,63,79, 84,135
Pigs, 255,279,281,354
Pinhel, 251
Pinto, 12
Pitt, Ensign W, 185
Plaisance, 120
Plough, 217
Pollos, 33
Pombal, 249
Pompepolis [see: Pamplona]
Pompey (Roman general), 59
Pontalegre, 208
　　Ramparts, 208
Pontoons [see under: Bridges]
Porter, Sir Robert Ker, 256
Portugal, 6,27,28,29,61,188,193,
　　194,196,199,205,211,218,219,220,
　　243,244,251,261,262,267,277,360,
　　364,367,368
　　[see also: **Battles, Campaigns,**
　　Wars - Peninsular War; individual
　　place names (eg Lisbon); Iberian
　　Peninsula in general section]
　　Frontier, 211,279
　　Peasantry, 193
Portuguese, 170,215,261,269,271,
　　283,365,367,370
　　[see also: UNITS AND
　　FORMATIONS - Portugal]
Poseda, 4
Prevost, Charles, 98
Prince of Orange [see: Orange, Prince of]
Prince Regent, 98
Pringle, Maj (later Lt Gen) Sir W H,
　　137,139, 147,151,154,160
Prisoners-of-War

British, 26
French, 34,113,214
Probyn, -, 178
Provisions, 60,81,113,194,226,230, 240,248,281,293
[see also: Stores, Supplies]
Pyrenees, 61,69,71,76,87,104,164, 258,269,343
[see also under: **Battles, Campaigns, Wars**]
Passes, 65,71,78,85,134
Donna Maria, 89

R

Ramsay, Capt (later Maj) [William] Norman, 110,111
Ranhadas, 263
Rations, 18,26,29,230,254,275,277, 282,350,351,386
[see also: Beef, Biscuit, Rum]
Recollections of the later war in Spain and Portugal (J Emerson), 205-242
Recollections of the Peninsula (Lt Col Wilkie), 243-259
Religious orders, 271
Revenge (play), 11
Rey, General [Louis-Emmanuel], 308
Rivers, 57,123,164,268
[see also: name of river (eg Tagus)]
Roads/routes, 4,12,14,19,20,22,26,30, 33,38,39,40,43,44,47,49,52,53,59, 60,61,62,64,65,67,68,69,71,79,80, 81,82,85,87,88,89,90,91,92,93,104, 106,112,115,117,119,120,121,122, 134,135,136,137,138,139,140,141, 142,144,146,147,151,171,178,180, 181,182,183,189,190,192,193,194, 195,201,202,207,213,226,228,231, 232,236,243,244,250,251,252,259, 261,265,272,273,274,275,277,278, 280,281,282,283,312,313,317,318, 335,344,351,352,353,354,359,360, 365,366,368,381,382
Scotland
Highlands, 244
Robe, Col, 280
Robe, Lt, 279
Rocio, 198

Roman Catholics, 215,216
Church, 216
Roncesvalles, 60,71,78,79,82,91
Mountain pass, 78
Rosas, 7
'Rosinante' (horse), 197
Ross, Lt Col Hew, 59,135,141,143,375
Rousseau, General, 357
Roverea, General, 348
Rueda, 14,33
Rum, 17,29,230,274,283
Ruty,-, 239
Rye, 218

S

Sabijana de Alva, 41
Sabugal, 278,279
Sacavan, 270
Sage, Alain Rene Le, 68
Saint...[see: St... at end of this letter sequence]
Salamanca, [1],15,17,18,19,26,30, 31,33,64,251,252,254,256,257,283, 372
[see also under: **Battles, Campaigns, Wars**]
Bridge, 254
Cathedral, 32
Square, 32,255
University, 254
Salamonde, 31
Salines, 69
Salvatierre, 104
San Munez, 23,30
Santa Barbara (heights), 71,81,94
Santarem, 29,249,273,274,275,359, 360
Magistrate, 361
Saragossa, 62,63
Sarnadus, 189,191,200,202
Sarre, 69
Saurorem, 84
Sauveterre, 118
Scottish Highlands, 66
Sebastiani, [Marshal Horace-Francois-Bastien], 359
Segovia, 4

INDEX 401

Seven weeks captivity in St Sebastian in 1813
(Lt Col Harvey Jones), 286-311
Seville, 231
Seymour, Pte, 262,263,264,268
Sheep, 53,54
Shiffner, Capt J B, 185
Shipping/Ships
  Boats, 166,167,290,292,297,302
  Corvette, 165,166
  Cruiser, 297
  Fire ships, 169
  Float, 211
  Gunboats, 165,169,366
  Lyra, 168
  Men-of-War, 168
  Transports, 311
  Woodlark, 168
Shoes, 20,24,29,64,82,208,214,343
Sicily, 247
Sierra de Alcoba (Mountain), 250
Sierra d'Estrella (Mountain), 260
Skerret, Col, 26
Skirmishing [see under: **Tactics**]
Smith, Capt Webber, 110
Smyth, Capt, 227
Smyth, Maj Henry, 155
Sobral, 366 [*see also:* Forts - Sobral]
Somerset, Col (later Gen) Lord Robert Edward, 378,379
Songeon, Mr, 294
Sor, Juana Ines de la Cruz
  Tomb, 247
Souham [Gen Joseph], 12
Soult, Marshal [Nicholas], 12,18,72, 78,79,80,82,84,89,90,91,96,113, 118,120,133,134,137,231,236,238, 239,297,308,322,323,326,331,347, 354,372
South America, 55
Spain/Spaniards,
  [*see also:* **Battles, Campaigns, Wars** - Peninsular War; individual place names; UNITS AND FORMATIONS - Spain]
  Agriculture, 216-217
  Coast, 297
  Farmers [*see:* Agriculture]
  Frontier, 28,69,211,279
  Houses, 291

Inquisition, 251
King [*see:* Joseph Bonaparte]
Ladies, 10,11,16,290
[*see also:* Women in general section]
Language, 253,255,263
Peasantry/peasants, 24,37,45,63,85,117, 173,200,202,219,260
Pizanos [*see:* Peasantry/peasants]
Provinces
[*see also:* individual provinces; eg Estremadura, Navarre]
Southern, 62
Spies, 213
Universities, 11 [*see also under:* Alcala, Salamanca]
Square [see under: **Tactics**]
Staffordshire, 353
Standards [*see:* Colours, Eagles]
Sterne, Laurence, 324
Stewart, Brig Gen (later Lt Gen Sir William), 135,139,145,148,159, 226,235,325
Stockings, 82,208,214
Stores, 52,54,114,169,191,226,297,337
[*see also:* Provisions, Supplies]
Straw, 7,116,170
Stretton, Col S
  The 40th Regiment in the Pyrenees, 347-349
Subaltern, 355
Sullivan, Lt Col Sir H, 185
Sunbilla [*see under:* Bidassoa (River) - Bridges]
Supplies, 113,287 [*see also under:* Provisions, Stores]
Swinney, Pte, 177
St Bernard (Mountain), 69
St Christoval (heights), 17,18
[*see also:* Forts - St Christoval]
St Christoval (valley)
[*see also:* Fort St Christoval]
St Esprit
  Fauxbourg [residential district], 180,181
St Estevan, 65,71,73,79,80,82,83,91,94
St Etienne, 171,181,182
St Fernando, 14
St Jean/John de Luz, 69,70,76,134, 168,333,349,354,355

St Jean/John du Port, 76,116,133,147
St Martha, 214
St Martin, 103
St Palais (house), 136,137,139,140,
 141,144,145,146
St Sebastian, 43,69,71,87,286
 [*see also under:* **Battles,
 Campaigns, Wars**]

T

Tabara, 33
Tactics
 Column, 13,15,20,21,22,23,24,40,
 43,44,45,47,48,49,53,56,59,68,70,
 79,91,105,110,135,136,138,139,
 140,141,143,144,145,151,152,154,
 166,167,237,238,239,302
 March, 84
 Line, 28,40,48,49,108,141,142,
 143,161
 Skirmishing, 110,139,140,146,
 147,171
 [*see also under:* UNITS AND
 FORMATIONS - Great Britain -
 Army - Skirmishers; France - Army
 - Skirmishers]
 Square, 12,22,34,61,100,374
Tafalla, 62
Tagus (River), [1],7,12,193,198,207,
 208,244,366
 Pontoon bridge, [1],207
Talavera de la Reyna, [1]
Tarbes, 164
Tartarus, 258
Tartas, 164
Teer, Jaen, 102
Telescope, 100
Tents, 29,31,38,64,70,71,73,208,321
Thomar, 205,207,208
Tolosa, 60,61,85,90
Tordesillas, 33
Tormes (River), 17,19,31,33,254,
 257,376
 Fords, 17,19,31,33,254,257,376
Toro, 33,34,35,64,97
Torrecilla della Orden, 375
Toulouse, 120,121,181
 [*see also under:* **Battles,**

Campaigns, Wars]
Townsend, Lt Col, 388
Transport, 362
 [*see also:* Carts, Horses, Mules]
Transportation, 223
Tras os Montes (River), 33
Trenches
 [*see also under:* **Battles,
 Campaigns, Wars** - Badajoz, Fort
 St Christoval, St Sebastian]
Tres Pontes [see under: Zadora
 (River) - Bridges]
Trousers, 16,24
Trumpets, 70
Truxillo Jacarejo, [1]
Tulloch, Lt Col, 135,143
Tumbrils, 55
 [*see also:* Carts; **Weapons and
 Ammunition** - Ammunition -
 Waggons]

U

Uniforms and accoutrements
 [*see also under:* UNITS AND
 FORMATIONS - France - Army -
 Hussars, Lancers: Infantry; Great
 Britain - Army - Corps - Engineers,
 Royal Military Artificers; Portugal -
 Army; Spain - Army]
 Badges
  27th Regiment, 216
 Belts, 25
 Canteens, 283,354,365
 Caps, 24
 Cartridge box, 225
 Cloaks, 21,355,369,373
 Cuirass, 127,128
 Epaulette, 25,287,291
 Gaiters, 64
 Greatcoats, 24,29,173,174,285
 Haversacks, 24,29,40,54,94,95,157,
 171,208,214,225,248,315,336,345,
 346,351,384
 Helmets, 21,35,48
 Knapsacks [*see:* Haversacks]
 Pelisse, 68
 Pouches, 111
 Tartans, 3

INDEX 403

Valises [*see:* Haversacks]
United Kingdom [*see:* Great Britain]
UNITS AND FORMATIONS
Allied armies (Napoleonic Wars), 182,236,238
Allied Army (Peninsular War), 114,134
[*see also:* Great Britain, Portugal, Spain]
Europe
   Cavalry, 128
France [*see also:* French, in general section]
   Armies, 18,24,26,29,34,42,50, 56,60,72,76,90,94,99,103,110, 111,113,114,118,120,137,138, 140,165,236,254,259,290,322, 333,335,337,343,374,375
   [*see also:* Tactics - Column]
   Army of the Centre, 104
   Army of Portugal, 104,114
   Army of the South, 104
   Artillery, 42,46,47,84,104,118, 141,146,147,237,239,259,299, 309,323, 326,330,376
     Batteries, 12,108,140,171
     Gunners, 47,49,51,110,290,292
     Siege artillery, 80
   Battalions, 375,377
   Brigades, 39,40,114,126,312, 329,378
     Cavalry, 120
     Infantry, 377
   Camps, 138
   Cavalry, 19,21,22,23,36,42,47, 84,91,93,102,104,109,322,323
   [*see also:* under Brigades]
     Chasseurs, 68,98,109,117,118, 119,120,122,123,124
     Cuirassiers, 127
     Dragoons, 21,35,46,99,100, 101,110,111,112,118,156,312, 317,382,383,387
     Heavy cavalry, 20,22,34
     [*see also:* Cuirassiers]
     Hussars, 126
       Uniform, 16
     Lancers, 126,236,237,238, 324,325
     Light cavalry, 21,43,88
     [*see also:* Chasseurs, Hussars, Lancers]
   Chasseurs [*see under:* Cavalry]
   Commanders, 114
   [*see also:* individual names]
   Corps, 62
     Observation, 84
     4th Corps, 259
   Cuirassiers [*see under:* Cavalry]
   Deserters, 177,329
   Divisions, 40,43,51,103,110,111, 118,137,138,159,326,357
   Dragoons [*see under:* Cavalry]
   Engineers, 169,290,297,303, 307,310
   Grand Army (Russia), 118
   Grenadiers, 287,288,291,303, 317,320
   Imperial Guard, 98
   Infantry, 23,31,47,68,98,99,100, 103,104,109,110,111,114,119, 126,140,148,312,338,373,377, 382
     Companies, 291
     Light Infantry, 41,95,141,151, 156,167,326
     [*see also:* Skirmishers]
   Joseph Bonaparte's army, 34
   Lancers [see under: Cavalry]
   Marshals [*see:* Commanders]
   Medical officers [*see:* Surgeons]
   Non-Commissioned officers, 291
   Officers, 16,35,53,54,98,118, 160,176,187,288,290,291,293, 295,298,299,301,305,305,307, 308,309,310,311,317,333,334, 335,344,345,348,353,353,383, 383,387
   Poles [*see:* Cavalry - Lancers]
   Regiments, 329,333,334
     2nd Regiment, 95
     27th Regiment (Chasseurs-a-Cheval), 318
     32nd Light Infantry, 344
     66th Regiment, 377
   Scouts, 88
   Skirmishers, 21,22,63,129,140, 141,142, 144,152,377
   [*see also:* Voltiguers]

Soldiers, 3,54,73,76,81,94,95, 98,99,100,102,103,105,113,116,117,178,135,136,137,145,159,176, 177,178,236,239,258,288,290, 292,293,302,303,304,305,306, 307,308,310,334,335,336,344, 352,354,379,384
   German, 318
   Italian, 318
   Swedes, 318
   Swiss, 318
Troops [see: Soldiers]
Uniform, 24,280,288,303,356
Insignia, 24
Videttes [see: Soldiers]
Voltigeurs, 291,356
Gendarmes, 121
Great Britain
  Army, [1],2,6,14,15,19,20,22,24, 25,28,29,34,36,37,43,45,48,50, 52,54,61,62,71,73,74,78,80,87, 93,94,99,102,103,110,111,113, 115,125,131,133,134,135,137, 151,153,161,163,168,175,182, 187,188,191,205,207,215,236, 238,239,252,256,262,263,270, 272,273,279,280,290,299,321, 322,323,328,330,333,337,338, 350,354,361,364,365,367,370, 375,376,378, 384
  Artillery, [1],31,35,48,58,62,73, 105,113,135,136,140,309,327
  [see also under: King's German Legion; see also: Regiments - Royal Horse Artillery]
    Batteries, 46,60,72,164,165, 213,223,224,227,229,291,292, 299,300,301,302,309,310
    Mirador, 300
    Brigades, 164,280,326
    Companies, 281
    Gunners, 166
    Horse artillery
    [see: Regiments - Royal Horse Artillery]
  Bands, 257,265
  Barracks, 131
  Batman, 14,321,354
  Brigades, 23,36,40,44,48,52,53, 84,89,93,109,110,112,135,139, 146,147,151,152,156,160,161, 211,214,226,227,254,313,321, 322,324,325,328,329,330,377, 378, 380,381,383,385,386
  [see also under: Artillery; King's German Legion; individual brigades]
    Dragoons, 43
    Fusiliers, 234,235,238,326,359
    Guards, [see also under: Regiments]
    Household Brigade, 28,30,33, 127,128
    [see also: Regiments - Life Guards, Royal Horse Guards]
    Hussars, 30,34,37,43,48,98, 106,107,108,116,120,125
    1st Brigade (Light Division), 7,27,71,81
    1st Infantry Brigade, 164
    2nd Brigade (Light Division), 7, 24,27,40,48,50,53,71,93
    2nd Infantry Brigade (1st Division), 166
    Brunswick-Oels Corps, 299
  Bugler, 173
  Camps
    Curragh, 107
  Cavalry, [1],22,31,36,42,52,53, 62,73,97,104,105,106,111,112, 114,115,121,125,126,127,128, 129,130,131,243,280,313,315, 329,330,374,375,377,378,379, 383,385
  Depots
    Maidstone, 388
  Heavy Cavalry, 33,43,373,374, 377,378,380
  [see also: Brigades - Dragoons, Household Brigade; individual regiments]
  Light Cavalry, 49,100
  [see also: Brigades - Hussar; individual regiments]
    Troopers, 33
  Commissariat, 29,95,275,282
  Commissary, 305,360,362
  Communications, 375
  Corps (ie Army Corps), 103,134
  Corps
    Engineers, 223,224,228,295 [see

INDEX 405

also: Pioneers]
  Uniform, 287
Royal Military Artificers, 17,299
  Uniform, 299
Divisions, 25,26,27,29,32,36,43,
  46,48,49,50,52,73,81,84,91,96,
  105,106,130,133,180,209,210,
  354,354,355
1st Division,
  12,18,36,43,49,71,80,84,
  164,169,350
2nd Division, [1],12,19,27,29,
  33,36,41,42,48,49,65,71,82,84,
  89,133,151,158,159,207,209
3rd Division, 7,12,36,44,46,47,
  48,51,62,63,72,80,84,89,373,
  374,375,376,377,378
4th Division, [1],12,36,41,42,43,
  47,49,51,62,72,85,89,103,138,
  144,205,323,326,330,345,347
5th Division, 36,38,43,49,72,78,
  80,84,115,351,352,377
6th Division, 43,73,79,82,83,
  85,89,133,138,143,144
7th Division, 23,36,43,44,47,50,
  71,80,81,82,84,87,89,90
Light Division, [1],2,10,11,13,
  14,17,18,20,21,22,23,26,27,28,
  29,30,31,34,35,37,40,42,43,44,
  48,50,55,56,58,63,65,81,82,84,
  85,87,88,89,90,91,92,106,375
Doctors [*see under:* Medical staff]
Dragoons, 31,43,49,100,105,
  112,118,120,121,128,375,377,
  384,385
[*see also under:* Brigades;
individual regiments]
  Heavy Dragoons, 23,36,127
  Light Dragoons, 36,114,375
  [*see also:* individual regiments]
Highlanders, 3
Hussars, 35,39,68,99,100,101,
  109, 119,123,124
[*see also under* Brigades: individual
regiments; King's German
Legion - Cavalry - Hussars]
Infantry, 21,28,36,52,92,93,105,
  107,110,111,112,114,115,116,
  120,128,130,131,135,147,162,
  174,315,374,377,378

[*see also under:* Brigades; King's
German Legion]
Battalions,
  35,59,179,265,268,331
[*see also:* individual battalions
under Regiments]
Companies, 16,21,24,29,46,67,
  108,169,171,173,174,177,260,
  331,350,351,358
[*see also:* Tactics - Column]
Grenadier, 320
  Light Companies, 152,156,
  164,166,171,179,227,314,332,
  333,356,351,352,353,355
Divisions (units within battalions)
  Sub-divisions, 233,234
Fusiliers, 236,239
Grenadiers,151,155,156
[*see also under:* Companies]
Light infantry,
  151,159,169,314,349
[*see also under:* Companies]
Sections, 234
King's German Legion, 31,323
Brigades, 36
Cavalry [*see also:* individual
regiments]
Hussars, 21,24,28,30,59,115,
  383,384
[*see also:* individual regiments]
Infantry
  Light Infantry, 280,323
  Riflemen, 236,333
  Regiments
    1st Hussars, 381
Medical staff,36,59,187,198
  Assistant Surgeon, 337
  Doctors, 2,277
  Surgeons, 178,188,271
Officers, 2,3,7,8,10,13,16,20,21,
  24,29,31,34,36,49,54,59,63,64,
  73,75,87,88,105,108,110,117,
  118,121,122,123,124,128,129,
  130,131,142,144,152,157,158,
  159,164,169,173,174,178,180,
  183,184,187,191,193,195,200,
  212,222,223,228,238,243,246,
  247,248,249,254,262,265,266,
  270,272,277,279,280,281,282,
  284,289,294,296,298,299,315,

317,318,319,325,327,329,332,
333,334,335,350,351,362,
372,373,387
  Mess, 13
Pipers, 143
Provost Marshals, 220
Quartermaster General
  Quartermaster General's
  Department
Quartermasters, 321,345
Regiments, 21,24,28,39,45,55,
109,137,142,153,228,235,238,
239,244,260,295,324,333,337,
338,342 [see also under: King's
German Legion]
  'Buffs' [see: 3rd Regiment]
  Cavalry, 131,209,378,387
  [see also: individual regiments]
  Heavy Cavalry, 127
  Coldstream Guards [see: 2nd
  Foot Guards]
  Foot Guards, 179
  [see also: individual regiments]
    Fusiliers [see: 7th
  Regiment]
  Guards [see: Foot Guards]
  Rifle Regiment [see: 95th
  Regiment]
  Royal Dragoons [see: 1st
  Dragoon Guards]
  Royal Fusiliers [see: 7th
  Regiment]
  Royal Horse Artillery,
  21,23,46,59, 135,139,279,375
  Brigades,28
  Royal Scots [see: 1st
  Regiment]
  Scots Guards [see: 3rd Foot
  Guards]
  1st Dragoon Guards, 129
  1st Foot Guards, 179
  [see also under: Monuments]
  1st Regiment (Royal Scots),
  182,289,308
  2nd Foot Guards, 184,185
  [see also under: Monuments]
  1st Bn, 180
  3rd Foot Guards,185,186
  [see also under: Monuments]
    3rd Regiment, 144,146,

235,322,324,331
4th Dragoon Guards, 377
5th Dragoon Guards, 377
7th Hussars, 116,117,120
7th Regiment, 345
9th Regiment, 287
10th Hussars, 28,120,125
13th Light Dragoons,
136,209,211,213
14th Light Dragoons,
136,380, 381,386,387
15th Hussars,
28,46,109,119,120,124,125
15th Light Dragoons [see:
15th Hussars]
18th Hussars, 120
18th Light Dragoons [see:
18th Hussars]
24th Regiment, 131
25th Regiment, 151
27th Regiment, 216
28th Regiment,
151,152,153,320,322
29th Regiment, 321,322,324,
328,329,331
31st Regiment, 235,322,331,
333
34th Regiment, 322
38th Regiment, 290
39th Regiment, 151,153,154,
155,156,157,158,159,160,322
40th Regiment, 344,345,346,
347,348
42nd Regiment, 141,254
48th Regiment, 235,324,325,
329
1st Bn, 321,322,328
2nd Bn, 322
50th Regiment, 139,140,141,
143,144,312,314
52nd Regiment,
16,39,40,107,108,358,359
60th Regiment, 155
[see also under: Monuments]
  66th Regiment,
146,235,322, 324,331
71st Regiment,
139,142,144,147,312,314,315,
317,319,372
92nd Regiment, 139,140,142,

143,145,312,314
95th Regiment, 11,39,46,59,
75,93,95
1st Bn, 45,46,95
Riflemen, 44,211
[see also: 95th Regiment]
Sappers [see: Corps - Royal
Military Artificers]
Scouts, 90
Skirmishers, 102,119,120,148,
221,317,327,350
Soldiers, 6,7,12,13,14,15,16,17,
18,20,22,25,26,29,35,49,53,54,
57,58,64,72,80,81,84,88,91,92,
94,95,106,113,117,121,124,136,
144,151,152,153,154,158,160,
162,163,173,174,180,188,189,
195,202,208,212,213,221,224,
225,227,233,235,244,248,254,
265,270,273,279,282,283,284,
289,293,294,299,313,317,318,
323,327,328,329,331,333,334,
349,351,352,359,363,364,365,
377,378,381,382,385,387
[see also: Cavalry - Troopers]
Surgeons [see under: Medical
staff] Troops [see: Soldiers]
Uniform, 55,265,330
Portugal
Army, 322,337,341,343
Artillery, 135,136,141,142
Brigades, 36,43,79,103,108,
135,136,137,139,140,143,144,
145
[see also under: Cavalry]
Cacadores, 16,139,140,143
[see also under: Regiments]
Cavalry, 211 [see also under:
Regiments]
Brigades, 36
Dragoons, 103,191,192,213
Commander-in-Chief, 341
[see also: Beresford, Marshal
Sir William Carr]
Conscription, 223
Conscripts, 223
Divisions, 133,135,329,338
Garrisons
Santarem, 275
Infantry, 108,135,147,222,338

Militia, 210
Officers, 48,219,222,272,296,
301,362
Regiments, 24,48
Cacadores,156,335
[see also: specific regiments]
Cavalry, 209
Elvas, 222
20th Regiment, 26
Soldiers, 190,215,222,223,
230, 283,335,359
Uniform, 339
Irregulars, 33
Russia
Army, 256
Cossacks, 16
Spain, [see also: **Spain/Spaniards**
in general section]
Army, 41,71,72,80,90,126,236,
237,253,321,322,323,324,325
Corps, 116,136
Divisions, 43,90,159
Generals, 32
Infantry, 136
Officers, 18,32,219,279,298
Regiments, 238,279,347,348
Royal Horse Guards, 37
Soldiers, 68,74,219
Uniform, 32   128
Guerrillas, 4,19,33,36,112

V

Vachell, Ensign F, 185
Valencia, 12
Valorosas, 108
Vane, Ensign W, 185
Vanzella, Dolores, 261,262,263,264,
265,266,267,269
Vanzella, Joaquina, 266
Vanzella, Maria, 266
Vanzella, Pedro, 261,265
Ventura, Senorita, 84
Vera, 67,68,69,70,71,76,81,82,87,90
Mountain pass, 78,94
Vigors Harvey, 184
Villa Franca, 244,360,363,364,365
Villalba, 61
Villate, General, 80

Villa Velha, 202
  Mountain pass, 277
Villoses, 44
Virgil (*Georgics*), 364
Viseu, 250,265,267
Vittoria, 41,42,46,47,50,51,52,53,
  54,55,62,77,103,111,345
  [*see also under*: **Battles,
  Campaigns, Wars**]
Vivian, Col [later Lt Gen Sir Richard
  Hussey), 120

W

Wade, Field Marshal [George], 244
Waggons, 52,53,110,339
  [*see also under*: **Weapons and
  Ammunition** - Ammunition]
Ward, Lt, 336
Ward, Maj, 226,231
Warre, Col, 338,339
Water, 9,24,295,302,304,353,354
Way, Maj, 329
Weapons and Ammuntion
Ammunition
  Balls [*see*: Musket balls, Cannon balls]
  Bombs, 224
    Fuses, 224
  ★Bullets, 23,50,51,68,234,309,
  341,342 [★Note: A term used interchangeably with musket ball]
  Caissons [*see*: Waggons]
  Cannister shot [*see*: Case shot]
  Cannon balls, 23,24,45,48,59,141,
  171,172,175,184,210,221,222,226,
  229,346
  Case shot, 110
  Grape shot, 110,226,227,229,238,
  280,287,299,301,358
  Gunpowder, 17,25,52,53,303,304
  Magazine, 301
  Mortar bombs [*see*: Bombs]
  Musket balls, 26,47,48,53,68,143,
  154,161,240,309,340,346,354
  [*see also*: Bullets]
    Cartridges, 25,29,52,111
  Powder
  [*see*: Gunpowder]
  Round shot

  [*see*: Cannon balls]
  Shell, 48,210,221,222,225,226,
  229,289,290,291,304,309,310,372
    Fuse, 225,306,309
  Shrapnel, 301,308,309,310
  Shot [*see*: Case shot, Round shot,
  Grape shot]
  Waggons, 52,55,282
  [*see also in general section*]
Artillery, 18,23,24,48,51,52,54,104,
  169,224,225,231,232,238,305,308,
  327
  Cannon
  [*see*: Guns]
  Guns, 15,19,23,31,44,46,49,51,
  52,55,59,67,80,109,110,111,113,
  114,115,120,135,136,139,140,141,
  143,147,148,150,151,152,164,168,
  169,214,226,227,228,229,231,233,
  238,258,259,305,326,327,337,346,
  347,366,378,379
    3 pr, 23
    6 pr, 135
    9 pr, 135,326
    18 pr, 164
    24 pr, 175,230
  Carriages, 12,202
  Howitzer, 135,230
  Mountain gun, 23
  Mortars, 222,305
  Rockets, 165,167
Bayonet, 22,44,48,50,84,95,106,142,
  154,155,156,160,161,162,234,318,
  344,348,349,353,377
Cannon [*see*: Artillery - Guns]
Carbine, 98,115,119
Firelocks [*see*: Musket]
Grenade, 291
Guns [see under: Artillery]
Hand-grenade [*see*: Grenade]
Lance, 234
Musket, 12,23,45,86,92,94,148,160,
  196,212,239,240,302,316,317,334,
  335,352
  Flints, 25
  Ramrod, 25
Ordnance [*see*: Artillery]
Pike, 36
Pistol, 6,383
Rockets

[*see under*: Artillery]
Sabre
[*see under*: Sword]
Small arms, 48,53,80,81,95,152,327
[*see also*: Bayonet, Carbine, Musket, Pistol]
Sword, 21,48,93,101,108,142,160, 178,191,194,199,287,288,289,311, 344,353,383,384,386
  Broadsword, 6
  Sabre, 31,36,43,57,190,199,311,317
Wellesley, Sir Arthur [*see*: Wellington, Duke of]
Wellington, Duke of, 11,14,19,22,23, 28,32,33,34,41,42,44,45,47,50,65, 79,80,84,87,89,91,96,97,99,100, 101,103,105,106,111,112,113,114, 115,118,134,138,144,147,148,150, 151,152,153,159,165,240,273,296, 308,323,331,344,345,347,348,354, 360,367,375,376,387
  Despatches, 387
    Bayonne, 147
    Salamanca, 374
    20 February 1814, 159
Wemyss, Bde Maj, 143
Wheat, 60,220
White, Lt Col, 329
White, Capt C, 185

Wilkie, Lt Col
  Recollections of the Peninsula, 243-259
Winterfield, Cpl, 124
Wodehouse, Capt, 119
Wolves, 5,241
Women, 16,38,53,74,304,305,360, 361,363,386
  [*see also*: Spanish/Spaniards - Ladies]
Wood, 26,63

Y

Yanzi [*see under*: Bidassoa (River) - Bridges]
Yeoman, [1]
Yruna (River), 45

Z

Zadora (River), 41,42,43,46,47,48,49, 50,52,105,288
  Bridges, 42,45,46,47,49
    Nanclara, 47
    Tres Pontes, 46,48
Zadora (Valley), 106
'Zanga' (character in *Revenge*), 11
'Zarya' (mule), 170
Zubieta, 85

www.ingramcontent.com/pod-product-compliance
Lightning Source LLC
Chambersburg PA
CBHW071647160426
43195CB00012B/1378